BID THE VASSAL SOAR

Say unto foul oppression, Cease:
Ye tyrants rage no more,
And let the joyful trump of peace
Now bid the vassal soar.
—George Moses Horton

BID THE
VASSAL SOAR

*Interpretive Essays on the Life and
Poetry of **Phillis Wheatley** (ca. 1753–1784)
and **George Moses Horton** (ca. 1797–1883)*

M. A. Richmond

HOWARD UNIVERSITY PRESS
WASHINGTON, D.C.
1974

Copyright © 1974 by Merle A. Richmond

All rights reserved. No part of this book may be reproduced or utilized in any form without permission in writing from the publisher. Inquiries should be addressed to Howard University Press, 2400 Sixth Street, N.W., Washington, D.C. 20001.

Printed in the United States of America.

LIBRARY OF CONGRESS CATALOGING IN PUBLICATION DATA

Richmond, Merle A.
    Bid the vassal soar.

    1. Wheatley, Phillis, afterwards Phillis Peters, 1753?–1784.   2. Horton, George Moses, 1798?–ca.1880.
I. Title.
PS866.W5Z68   811'.009   73-85493
ISBN 0-88258-001-9

Acknowledgments

With gratitude I acknowledge the courtesy and assistance of the curators and library personnel at the following institutions: Manuscript Department and Southern Historical Collection of the Library of the University of North Carolina; Massachusetts Historical Society; Boston Athenaeum; Rare Book Room, Boston Public Library; New-York Historical Society; New York Public Library, Schomburg Collection; Library Company of Philadelphia. I am grateful, too, for permission to quote from the various items in their custody, mentioned with specificity in the Notes.

Thanks are also due the following publishing houses for permission to quote from their respective publications, mentioned more particularly in the Notes: University of North Carolina Press, Chapel Hill; Harcourt, Brace & Jovanovich, New York; Philosophical Library, New York.

My grateful appreciation is owing to the editorial staff of Howard University Press for their sensitive and careful reading of the manuscript. In this regard I am especially indebted to my editor, Paula Giddings, whose valuable suggestions and critical comments vastly improved this study.

M.A.R.

TO LOUISE

Contents

Introduction ix

Phillis Wheatley
1. The Poet and the General 3
2. From a Fancied Happy Seat 11
3. A Child Prodigy 15
4. Poetry and Fame 24
5. Triumph in London 31
6. War, Revolution, Freedom 37
7. Marriage 43
8. Tragedy and Death 48
9. The Critics 53
   Notes 67

George Moses Horton
1. A Natural Poet 81
2. The Slave and the Citadel 84
3. Poet Laureate 97
4. *Hope of Liberty* 105
5. Years of Reaction 115
6. *Poetical Works* 126
7. Vain Appeals 135
8. The Eve of War 149
9. War and Emancipation 157
10. *Naked Genius* 163
11. Oblivion and Death 170
12. Critical Appraisals 178
    Notes 199

Introduction

When the Abolitionists published a volume of verse by Phillis Wheatley and George Moses Horton in Boston in 1838, it was not to praise poetry but advance the Abolitionist cause. Their purpose is suggested by the cumbersome title: *Memoir and Poems of Phillis Wheatley, a Native African and A Slave; Also, Poems by A Slave.* Twice it is said in the one title that the poems were written by slaves, and the Abolitionist argument was that people with the sensitivity and intelligence to compose verse ought not to be slaves, that the Wheatley–Horton accomplishments belied the slavocracy's dogma that Africans were cursed with an innate brutishness, which rendered them fit for no more than chattel.

Thus it was politics rather than art that made volume companions of Wheatley and Horton, and strange companions they were. To be sure, both were black, both were slaves, both were poets, and these are powerful bonds of community; but there are also contrasts. Female and male, native of Africa and native of these United States. She a "house nigger" reared in the fashionable New England urbanity of the late eighteenth century, he a "field nigger" reared in rural North Carolina in the early nineteenth. Their times were different. The big historic event in her lifetime was the Revolutionary War, in his the Civil War. In her time the institution of slavery was still tentative, the gin was yet to crown cotton king, and although learning was not encouraged among slaves, neither was it prohibited by law. In Horton's time the repressive superstructure of slavery attained all its monstrous dimensions and even the learning of letters by a slave was prohibited by law, subject to harsh penalties. A black poet in the South was, by legal definition, a potentially dangerous criminal. The two poets differed, as well, in their venture. She was seemingly too timorous to avow the goal of freedom (except on one memorable occasion, but even then she circumscribed the avowal with qualifications);

he was remarkably constant and tenacious in his declared pursuit of freedom. Their personal styles were opposite. She was immersed in Christian piety, he confessed to a weakness for the bottle. He had some sustenance of family, mutilated and deformed as it was by slavery, and there is evidence that in his literary passion he received sympathetic encouragement from his mother and the stimulus of competition from a younger brother. She was alone, the memory of family in Africa obliterated, and if any of her kin were brought into slavery in America she had no knowledge of them. Since family is the primary school in human relations, it might account for his greater adeptness and aggressiveness in such relations; she was stilted and inhibited, filling the human void with the austere grace that Puritan New England called Christian. Inevitably then their work differed, the contrast being sharp in what was requested of them. She was commissioned to write elegies, he to compose love lyrics.

So Wheatley, in the clear, mannered strokes of what was proper penmanship in the Boston of her time, wrote:

> Thy Church laments her faithful Pastor fled
> To the cold mansions of the silent dead . . .
> As the sweet Rose, its blooming beauty gone
> Retains its fragrance with a long perfume:
> Thus Cooper! thus thy death-less name shall bloom . . .

And Horton, in the barely legible scrawl of the hand that knew the plow early and held the pen late, wrote in *Hope of Liberty*:

> Thus oft in the valley I think and wonder:
> Why cannot a maid and her lover agree?
> Thy looks are so pleasing, thy charms so amazing,
> I pine for no other, my true-love, but thee . . .

Yet, for all the differences in theme and meter, there is an underlying similarity. Both wrote for whites. She composed her elegies for dead white elders, mostly men of the church. He wrote his lyrics for young white swains, mostly sons of the Southern aristocracy.

To write, Camus said, is already to choose. This seems so profound and so true, and yet implicit in it is some freedom to choose. What freedom of choice did Wheatley and Horton possess? They chose, it would seem, as countless poets have, before and after them, two themes that are fundamental to the human condition: death and love. Such is the grand generalization, but in its specifics it always turned out to be a white master's death and a white master's love.

Introduction / xiii

There is fine irony here: white mourners and white lovers turning to black slaves to articulate their sentiments. Indulgence in irony is not enough, however, because the tragedy overshadows the irony. What happened to the blacks in the process? What happened to black identity? To the vast degree that the latter question is contemporary, so are Wheatley and Horton.

For the Abolitionists of 1838, still contesting against the primitive evil of chattel slavery, it was prize enough to proclaim to the world simply that black slaves could write poetry. In the latter third of the twentieth century the issue is more complex: what did the poetry reveal? If it is true that poets are possessed of unique sensitivity and of an unusual gift for expressing human perception and emotion, then this very different woman and man, separate in all except their blackness and their bondage, ought to afford some insight into what slavery did to black identity and what mark it left on black-white relationships in this country.

This is not to say that either was a great poet. Neither was. In this respect the Abolitionists displayed a wisdom that still is exemplary. Their poetry as poetry is not the main thing. Their influence on American poetry is closer to nil than negligible, and if your interest is in poetry as such, you need pay them no more mind than those other minor poets who clutter the footnotes of literary histories. What is important about the poetry is what it reveals or suggests about the slaves who wrote it, and, by extension, what it reveals about the institution of slavery. Because of the censorship implicit in the slave condition, quite often what is left unsaid is more significant than what is said, and even what is said may be more important for what it masks than what it lays bare.

Each of the poets represents something of a mystery. There are some clues scattered in their verse and in the available facts about their lives; with these an effort has been made to reconstruct the human identity that was or might have been. In the conviction that this modest effort is relevant to the larger endeavor to discover the roots of black identity and to delineate its contemporary content and meaning, these studies of Phillis Wheatley and George Moses Horton are offered. Once again, after an interval of 136 years, they are volume companions.

Phillis Wheatley

1

The Poet and the General

So many visitors came flocking to General Washington's headquarters at Cambridge early in 1776 that one chronicler of the proceedings there chose apologetically not to set down the long list.

"I cannot refrain, however," he interjected, "from noticing the visit of one, who, though a dark child from Africa and a bondwoman, received the most polite attention of the Commander-in-Chief. This was Phillis, a slave of Mr. Wheatley, of Boston. . . . She passed half an hour with the Commander-in-Chief, from whom and his officers, she received marked attention."

Having then just attained the age of twenty-three, Phillis Wheatley was no child, but she was definitely dark, an African, and a slave, attributes sufficiently unique among Washington's visitors to prompt the chronicler's departure from his resolve not to clutter the record with an account of those who came to Cambridge. The uniqueness of the visit is underscored by the circumstances.

Washington was an uncommonly busy man at the time, having been designated by the Continental Congress only a few months earlier as Commander-in-Chief of the Armies of North America, and being occupied with the effort to fashion a reality that approximated the grandiloquence of his title. The armies were still to be created out of scattered bands of armed irregulars, and were still to face the major tests of battle against the imperial might of the British Crown.

With this burden of military duties, Washington could hardly have welcomed civilian visitors, making an exception perhaps for those who came on relevant business; that is, influential politicians, financiers, or potential suppliers and provisioners of his troops. Surely, one least likely to be welcomed at general headquarters might well have been a "dark child from Africa," who was a slave, a poet, and a woman. As a Virginia plantation owner with two hundred slaves Washington was hardly predisposed to the polite entertainment of a slave. Nor were his intellectual interests such as to impel him to seek out the company of poets. And the male prejudices implicit in Southern chivalry would not have deemed a wartime military camp the proper haunt for a young woman, although in this instance Southern chivalry might be irrelevant because Miss Wheatley was black.

Just the same, against all the odds, the Father of His Country did grant a civil audience to the slave poet who just as fittingly may be christened the Mother of Black Literature in North America.

Events leading up to the curious encounter are shrouded with choice ambiguities. The opening shot, however, clearly was fired by Miss Wheatley with a letter and poem addressed to Washington at his Cambridge headquarters. The letter follows:

> Providence,
> October 26, 1775
>
> SIR.
>
> I have taken the freedom to address your Excellency in the enclosed poem, and entreat your acceptance, though I am not insensible of its inaccuracies. Your being appointed by the Grand Continental Congress to be Generalissimo of the Armies of North America, together with the fame of your virtues, excite sensations not easy to suppress. Your generosity, therefore, I presume, will pardon the attempt. Wishing your Excellency all possible success in the great cause you are so generously engaged in, I am,
>   Your Excellency's most obedient and humble servant,
>   Phillis Wheatley

For the next four months then there was silence, with no record that the General had received or noted the poet's offering. Finally, on February 10, 1776, writing at some length about other matters to his military secretary, Colonel Joseph Reed, Washington added almost as an afterthought:

> I recollect nothing else worth giving you the trouble of unless you can be amused by reading a letter and poem addressed to me by Mrs. or Miss Phillis Wheatley. In searching over a parcel of papers the other day, in order to destroy such as were useless, I brought it to light again. At first, with a view to doing justice to her great poetical genius, I had a great mind to publish the poem; but not knowing whether it might not be considered rather as a mark of my own vanity, than as a compliment to her, I laid it aside, till I came across it again in the manner just mentioned.

Several questions are provoked by this brief passage, chiefly: Did Washington know who his correspondent was? Were the Wheatley letter and poem saved from destruction as useless by the chance thought that they might amuse Reed?

Historians are divided in their answer to the first question. True, Phillis Wheatley had by then achieved fame as a slave poet—but it is also true that Washington's interest in poetry was so slight that she might have escaped his notice, and the reference to her "poetical genius" could rest on the one poem rather than on a knowledge of her prior work. More intriguing is his use of "Mrs. or Miss," for it was not the custom then among whites, most especially slaveowners, to dignify slaves with such titles. The chronicler who recorded the meeting between the general and the poet employed the common usage, "Phillis [no Miss or Mrs.], a slave of *Mr.* Wheatley," and he *was* aware of her reputation as a poet. It would seem that the "Mrs. or Miss" is evidence not only of Washington's uncertainty about his correspondent's marital status but of a more fundamental ignorance of her identity—except for the suggestion that the secretary might be amused by the letter and poem, flavoring the entire passage with condescension and irony, which was common white sport at the expense of slaves (and, indeed, this sort of entertainment survived emancipation in white American lore). If this was the vein of the memo, there could be more mockery than courtesy in the usage of "Mrs. or Miss." However, Washington's suggestion of amusement may be attributed more charitably to modesty or the affectation of it. A general is no more likely to be a hero to his secretary than to his valet, and the Wheatley poem was so fulsome that Washington might well have been constrained to inject a deprecating note when transmitting it to Reed, especially since he was concerned with the appearance of vanity.

The controversy cannot be resolved conclusively, but its very existence says something about the black-white relationship, involving in this instance the most renowned slave and the most highly esteemed slaveowner of 1776.

However the communication to the secretary is interpreted, its tone certainly did not foreshadow what Washington was to write little more than a fortnight later, this time directly to the poet. Dated from Cambridge, February 28, 1776, the letter reads:

> Miss Phillis, Your favor of the 26th of October did not reach my hands till the middle of December. Time enough—you will say, to have given answer ere this. Granted. But a variety of important occurrences, continually interposing to distract the mind and

> withdraw the attention, I hope will apologize for the delay, and plead my excuse for the seeming, but not real neglect. I thank you most sincerely for your polite notice of me in the elegant lines you enclosed; and however undeserving I may be of such encomium and panegyric, the style and manner exhibit a striking proof of your poetical talents; in honor of which, and as a tribute justly due you, I would have published the poem, had I not been apprehensive that, while I only meant to give the world this new instance of your genius, I might have incurred the imputation of vanity. This, and nothing else, determined me not to give it a place in the public prints.
>
> If you should ever come to Cambridge, or near head-quarters, I shall be happy to see a person so favored by the Muses, and to whom nature has been so beneficent in her dispensations. I am with great respect, your obedient and humble servant.

The internal evidence is overwhelming that the General knew the identity of the poet. The reference to "this new instance of your genius" presupposes awareness of prior instances of it, and the open invitation to visit his headquarters also suggests acquaintance with whom his correspondent was. This time there is no ambiguity about her unmarried state, and the use of "Miss Phillis" seems like a knowing compromise: the overall tone of the letter dictating the common courtesy of "Miss" in the salutation and the first name only drawing the line of caste differentiation. One historian, whose focus is on Washington's relationship with the Negro, observed, "This . . . is probably the first time in his life that he ever accorded the civility of 'Mrs.' or 'Miss' to one of her race, or gave a Negro the unusual distinction of an invitation to pay him a social visit."

As plausible a speculation as any is that between February 10, when he wrote to Reed, and February 28, when he wrote to Phillis Wheatley, Washington was briefed by someone, possibly Reed, about his correspondent's identity, thus accounting for the striking change in attitude.

In any event, acceptance of the invitation was much more prompt than its issuance. In March, four months before independence was declared, the General and the poet met in Cambridge, neither knowing what the still infant war had in store for them. They should have been guided by the prescience that wars make generals and destroy poets.

Although the General was then forty-four and the poet only twenty-three, his former service as a secondary officer in a minor war had

The Poet and the General / 7

hardly tested his mettle as a commander of armies and a leader of men, and all the accomplishments that were to establish his place in history and legend were still before him; she, on the other hand, had completed the main body of her published literary work. The tall, physically robust soldier still had twenty-four years of life left; the slender, frail poet had less than nine.

In a sense, the poet anticipated the Washington legend, the effulgent tones of her poem seeming more in harmony with the successful conclusion of the war than with its uncertain beginning. Aside from this, an interesting claim is made for the poem: that she originated the phrase "first in peace." This seems doubtful, since in the poem's context "first in place and honours" fits better than does "first in peace and honours," although both renditions have been published.

Despite Washington's protestation that publication of the poem could be misunderstood as a token of his vanity, the poetic tribute from the black slave to the white general appeared in the April, 1776, issue of the *Pennsylvania Magazine,* then edited by Thomas Paine. Presumably Reed, residing in Philadelphia at the time, arranged for its publication. The poem follows in full, for its historical interest and as a fair example of Miss Wheatley's poetic output, both in literary form and intellectual content, at the peak of her fame.

To His Excellency General Washington

Celestial choir! enthron'd in realms of light,
    Columbia's scenes of glorious toils I write.
While freedom's cause her anxious breast alarms,
She flashes dreadful in refulgent arms.
See mother earth her offspring's fate bemoan,
And nations gaze at scenes before unknown!
See the bright beams of heaven's revolving light
Involved in sorrows and the veil of night!
    The goddess comes, she moves divinely fair,
Olive and laurel bind her golden hair:
Wherever shines this native of the skies,
Unnumber'd charms and recent graces rise.
    Muse! bow propitious while my pen relates
How pour her armies through a thousand gates,
As when Eolus heaven's fair face deforms,
Enwrapp'd in tempest and a night of storms;
Astonish'd ocean feels the wild uproar,
The refluent surges beat the sounding shore;
Or thick as leaves in Autumn's golden reign,
Such, and so many, moves the warrior's train.
In bright array they seek the work of war,
Where high unfurl'd the ensign waves in air.

> Shall I to Washington their praise recite?
> Enough thou know'st them in the fields of fight.
> Thee, first in place and honours,—we demand
> The grace and glory of thy martial band.
> Fam'd for thy valour, for thy virtues more,
> Hear every tongue thy guardian aid implore!
>   One century scarce perform'd its destined round,
> When Gallic powers Columbia's fury found;
> And so may you, whoever dares disgrace
> The land of freedom's heaven-defended race!
> Fix'd are the eyes of nations on the scales,
> For in their hopes Columbia's arm prevails.
> Anon Britannia droops the pensive head,
> While round increase the rising hills of dead.
> Ah! cruel blindness to Columbia's state!
> Lament thy thirst of boundless power too late.
>   Proceed, great chief, with virtue on thy side,
> Thy ev'ry action let the Goddess guide.
> A crown, a mansion, and a throne that shine,
> With gold unfading, WASHINGTON! be thine.

Surely Washington may be forgiven if from a reading of this poem he could not divine that its author was either an African or a slave. The ornate style was clearly an imitation of Alexander Pope's, which was then the fashion and had, therefore, many imitators. The thought was mercantile Whig, preferred by the fashionable New England society in which the poet's owners, the Wheatleys, moved, and the suggestion of a golden throne and crown for Washington at the poem's end might easily have been no mere poetic image but an expression of political belief.

The poem poses a mystery more profound than Washington's awareness or nonawareness of the poet's identity. How did the poet comprehend her own identity? Relevant to this question is the larger background of the Wheatley–Washington exchange, a background that concerned the relationship of the Continental Army to all blacks.

On October 18, 1775, just eight days before Miss Wheatley wrote her letter to Washington, the Continental Congress adopted a resolution that barred all blacks from the Revolutionary armies. As happens so often, the Congressmen did not make policy; they merely approved a policy that the generals had already put into effect. With Washington's sanction, his council of general officers had already determined that no blacks, free or slave, were to be soldiers.

Eleven days after the Wheatley letter, on November 7, the royal governor of Virginia, Lord Dunmore, issued a proclamation that said:

> I do hereby further declare that all indented servants,
> Negroes, or others (appertaining to rebels) free, that
> are able and willing to bear arms, they joining his
> Majesty's troops as soon as may be.

Note that the proclamation did not refer to all slaves, only to those owned by rebels. Slaveowners loyal to the king were safe in the possession of their chattels (at least as far as Lord Dunmore was concerned, although slave rebellions and escapes, which were numerous in those unsettled times, did not await his royal dispensation). Later, the British Army did not always keep its promise of liberty, and many of its black volunteers were afterward sold into bondage elsewhere in the British colonies. But all this was later and did not affect the potential impact of Lord Dunmore's proclamation at the time of its issuance. A half-million blacks, a few free and the rest slaves, inhabited the Colonies. Their disposition could be decisive in determining the outcome of the still gathering contest. Apparently the king's governor in Virginia thought so, and his prime adversary from Virginia, General Washington, was impelled to counter this bold stroke.

Without consulting either his general officers' council or the Continental Congress, and ignoring his prior concurrence with their decisions, on December 30, 1775, Washington issued the following order from his Cambridge headquarters:

> As the General is informed, that Numbers of Free
> Negroes are desirous of inlisting, he gives leave to
> the recruiting officers to entertain them, and promises
> to lay the matter before the Congress, who he doubts
> not will approve it.

The next day Washington sent a letter to the Continental Congress with the explanation that "free Negroes who have served in this Army, are very much dissatisfied at being discarded," and that therefore he had run counter to his previous instructions from the Congress and permitted blacks to enlist. Note the date of these communications— the end of December—and then recall that in his letter to Phillis Wheatley, Washington said that hers, dated October 26, somehow did not reach his hands "till the middle of December." Was this purely coincidental, or did subordinates in his entourage consider the poet's message of insufficient importance for his attention until a change in policy on black enlistments was under consideration?

Once again, Congress voted after the fact of military action. Early in January, 1776, the Congress approved Washington's unilateral reversal of its policy, stating in its resolution:

> . . . the free Negroes who have served faithfully in the army at Cambridge, may be re-enlisted, but no others.

More mincing than the royal governor, who promised freedom to slaves who fought for the king, the Colonial Congress promised them nothing, and even for freed blacks Congressional generosity was limited to conferring the right to bear arms only upon those who had already exercised it. Congressional apprehension at Lord Dunmore's thrust was overshadowed by solicitude for the slaveowner's property rights. After all, Washington was not the only large slaveholder among the leaders of the independence forces. Several Colonies, however, went beyond the Congress and passed laws providing freedom for slaves who fought with their armies. So it was that at least five thousand blacks fought in the armies of the American Revolution. The pressures of military necessity played a part similar, if not comparable in scope, to the part they were to play four score and seven years later, when Lincoln issued the Emancipation Proclamation.

Congressional approval of Washington's policy change came, as has been noted, in January. What effect, if any, did this have on creating the climate for Washington's gracious note to Miss Wheatley in the subsequent month? Granted, this is a question of conjecture, but it is not far-fetched. Presumably, in his position Washington was guided by considerations of state in small matters as well as large, and a modification of policy toward blacks in general would have influenced the relationship with one particular black poet.

If Phillis Wheatley was aware of the political maneuvers of Lord Dunmore and General Washington in relation to blacks and the rival armies, there is no trace of it in her communications, rhymed or prose, to the General. And if her feeling toward the Revolutionary War was in any way shaped by her condition as a black and as slave, there is no hint of it in her writing.

Who was she then? There are bone-bare facts to answer this question. Who did she think she was? Here the answer is more obscure, more complex, reflecting self-awareness, a sense of self-identity, all the influences, crude or subtle, that fashion a human mind and spirit. Traces of such influences must be sought along the path she traversed from Africa to Cambridge.

2

From a Fancied Happy Seat

On this day in 1761 Susannah Wheatley, responding to the advertisement for a sale, surveys the wares displayed on a Boston dock. She is the wife of John Wheatley, a tailor sufficiently affluent to reside on fashionable King Street, and she is shopping for something special, for a providential purchase to meet the contingencies of her household some years hence.

The household consists of the two elder Wheatleys, their eighteen-year-old twins Mary and Nathaniel, and their several slaves, who clean, cook, and serve and one of whom drives Mrs. Wheatley about in her carriage. Looking forward to the day not too distant when her daughter would leave the household, Mrs. Wheatley is shopping for a companion, but being of a practical Puritan bent she is also aware that age will soon slow her incumbent slaves in the performance of their domestic chores and someone will be needed to take up the slack.

To discern the delicate combination of companion and domestic among the strange blacks, who cannot be interviewed because they speak no English, requires a sharp eye. Mrs. Wheatley's eye passes over "several robust, healthy females" (in one chronicler's[*] words) and lights upon a child "of a slender frame, and evidently suffering from a change of climate." Perhaps the suffering would not be so evident if the child were not barefoot and all but naked—"she had no other covering than a quantity of dirty carpet about her." The child might have been a "refuse" Negro, as some historians have suggested, for it was a custom among slave merchants to sell their prize specimens in the West Indies and Southern plantation colonies, where physical strength and vigor commanded premium prices, so that the human culls were left for the lesser demands and lower prices of the New

---

[*] This chronicler (frequently referred to hereafter as Phillis Wheatley's "chief biographer") is Margaretta Matilda Odell (see Notes, pp. 67–68).

England market. To buy or not to buy? The question is resolved by the "humble and modest demeanor and the interesting features of the little stranger." Mrs. Wheatley buys herself a slave.

The child was given the Christian name of Phillis and in keeping with the custom of slavery, the family name of her masters automatically became hers. So Phillis Wheatley came into being, and such other name as the child answered to before vanished. Much else also vanished. Where on the vast African continent she came from, what her tribe was, or how she got from Africa to New England—none of this is known. Her own memory of her African birthplace was obliterated, except for one image of a sunrise ritual. She retained the vision, writes a biographer, "of her mother, prostrating herself before the first golden beam that glanced across her native plains."

Memory's void can now be filled only with the flimsy, uncertain material of conjecture. It is generally thought that she came from a region then known as Senegambia, now comprising the modern African states of Senegal and Gambia on the westernmost projection of Africa, where the Senegal and Gambia rivers flow into the Atlantic on either side of Cape Verde. Less certain is the identity of her people, although the available evidence suggests that of the several peoples inhabiting Senegambia, hers probably were the Fula. They were Moslems, and her one early memory of her mother's sunrise ceremony suggests the Moslem ritual welcome to the new day. Moreover, with their Mohammedan religion the Fula also possessed a knowledge of Arabic script, and childhood familiarity with a written language might help explain the remarkable aptitude she displayed for mastering reading and writing in a foreign tongue. Finally, the only extant portrait of her reveals the sharper features of the Fula and a skin hue closer to theirs than to the equatorial black of the other peoples of Senegambia.

So much for her origin. She herself reasonably assumed that she was kidnapped into slavery, and it may also reasonably be assumed that she was brought to North America aboard a slaving vessel on the Middle Passage. Since she did not record her experiences, these may only be generalized from typical recollections of others who witnessed or experienced the same ordeals.

As authentic a personal memoir as any of child-slave kidnapping was written by Oloudah Equiano (or Gustavus Vassa), who was kidnapped into slavery from his native Nigeria at age eleven, just five years before Phillis Wheatley's abduction. He wrote:

> Generally, when the grown people in the neighborhood were gone far in the fields to labour the children

> assembled together in some of the neighbors' premises to play; and commonly some of us used to get up a tree to look out for any assailant or kidnapper that might come upon us; for they sometimes took those opportunities of our parents' absence, to attack and carry off as many as they could seize. . . . They (kidnappers) stopped our mouths and ran off with us to the nearest wood. Here they tied our hands, and continued to carry us as far as they could, till night came on, when we reached a small house, where the robbers halted for refreshment, and spent the night. We were then unbound, but were unable to take any food; and, being quite overpowered by fatigue and grief, our only relief was some sleep, which allayed our misfortune for a short time. The next morning we left the house, and continued travelling all the day.

Was the experience any less terrifying for a girl of seven than for a boy of eleven? If she was thus abducted, Phillis Wheatley was likely taken to a barracoon, or factory as it was sometimes called, one of those slave pens that dotted the African west coast from the Senegal River to the Niger to store the human cargo until a slave ship arrived and there was enough cargo for a profitable payload. These were barricaded areas, fortresses really, inside of which was another barred area whose only shelter was a rude structure along the middle. Here the slaves were kept, the men fastened to a long chain attached to stakes grounded at both ends of the enclosure. Women and children were spared the shackle; presumably they would not attack their guards, and the two barriers were formidable guarantee against their escape.

The horrors of the Middle Passage, a voyage that lasted anywhere from three weeks to three months, the slaves shackled on crowded shelves in the ship's hold, stinking with human excrement, reeking with disease and death, have been sufficiently chronicled and need not be elaborated here. There may be some morbid speculation as to whether the ship's master was a "tight" or "loose" packer, there being a difference of opinion among slave traders as to which was the more profitable, some arguing for the loose pack because the rate of loss by death was smaller, and others countering that if you packed them tight enough, the higher mortality rate was more than offset by what was left of the cargo at the time of arrival.

Since Phillis Wheatley was transported after 1750, the odds are that she was in a tight pack; by then the prevailing practice was to use bigger and faster ships with the tightest pack possible. This happened to hundreds of thousands of slaves, of course, although it might be worth noting that in this instance the child was unusually young and, as subsequently revealed, unusually sensitive and intelligent. Sensitivity and intelligence were of no account to slave traders, having no bearing on the price in their particular commerce. Age was something else, and the question might well arise as to why slave traders would go through all the cost and trouble of kidnapping in Africa and transporting across the ocean a seven-year-old girl who was still too frail for labor and still too young for breeding purposes.

Some Colonial ladies, it seems, preferred very young girls because they were still unformed and malleable—more easily trained, therefore, in the minimum requirements of Christian civilization, in the proper manners and requisite servility, to make a superior domestic servant in a fashionable household. The near-naked, shivering child on the Boston dock fitted those specifications. "She is supposed to have been about seven years old, at this time," her biographer wrote, "from the circumstance of shedding her front teeth."

3
A Child Prodigy

As the Wheatley women, mother and daughter, proceeded to train the newly acquired child slave as a domestic and companion, it quickly became apparent that Mrs. Wheatley had bought more than she had bargained for in the Boston slave market. The child not only learned to understand and speak the alien language with remarkable rapidity but also displayed an aptitude for mastering its written form. "She gave indications of an uncommon intelligence," her biographer wrote, "and was frequently seen endeavoring to make letters upon the wall with a piece of chalk or charcoal."

Mary Wheatley, eighteen when the dark child was brought into the Wheatley household, was her instructor. Nothing in the record indicates that the teacher's skills or talents approximated the pupil's aptitude. Indeed, there is no hint that Mary was an exception to the dour judgment of the poet's biographer: "The great mass of American females could boast of few accomplishments save housewifery. They had few books besides the Bible. They were not expected to read—far less to write."

If the judgment was valid, then the African child soon surpassed in literacy New England's white womanhood. After sixteen months she not only read English but managed to negotiate the most difficult passages in the Bible. At the age of twelve she embarked upon the study of Latin, simultaneously immersing herself in English literature with Alexander Pope as her model. Her facility in both pursuits was soon exhibited in a translation of Ovid in the meticulous heroic couplet that then reigned as correct poetic form. At fourteen she was a poet, as full-fledged in the art as any of her contemporaries. Her attainments are the more impressive when set against the Boston background.

> She had no brilliant exhibition of feminine genius
> before her, to excite her emulation [her biographer

remarked]; and we are at a loss to conjecture, how
the first strivings of her mind after knowledge—her
delight in literature, her success even in a dead
language, the first bursting forth of her thoughts in
song—can be accounted for, unless these efforts are
allowed to have been the inspirations of that genius
which is the gift of God.

The biographer's assessment of the feminine cultural condition in Massachusetts Colony might have been accurate, but no allowance was made for rule-proving exceptions. About a century before Phillis Wheatley's arrival, Anne Bradstreet, the English-born daughter of well-to-do Puritan immigrants, wrote poetry in Boston, and a volume of it, entitled *The Tenth Muse,* was published in London on July 1, 1650. This was the first published verse by a woman in the Colonies. The title of the volume was also attached to its creator, which was an extravagant encomium, attesting less to the talent of the poet than to the poverty of native culture in the rigors and hardships of Colonial life in the decades after the settlement at Plymouth. In those circumstances, which dictated more elemental preoccupations, the very pursuit of the poetic Muses, even if faltering, was an impressive venture.

A third edition of *The Tenth Muse* appeared in Boston in 1758, a scant three years before Phillis was purchased. No evidence exists that she read the volume, and yet the rarity of the precedent invites the speculation that she might have. There is a marked similarity between the two poets in the accent on personal humility and deep religious feeling. Of her own poetry Anne wrote, "I have not studied in this you read to show my skill, but to declare the Truth—not to sett forth myself, but the Glory of God." Phillis's verse was also replete with disclaimers of personal vanity in the service of God's glory, but such coincidence is easily attributed to the similarity in intellectual environment, without any inference that black Phillis was influenced by the prior example of white Anne. In aesthetic quality critical comparison has demonstrated that the black poet had nothing to learn from her white predecessor.

Among Phillis's contemporaries sharing the same social status was a remarkable black woman named Lucy Terry, the slave of Ensign Ebenezer Wells of Deerfield, Massachusetts. Terry tried her hand at verse, and did so early enough (1746) to upset a common assumption that a slave named Jupiter Hammon was the first Afro-American to write poetry. However, by the exacting standards of the Wheatley biographer Terry's poetry would not have qualified as "a brilliant exhibition of feminine genius." By all accounts she was much more apt with the spoken word than the written, a much better raconteur and orator than poet. Her pioneering poem, an account of an Indian raid on Deerfield in 1746, has been described as the best and most comprehensive contemporary account of that incident, but its quality as verse may be gathered from these typical lines:

> Eunice Allen see the Indians comeing
> And hoped to save herself by running
> And had not her petticoats stopt her
> The awful creatures had not cotched her
> And tommyhawked her on the head
> And left her on the ground for dead.

Terry's more solid reputation as raconteur and orator was established about a half-century after her ballad of the Deerfield raid. By then she was free, married to a black freedman, and a landowner in Vermont. Her home was said to be a gathering place for young auditors attracted by her storytelling prowess. Her most unusual oratorical feat was performed before the United States Supreme Court, when she brushed her lawyer aside and pleaded her own case in a land-boundary suit against Colonel Eli Bronson, her neighbor in Sunderland, Vermont. Justice Samuel Chase, who presided at the hearing, remarked later that Terry's pleading surpassed that of any Vermont lawyer he had ever heard.

Terry's eloquence might have impressed the court, but it did not affect Phillis Wheatley. By then, in her own poetic image, Phillis had ascended to "the seat on high." Even during her lifetime it is unlikely that she was influenced by Terry. There is no evidence that the Boston poet had even heard of her Deerfield contemporary. Deerfield, in the northwestern part of Massachusetts, near the Vermont boundary, was on the frontier during Phillis' formative years, as the Indian episode suggests. Terry's boldness and independence, her much greater fluency in speech than in writing, and even her physical stamina, indicated not only by her longevity but by the remarkable command of her faculties in the Supreme Court episode, when she was likely past three score and ten, are all suggestive of a frontier environment. In such attributes she was the opposite of the poet who was fashioned in the shelter of a middle-class Boston household.

Still, perhaps, the Terry story might be relevant as another indication that the black condition in pre-Revolutionary America did not preclude the rare cultivation of a black talent. Straining the point, a similar relevance may be assigned to Benjamin Banneker of Maryland.

He also contributes to the diversity of the black mosaic in Colonial times, for he was born male, free, a third-generation American, descended from a white grandmother and a black grandfather. His achievements were also different, consisting of scientific explorations (from stars to locusts) and bold ventures, some innovative, into the realm of social thought (ranging from an appeal to Jefferson for the abolition of slavery to proposals designed to promote the abolition of war and capital punishment). Although his birth antedated Phillis' by some twenty-three years, his first claims to public attention came long after hers. He joined the surveying party in what was to be the District of Columbia in 1789, five years after her death, and his almanacs did not begin to appear until 1791.

Post-Wheatley as a public figure, Banneker patently did not intrude into her consciousness, and yet he, too, was symptomatic of a general ambience in which "the talented tenth" of black folk, in the later phrase of William E. B. Du Bois, began to make its debut. The most thorough historian of the black experience in Colonial New England adduced evidence that white rule was less repressive there than in the other Colonies, and presumably New England afforded more opportunity for black achievement. However, Lorenzo Johnston Greene also observed that "in spite of the mildness of New England slavery, there were Negroes who found their bondage so intolerable that they committed suicide."

The trace of irony in this observation derives from the juxtaposition, which might be contrived. The "mildness" is a regional generalization, but the master-slave relationship was also particular and individual, so that some Negroes may have been driven to suicide, not in spite of the mildness, but because of the cruelties and humiliations of specific masters. Phillis' owners, however, were guided by the tradition and norm of mildness; their benevolence was nourished by an appreciation of the black child's unique gifts.

The Wheatleys had intended to train a servant and would-be companion for domestic utility, but what they got was an intellectual adornment. They were not equipped to instruct her in Latin or in the composition of verse, but they were sufficiently appreciative of such distinctions to encourage the girl—and to show her off! Boston society came to the Wheatley household to see this phenomenon, this Negro girl who wrote poems, to marvel at her, and sometimes to lend her books and encouragement. She became an exotic curiosity in Boston's fashionable drawing rooms, invited there to converse with learned men about literature and significant topics of the day, gaining a reputation as a lively and brilliant conversationalist. Puritan dominance permitted Boston few diversions, and despite its pretensions, Boston was not then graced with literary distinction. Phillis Wheatley filled those two voids. She was, in short, a sensation, the more so, of course, because she was a black African.

Indeed, etched against the African blackness of her physical being, the Puritanical whiteness of her thoughts must have seemed all the more dazzling to Boston society. The Wheatley mistresses may be forgiven a lapse into the sin of pride at what they and God had wrought. True, what they created was not exactly what they had originally conceived, but this does not deny the force and effect of their original conception. They had set out to fashion a serviceable domestic and companion. There was no diabolic intention in this. By Mrs. Wheatley's Puritan lights, it was a meritorious labor, pleasing to God, to transform a young African heathen into a Christian servant, giving this last word a dual meaning: a servant of Jesus and of the Wheatley household. Being confirmed in the Puritan belief in the immediacy and practicality of divine justice, Mrs. Wheatley would have no reason to doubt that the better Phillis served one of her masters, the better she would also serve the other.

However Mrs. Wheatley apprehended her own motivation, all the formidable Puritan powers of indoctrination were unloosed upon the "dark child from Africa," uprooted, transplanted, defenseless, to transform her into something other than what she was. But transform her into what? This is the enigma. Her dark skin and slave status precluded her re-creation in Mrs. Wheatley's own image. Skin and status were sharp chisels to shape her. Less tangible was the influence of her African nativity, which she had forgotten in the particular and yet recognized in general. Overshadowing all was the weight of Puritan teaching and environment. To list these primary influences is to conjure up an image of an African, black, slave, New England Puritan hybrid, a mix not designed to simplify the answer to that troublesome question: who am I? As the young Phillis grew, you might think her poetic gift would have spurred and helped her in the quest for an answer to that question, but as it turned out, her talent rendered her identity more equivocal.

The cost of being a child prodigy was incalculable, for as she grew into adolescence it fashioned a special—and peculiar—status for her that set her apart from all other human beings, black or white. Mrs. Wheatley, the poet's biographer relates, "did not require or permit her services as a domestic, but she would sometimes allow her to polish a table or dust an apartment . . . or engage in some other trifling occupation that would break in upon her sedentary habits; but not infrequently, in these cases, the brush and duster were soon dropped for the pen, that her meditated verse might not escape her." In all this solicitude the patronizing nexus of owner-slave relationship is conveyed in the phrase "require or permit." It may be assumed the poet preferred the book to the brush and the pen to the duster, but the option was not hers. It being a dispensation of Mrs. Wheatley's, the owner's supremacy was clearly maintained, and the poet, being the recipient of such favor, was just as clearly set apart from the other slaves in the household.

Such solicitous dispensation was operative during the night as well as the day. As with others, Phillis Wheatley's inspirations were frequently nocturnal. The felicitous line or striking image that seemed so vivid at night tended, however, to fade away by morning. To guard against such loss, the poet was permitted by her mistress to keep a light by her pillow and pen and ink at hand to record her inspirations before sleep and dawn erased them. In the cold New England winters she was permitted to keep a fire burning throughout the night to warm her when she wrote.

Most revealing, perhaps, of her peculiar status is a specific incident. The weather having turned cold and damp suddenly, as it sometimes does in Boston, Mrs. Wheatley sent her own carriage, driven by her own black coachman, Prince, to bring the young poet home from one of her showpiece visits to a distinguished household. The carriage drew up at the Wheatley residence on King Street, Phillis riding up front with Prince.

"Do but look at the saucy varlet," Mrs. Wheatley exclaimed, "if he hasn't the impudence to sit upon the same seat as my Phillis." The coachman was severely reprimanded.

The direct confrontation is between the outraged mistress and the humiliated coachman, but the scene describes a triangle and the central role belongs to the third actor, "my Phillis," who remains silent. If in the Wheatley scheme it was impudent of the coachman to share a seat with the poet, it is unlikely that he determined the seating arrangement. It was she, then, who made the choice that provoked Mrs. Wheatley's displeasure, and the explicit reprimand to the coachman contained an implicit rebuke to the poet. In putting Prince in *his* place the mistress was just as surely reminding "my Phillis" of *hers*.

In the gradations of place, Phillis' was, in many respects, the most difficult and cruel. Hers was a place in which she could not mingle with other black slaves as equals, nor could she encounter whites on terms of equality. She inhabited a strange, ambiguous twilight zone between black society and white society, cut off from any normal

A Child Prodigy / 21

human contact with either, denied the sustenance of group identity, doomed to a loneliness that, being particular and peculiar, was more tragic than the existentialist generalizations about the human condition. Assume, for instance, that in the incident of the carriage she was prompted by the impulse toward an elementary human contact. Even this was abruptly, humiliatingly, cut off. And not by the coachman, but by the mistress. It was white society that designated Phillis' place.

This consciousness of place was ever present in her frequent encounters with white society. Her biographer relates that having become acquainted with many of the best people of Boston, "she was often invited to their homes." This entailed recurrent crises—for her and for her hosts—about the nature of her reception, especially at teatime or with the service of some other meal. She developed the habit of always declining "the seat offered her at their board, and, requesting that a side-table might be laid for her, dined modestly apart from the rest of the company." The biographer elaborates: "She must have been painfully conscious of the feelings with which her unfortunate race were regarded. . . . Respecting even the prejudices of those who courteously waived them in her favor, she . . . placed herself where she could certainly expect neither to give or receive offense."

Intelligent and perceptive as she was, the poet must surely have known that she was at least equal, and most often superior, to the Boston Brahmins in conversation and intellectual accomplishment. But she was not their social equal at the dinner table. She could break bread neither with white masters nor with black slaves. She ate alone. Even in this elemental nourishment she was alone. What did she make of it? We can only surmise. Her discretion in placing "herself where she could certainly expect neither to give or receive offense" extended from the dining table to the writing desk.

Literary sensitivity to white prejudice may account for her most striking lapse in the imitation of Alexander Pope. She imitated him in meter and rhythmical form, in the profusion of classical allusion and image, in the classical discipline that eschewed any first-person intimacy, but not in the employment of satire. Pope's most celebrated works were satirical in vein, directing irony and thinly disguised barbs at literary critics and rivals, at intellectual adversaries, at sundry individuals who incurred his displeasure. It was this aspect of his work that was most zealously copied by his imitators in the Colonies. Political passions became more intense as the Revolutionary War drew nearer, and the most popular verse in the Colonies was political, couched in satirical vein. If it did not match Pope's in subtlety and deftness, it certainly yielded nothing to him in acidity and venom. This is one vein of her model that Phillis Wheatley did not tap. There may be some uncertainty as to whether her temperament would have inclined her to the satirical form, but if this had been her inclination, she would have been at a loss for targets. White society was willing to accept elegies and panegyrics to its famous men from a slave poet, but its tolerance of black wit at the expense of white sensibilities was dubious. For a black poet whites were above the shaft of satire—just as other blacks were beneath it. The critics who reproach Phillis Wheatley for her anemic imitation of Pope do not reckon with the white prejudice that did not give her the option to imitate what one critic has called his "slightly viperish dispositon."

Here again she was in the gray twilight zone. However, this denial of freedom to express anger or scorn may be considered among the lesser of her crosses. She was then in adolescence, highly intelligent and sensitive, with all the attendant hunger for the companionship of one's contemporaries, with the virginal stirring of sexual awakening and the longing for tenderness and love. An avid reader, especially of poetry, the possessor of a fertile imagination, who can tell what romantic embellishments she spun around the natural longings of adolescence and youth? When she awakened at night what other thoughts mingled with the poetic images and rhymes that came to her mind and were set down on paper? Puritan injunctions against sin were formidable enough, but in the conventlike cell of her twilight zone there was small opportunity for the pleasurable torment of grappling with tangible temptation and even less hope for the fulfillment of adolescent desire.

Coincidentally, it is hardly conceivable that her young, fresh, bright mind could have performed as it did without a passion for learning, without the excitement of intellectual discovery and literary creation. Cut off from the gratification and fulfillment of normal human relations, constantly lacerated by indignities, there was always the lonely shelter of learning and creativity. Here there was a measure of fulfillment, a sense of one's own worth. So the repressive flagella of her existence might have driven her to burrow deeper into her solitary shelter, to delve into a dead language, to immerse herself in the work of Pope, the Catholic poet who had died a decade before the estimated date of her birth and whose poetry mirrored an existence as distant from her own reality as New England was from her native Africa. What else was there for this adolescent with her unique mind and passion? There was Christian religion of the Puritan variety, a suffusive influence in her environment, drilled into her by her Wheatley mis-

A Child Prodigy / 23

tresses, the mother and the daughter. It offered consolation and made a virtue of repression, one of God's ways that needs must be justified to man.

All these circumstances of her existence left their heavy mark upon her work. One of her earliest poems, written when she was fourteen, contained fifty-six lines crowned with the title "An Address to the Atheist." The lines include these:

> Thou who dost not daily feel his hand and rod
> Darest thou deny the essence of a God!
> If there's no heav'n, ah! whither wilt thou go
> Make thy Ilysium in the shades below?
> If there's no God from whom did all things spring?
> He made the greatest and the minutest Thing.
> Angelic ranks no less his power display
> Than the least mite scarce visible to Day.

The Wheatleys could be proud. After only seven years in their household, the near-naked African child, who knew neither English nor Christianity when she was purchased, now produced this display of English poetry and Christian piety.

4

Poetry and Fame

The very title was constructed like a cathedral: "An Elegiac Poem on the Death of the celebrated Divine, and eminent Servant of Jesus Christ, the late Reverend, and Pious George Whitefield, Chaplain to Right Honourable the Countess of Huntingdon, &c, &c, Who made his exit from this transitory State to dwell in the Celestial Realms of Bliss, on Lord's Day, 30th of September, 1770."

Phillis Wheatley had been writing verse for several years, but it was the spectacular success of this elegy that catapulted her from the level of local celebrity to the plateau of poet with a reputation throughout the Colonies and in what still was the mother country overseas. The poem was published as a broadside with the legend "By Phillis, a Servant Girl of 17 Years of Age, belonging to Mr. J. Wheatley, of Boston:—And has been but 9 Years in this Country from Africa." Within a few months it appeared in Boston, Newport, Philadelphia, and New York in at least several editions, and in London in two.

The popularity of the elegy derived, in measure, from its subject, and since the poem was to play so significant a part in Phillis Wheatley's life it is permissible to dwell a while on the Reverend George Whitefield. An evangelist of the Methodist church in its nascent years, he was, as the elegiac title said, chaplain to Lady Huntington, but not a private chaplain in the ordinary sense. Lady Huntington was founder, spiritual leader, and financial patron of an early Methodist circle, which then still functioned within the Anglican church to further greater piety, personal and "methodical." As a peeress the good lady insisted she had a right to maintain as many clergymen as her ample financial means could support, and she exercised this right by appointing clergymen who shared her zeal to as many as sixty chapels in various parts of England and Wales. Her devout concern extended to the Christian state of the American Colonies and there she dispatched the Reverend Whitefield as her chaplain-missionary.

Foreshadowing latter-day revivalists, Whitefield preached the gospel in the Colonies, from Georgia to Massachusetts. His powers were attested to by very sophisticated contemporary witnesses, worldly men whose judgment was not influenced by any share in the Reverend's religious fervor.

In England the crusty Samuel Johnson said, "His popularity, Sir, is chiefly owing to the peculiarity of his manner. He would be followed by crowds were he to wear a night-cap in the pulpit, or were he to preach from a tree."

More acid was Wheatley's poetic model, Alexander Pope, who paid his respects to the preacher and a lesser-known newspaper writer named Webster in *The Dunciad:*

> Ass intones to Ass;
> Harmonic twang! of leather, horn, and brass;
> Such as from lab'ring lungs th' Enthusiast blows,
> High Sound, attemper'd to the vocal nose;
> Or such as bellow from the deep Divine;
> There, Webster! peal'd thy voice, and Whitfield thine.

In the Colonies, the frugal Benjamin Franklin related, "His [Whitefield's] eloquence had a wonderful power over the hearts and purses of his hearers, of which I myself was an instance. . . . I silently resolved he should get nothing from me. I had in my pocket a handful of copper money, three or four silver dollars, and five pistoles of gold. As he proceeded I began to soften, and concluded to give the coppers. Another stroke of his oratory made me ashamed of that, and determined me to give the silver; and he finished so admirably, that I emptied my pocket wholly into the collector's dish, gold and all."

One other witness was Oloudah Equiano, the black man who was kidnapped from his native Nigeria and sold into slavery in the West Indies, later securing his freedom, in which status he heard Whitefield preach in Philadelphia. "When I got into the church," Equiano related, "I saw this pious man exhorting the people with the greatest fervor and earnestness, and sweating as much as I ever did while in slavery on Montserrat beach. . . . I was very much struck and impressed with this; I thought it strange that I had never seen divines exert themselves in this manner before, and was no longer at a loss to account for the thin congregations they preached to."*

---

* "I would give a hundred guineas," said David Garrick, "if I could only say 'Oh' like Mr. Whitefield" (*Dictionary of American Biography* [1936], vol. 10, part 2, "Whitefield," p. 128).

An elegy for this preacher was a natural vehicle for the pious sentiments that were transported by Phillis Wheatley's earlier verse, but at seventeen her poetic line is more assured, firmer, and more vigorous:

> "Take him, ye wretched, for your only good,
> "Take him, ye starving sinners, for your food;
> "Ye thirsty, come to this life-giving stream,
> "Ye preachers, take him for your joyful theme;
> "Take him, my dear Americans, he said,
> "Be your complaints on his kind bosom laid:
> "Take him, ye Africans, he longs for you;
> "Impartial Saviour is his title due:
> "Washed in the fountain of redeeming blood,
> "You shall be sons, and kings, and priests to God."

Amid the praise for God, the Son, and the preacher, there is also a note of sympathy for the patron lady:

> Great Countess, we Americans revere
> Thy name, and mingle in thy grief sincere . . .

This elegy was to serve as her passport to England, to her patronage by the Countess of Huntingdon, and was instrumental, perhaps decisive, in the publication of a volume of her verse. All that came later. Before following her on her journey to England, there are some important matters in the Colonies to be considered.

The year of Whitefield's death was also the year of the Boston Massacre. This first fatal volley by British troops against American colonists was fired on King Street, only a few blocks from the Wheatley residence, close enough so that the poet perhaps heard the musket blasts, and if she did not hear these, there were other alarms to shatter the stillness of the March evening, for as one witness, Ebenezer Bridgham, testified, "all the bells in town were ringing, I heard the Old South first."

Surely Phillis Wheatley must have been aware that among the five colonists killed was a fugitive slave, who apparently had changed his white-given name, Michael Johnson, to one of his own choosing, Crispus Attucks. She might even have been acquainted with the inquest ("taken in Boston . . . the Sixth Day of March in the tenth Year of the Reign of our Sovereign Lord, George the Third"), which read: "The said Michael Johnson was willfully and feloniously murdered at King Street in Boston . . . on the evening of the 5th instant, between the hours of nine & ten by the discharge of a Musket or Muskets loaded with Bullets, two of which were shot thro' his body, by a party of soldiers to us known, then and there aided and commanded by Captain Thomas Preston of his Majesty's 29th Regiment. . . ."

Surely she was aware of the agitation among the colonists against the Quartering Act and the subsequent billeting of British troops in their midst, which was the immediate cause of the tensions that led to the fatal encounter on the evening of March 5. In weather-conscious Boston, especially so in the vagaries of March, she might have noted that the evening in question was cold and clear, the moonlight reflected in the blanket of snow and ice, spotted with oyster shells, that covered the ground. According to eyewitnesses, in the tense prelude to the fatal volley some of the townspeople on the scene, aroused beyond verbal sallies at the troops, may have hurled snowballs, ice, and oyster shells. In the Wheatleys' social milieu one can readily imagine impassioned discussion about the propriety and prudence of the colonists' behavior, and about the related question: did or did not the king's soldiers overreact?

Even as Phillis Wheatley was composing her elegy for Whitefield, who died September 30, Boston was agog with the forthcoming murder trial of the British soldiers, which finally opened in November. According to eyewitness testimony at the trial, the fatal confrontation (like so many confrontations to come) was triggered by teen-age boys.

"I saw a number of boys around the sentry," James Bailey testified, describing the scene in which a group of colonists was taunting a dozen British soldiers on duty close to the nearby State House, its roof adorned with two lions rampant.

"How many?"

"Twenty or thirty."

"Were they all boys?"

"Yes, none more than seventeen or eighteen years old."

Youth was in the van, a black man fell—and Phillis Wheatley, young and black, neighbor to these events, wrote an elegy for an old, white preacher. Not until two years later could anything she wrote be understood as an allusion to the Boston Massacre, and even then it was so veiled as to be susceptible of other interpretations. This allusion was contained in a letter, dated October 10, 1772, to the Earl of Dartmouth, accompanying a poem upon his appointment as Secretary of State for the Colonies.

"Nor can they [the colonists] my Lord be insensible of the Friendship so much exemplified in your Endeavours in their behalf during the late unhappy Disturbances. I sincerely wish your Lordship all possible success in your Undertaking for the interest of North America," she wrote.

"The late unhappy Disturbances" might have been the Boston Massacre, or, since the disturbances are linked to his endeavors on the colonists' behalf, the allusion might have been to much earlier protests against the Stamp Act. To the colonists generally, Dartmouth was known for his active and prominent part in the repeal of the Stamp Act in 1766 during his brief tenure as president of the Board of Trade in London. As a consequence, he was reputed to be "a friend of the colonies" and his appointment was welcomed by Colonial leaders, Benjamin Franklin among them.

Phillis Wheatley had been aware of the Stamp Act's repeal, although she was only twelve or thirteen at the time, for she celebrated the event with a panegyric to the king, reflecting in this the then-prevalent Puritan calculation of the accounts due, respectively, to God and Caesar. In the Puritan scale of the 1760's the king still occupied a place near God's. All the petitions then addressed by the colonists to the Crown were grounded on the premise that what they asked was their due as loyal subjects of His Majesty. With this premise, the more they asked the more fervently they professed their loyalty. Mirroring this state of mind, the child poet added loyalty to piety in a thanksgiving hymn to the king upon repeal of the Stamp Act:

> But how shall we the British King reward?
> Rule thou in peace, our father and our lord!
> 'Midst the remembrance of thy favors past,
> The meanest peasants most admire the last.
> May George, beloved by all the nations round,
> Live with heaven's choicest, constant blessings crowned.
> Great God! direct and guard him from on high,
> And from his head let every evil fly;
> And may each clime with equal gladness see
> A monarch's smile can set his subjects free.

Dartmouth had been the king's instrument in effecting the deed that evoked such gratitude, but for Phillis Wheatley he had a significance that transcended temporal matters. He was a leading figure in Lady Huntingdon's religious circle; so prominent, in fact, that at one time, when Lady Huntingdon took ill, he seemed destined to become the leader of the group, a fate from which he was spared by her recovery. Whitefield called him "the Daniel of the age, the truly noble Dartmouth." (Another contemporary, less pious and more scornful, called him the "Psalm-Singer.")

It is not at all strange, then, that Phillis Wheatley wrote a congratulatory poem to Lord Dartmouth. What is strange is that this poem, apparently planned to be the most formal of eulogies, contained the most unusual passage in all her verse:

> Should you, my lord, while you peruse my song,
> Wonder from whence my love of Freedom sprung,
> Whence flow these wishes for the common good,
> By feeling hearts alone best understood,—
> I, young in life, by seeming cruel fate
> Was snatched from Afric's fancied happy seat:
> What pangs excruciating must molest,
> What sorrows labour in my parent's breast!
> Steeled was that soul, and by no misery moved,
> That from a father seized his babe beloved:
> Such, such my case. And can I then but pray
> Others may never feel tyrannic sway?

Critics have pointed to the qualifications: *seeming* cruel fate . . . Africa's *fancied* happy seat; and the burden of anger is for the bereavement of the parent, not the bondage of the child. It is also true that by 1772 the Colonial air was rent with agitation for freedom and against tyranny, and the cynical might say that Phillis Wheatley, ever the conformist, now conformed to the new spirit of the times.

Nonetheless, this remains the one explicit statement that her condition as an African slave made her a particular partisan of freedom. In this rare departure from Pope's classical strictures, speaking as protagonist, in a highly personal vein, she brands slavery as tyranny. To be sure, she must have been affected by the general spirit of revolt that then animated the Colonies, but this is no general testament, as the later poem to Washington was, for instance. She writes from the specific, unmistakable vantage point of an African and a slave. Here for the first time is a spark amid the ashes of piety, a spark of independence, of self-awareness that suggests, however fitfully, a sense of distinct identity.

The poet was then nineteen, a volatile age for such sparks, but at this juncture she was caught up by a head-turning diversion, the prospect of a trip to England. To a provincial in the Colonies England was the great world, the metropolis; to a poet it was Mecca. Maybe it was the voyage, maybe the spark was foredoomed by feebleness to expire swiftly; whatever it was, the spark never kindled a flame, to employ a phrase associated with another poet of African origin. There was no later glimmer of it.

Shortly after she wrote the lines to Dartmouth her imagination was companion to her mistress somewhere on the waters of the Atlantic. She composed an "Ode to Neptune—On Mrs. W------'s Voyage to England," containing the line, "while my Susannah skims the watery way." The timing of Mrs. Wheatley's voyage suggests that she might have been the bearer of the letter and poem to the king's Secretary of State for the Colonies and that once in England she paved the way for her protégé's transatlantic journey the following spring.

5

Triumph in London

It was spring and she was in her twentieth year and she was embarked on her second transatlantic crossing, so different from the first a bare dozen years earlier. This voyage was intended, in part, to repair the physical damage consequent upon the other. The body had proven to be less adaptable than the mind in the transplantation from Equatorial Africa into New England's more rigorous climate. The poet was sickly and exposure to sea air in mid-spring was prescribed for its medicinal value.

If she was exhilarated by her destination, or if she savored the contrast between the therapeutic passage and the earlier transport as human cargo, she did not record either reaction. Exhilaration and irony were not among her literary gifts. Yet she was no longer a near-naked child, frightened and bewildered by the terrors of abduction and the horrors of the slave ship, embarked upon an uncertain journey to an unknown destination. Now she knew where she was going, now she was endowed with money to purchase appropriate dress in more fashionable London and outfitted with the intellectual accessories to encounter English society, but she was still black and a slave. Now she journeyed into the rising sun, to which her mother paid homage each morning, but she was not going home.

Heralding the voyage, the mistress in Massachusetts wrote to the Countess in England, "I tell Phillis to act wholly under the direction of your Ladiship. I did not think it worth while nor did the time permit to fit her out with cloaths; but I have given her money to Buy what you think most proper for her, I like she should be dress'd plain. . . ."

About a fortnight before she sailed the poet composed twelve stanzas of verse entitled "A Farewell to America" and addressed "To Mrs. S.W." (Susannah Wheatley). Typical of these sentimental quatrains, dated May 7, 1773, was this:

> Susannah mourns, nor can I bear
> To see the crystal shower,
> Or mark the tender falling tear,
> At sad departure's hour;

These lines are hardly suggestive that the sadness of departure eclipsed the excitement of it. Whatever her anticipations were, they seemed to have been fulfilled and (with one possible exception) exceeded. In London she was presented to the society in which her patron, the Countess of Huntingdon, moved. She wrote about it to a black friend, Obour Tanner (there is no trace of correspondence with any other blacks; no trace, indeed, that she had any other black friends with the sole exception of the man she later married).

"The friends I found there among the Nobility and Gentry" she wrote to Miss Tanner, "Their Benevolent conduct towards me, the unexpected and unmerited civility and Complaisance with which I was treated by all, fills me with astonishment, I can scarcely Realize it. . . ."

So brief a passage, and it is all that remains now to convey her own impressions of the sojourn in England. The modesty of the memoir is no measure of her emotion. Compared with the painful reticence of her other correspondence to Miss Tanner that has been preserved, this letter about London is an outburst of enthusiasm. Complementing this letter, there is one fugitive souvenir of her pilgrimage, a copy of Milton's *Paradise Lost* given to her by the Lord Mayor of London, a memento of her most triumphant days that was to figure in a pathetic postcript to her death.

Her gladsome time in London turned out to be brief, tragically truncated. Not until almost two centuries after the event did documents come to light that fix the time with fair precision and indicate that one encounter, which must have aroused her greatest expectations, did not occur.

The first of these documents, dated at London, June 27, 1773, is a letter addressed to the Countess of Huntingdon. "It is with pleasure," the poet wrote, "I acquaint your Ladyship of my safe arrival in London after a fine passage of 5 weeks in the Ship London with my young master. . . . I should think myself very happy in seeing your Ladyship. . . ."

(The "young master" referred to was Nathaniel Wheatley, who had come to London on business. In prior correspondence to the Countess, Mrs. Wheatley suggested that her son's planned business trip was a prime factor in deciding upon the poet's voyage. It was meet that the slave be accompanied by a master on her travels.)

The second document, also a letter to the Countess, dated at London, July 17, reads: "I rec'd with mixed sensations of pleasure & disappointment your Ladiship's message . . . acquainting us with your pleasure that my Master & I should wait upon you in So. Wales. . . . Am sorry to acquaint your Ladiship that the Ship is certainly to Sail next Thursday [on] which I must return to America. I long to see my Friend there. [I am] extremely reluctant to go without having first seen your Ladiship. . . ."

The Thursday on which the ship was to sail was July 22. It may be assumed reasonably that the first letter, dated June 27, was written immediately upon arrival. The poet was in England less than a month, a summer month when, as her biographer noted, "the great mart of fashion was deserted." The biographer relates that she was therefore "urgently pressed by her distinguished friends to remain until the Court returned to St. James's, that she might be presented to the young monarch, George III." Had this design been executed she would have acquired the double distinction of receptions by King George and George Washington.

She did not get to see the King, but did she see the Countess? There is only the anticipation in the first letter, the regret in the second, and the telling absence of any reference to a visit. Before the 1972 publication of the poet's letters, "recently discovered" among the papers of the Countess of Huntingdon at Churchill College in Cambridge, England, all biographies of Phillis Wheatley had accepted her primary biographer's assurance that she "was presented to Lady Huntingdon." Now, it seems, they were mistaken.

The crowning legacy of the poet's time in London was a volume of her verse, the first book by a black woman to be published. It was entitled *Poems on Various Subjects, Religious and Moral* and dedicated to her patron, Selina Shirley (Lady Huntingdon). Her Ladyship graciously permitted the dedication, and for this dispensation the poet and her mistress were effusive in their gratitude.

The poet's thanks included a shrewd calculation and a jolting lapse from her literary style. "Under the patronage of your Ladyship," she wrote, ". . . my feeble efforts will be shielded from the severe trials of uppity Criticism. . . ." Uppity?

If one realizes that the Wheatley volume, appearing more than a century and a half after the first Pilgrim landing at Plymouth, was still among the first volumes of verse by a colonist to be published, one may appreciate how rare a phenomenon it was. For a woman slave, barely turned twenty, it was a dazzling triumph. But even this moment of triumph was disfigured. The gift of the black slave could not be placed on the market without a white testimonial that it was genuine.

Appended to the volume was a statement by eighteen prestigious residents of Boston, attesting its authenticity. Among the eighteen were Thomas Hutchinson, royal governor of Massachusetts Colony; James Bowdoin, who was to be governor of the state of Massachusetts; John Hancock, possessor of the most celebrated signature in American history; and seven ministers. Men of substance all, conscious of it, affixing their valuable signatures to the ponderously drawn affidavit designed to impress even the most skeptical with its judicious restraint. It was a strange introduction to poetry:

> We, whose names are under-written, do assure the World, that the Poems specified in the following Page were, (as we verily believe) written by Phillis, a young Negro Girl, who was but a few years since, brought an uncultivated barbarian, from Africa, and has ever since been, and now is, under the disadvantage of serving as a slave in a Family in this Town. She has been examined by some of the best Judges, and is thought qualified to write them.

The signature of "Mr. John Wheatley, her master" was affixed to this statement, but he also appended another, all his own, exercising the prerogative and responsibility of master. This one read:

> PHILLIS was brought from Africa to America in the Year 1761, between seven and eight years of Age. Without any Assistance from School Education, and by only what she was taught in the Family, she, in sixteen Months Time from her Arrival, attained the English Language, to which she was an utter stranger before, to such a degree as to read any, the most difficult Parts of the Sacred Writings, to the great astonishment of all who heard her.
>
> As to her Writing, her own Curiousity led her to it; and this she learnt in so short a Time, that in the year 1765, she wrote a letter to the Rev. Mr. Occum, the *Indian* Minister, while in England.
>
> She has a great inclination to learn the Latin Tongue, and has made some progress in it.
> This Relation is given by her Master, who bought her, and with whom she now lives.

Reinforced by such testimonials, the London publishers put the book on sale on both sides of the Atlantic. An advertisement in the Boston *Gazette* on January 24, 1774, read:

This Day Published

Adorn'd with an Elegant Engraving of the Author,
(Price 3s 4d L.M. Bound)

POEMS

on various subjects—Religious and Moral,

By Phillis Wheatley, a Negro Girl
Sold by Mess'rs Cox & Berry

at their Store, in King-Street, Boston

N.B. The Subscribers are requested to call for their copies.

The "elegant engraving" shows a slender, handsome, young woman seated at a desk. The thoughtful, fine eyes and face are framed by a white ruffled cap, a necklace, and a wide kerchief collar. She holds a quill pen in her hand, and on the desk are paper, an inkpot, and a book. The portrait is thought to be a good likeness because her biographer records: "It is supposed that one of these [engraving] impressions was forwarded to her mistress, as soon as they were struck off; for a grand-niece of Mrs. Wheatley's informs us that, during the absence of Phillis [in England], she one day called upon her relative, who immediately directed her attention to a picture over the fireplace, exclaiming—'See! look at my Phillis! does she not seem as though she would speak to me!'"

Whatever opinion the poet had of the introduction to her volume, she busily promoted its sale, enlisting in this the help of her friend Miss Tanner. Apparently this salesmanship was stimulated by economic incentive. In one letter to Miss Tanner, a resident of Newport, the poet said she would "beg you'd use your interest to get subscriptions, as it is for my benefit." In another she acknowledged receipt of money for books sold, adding, "Your tenderness for my welfare demands my gratitude." A postscript to this letter adds, "I have received by some of the last ships 300 more of my Poems."

Seemingly the book was selling well, but just then history intruded upon poetry. The letter referring to the receipt of 300 volumes was dated May 6, 1774. She was very lucky to get those shipments, for on June 1 Boston Harbor was blockaded on orders of the British Parliament in retaliation for the celebrated Tea Party of December 16, 1773. The world of Phillis Wheatley was coming apart. Symptomatic of it, primary antagonists in the Tea Party were two men who had made common cause to vouchsafe that the "uncultivated barbarian from Africa" could, and did indeed, write poems. Hancock was a mastermind of the tea-dumping spree, Hutchinson was its immediate butt, leaving his post shortly after, the last civilian to serve as royal governor of Massachusetts.

Amid this gathering turbulence Susannah Wheatley died in March, 1774. Her death inspired no poetic elegy. This void is attributed by the biographer to a deathbed request by Mrs. Wheatley, but she is not certain of it, saying only that "it appears" that "Phillis was forbidden this indulgence of her grief." The poet's sorrow was expressed in a letter to Miss Tanner and the emotion is the more authentic for the privacy of it, for the absence of the constraints and embellishments of the heroic couplet. She wrote: "I have lately met with a great trial in the Death of my mistress; let us imagine the loss of a Parent, Sister or Brother, the tenderness of all these were united in her.—I was a poor little outcast & stranger when she took me in. . . . I was treated by her more like a child than her servant. . . ."*

Mrs. Wheatley's death was preceded by a long illness, another unfortunate coincidence for the poet. It was this illness that compelled her abrupt departure from England. She returned in the summer of 1773 from the benevolent civility she had encountered to the public turmoil in the Colonies and the personal vigil over the slow death of her owner-patron. One year after Mrs. Wheatley died, the shot was fired at Lexington. The long war was begun.

---

* Wheatley was not unique in expressing such sentiments about a humane mistress. Even the militant Frederick Douglass recalled that one of his mistresses was so "kind, gentle and cheerful" that he "soon learned to regard her as something more akin to a mother, than a slaveholding mistress." For this and similar expressions see John W. Blassingame, *The Slave Community* (New York: Oxford University Press, 1972), pp. 192–193.

6

War, Revolution, Freedom

It was a poor time for poetry, the public mind being preoccupied with other things. The time was especially bad for a poet of Phillis Wheatley's style and temper. Not for her was the rhythm of fife and drum, the beat of booming cannons. Her poetic meter and concerns were attuned to a bygone age. Gone, too, were her readers, who were among the elite of Colonial society. Some literally gone, fled behind the British lines, many then proceeding to Canada or beyond, to some haven of the Crown; and those remaining, most of them, being equally remote from the poet's voice, beset by anxieties, uncertainties, perils.

Early in the war Phillis Wheatley attempted a poetic response to it. There is her poem to George Washington, and yet, despite its publication in the radical Tom Paine's magazine, its sonorous tones are not in harmony with the times. It is not stuff written on a drumhead, as Paine's was. These were times of conflict and passion, much too intense to be contained in the ornate vaults of her imitation of Pope's classical style.

Her ode to Washington was followed a year later by one addressed to Major General Charles Lee on the occasion of his capture by the British. Dated December 30, 1776, seventeen days after Lee's mishap in New Jersey, the poem was entitled "Thoughts on His Excellency Major General Lee Being Betray'd into the Hands of the Enemy by the Treachery of a Pretended Friend." In one passage Lee is evidently addressing the British commander who captured him.

> What various causes to the field invite!
> For plunder *you*, and we for freedom fight.
> Her cause divine with generous ardor fires,
> And every bosom glows as she inspires!
> Already, thousands of your troops are fled
> To the drear mansions of the silent dead:
> Columbia too, beholds with streaming eyes

> Her heroes fall—'tis freedom's sacrifice!
> So wills the Power who with convulsive storms
> Shakes impious realms, and nature's face deforms;

Compare this with the poem to Washington. In the year of war that intervened, marked by clarification of Colonial war aims in the Declaration of Independence, the poet's sense of conflict was sharpened; the tone is now more combative, although once again nothing in the poem suggests that its author is an African and a slave. After this there is a long silence. No other poem of hers was published during the Revolutionary War, and no other of this period has been preserved. There is evidence that she continued to write—but not on war themes. The war dragged on through its several campaigns and many battles, through trials at Valley Forge and elsewhere, becoming a test of attrition, grim and relentless, rendering Colonial life ever more chaotic and more difficult. It may be assumed that Phillis Wheatley's poetic inspiration did not march with such events, could not keep pace with them, fell hopelessly out of step after the effort to keep abreast in the poem to Lee. (Historically, Lee proved to be a poor choice for eulogy, but she could not have known at the time, any more than her Colonial contemporaries did, that he was to establish treasonous contact with the British. His consuming envy at being passed over by the Continental Congress in the appointment of a commander-in-chief for the Colonial armies imparts a special irony to the conclusion of her poem, in which she has Lee speaking in

> . . . praise of Godlike Washington.
> Thrice happy chief! in whom the virtues join,
> And heaven-taught prudence speaks the man divine!)

In the general uncertainty of the times her own life was unsettled. She had occupied a unique sanctuary, part prison and part cloister, and now into this orderly pattern—flight, death, and pillage intruded, touching familiar places, people, and landmarks of her existence.

She was tossed about by the military tides. October, 1775, found her in Providence (where she wrote the letter to Washington), most probably there with John Wheatley's household, as a refugee from Boston, which then was in military contention. The Battle of Bunker Hill had been fought in Boston in June of that year. In its wake, the British reinforced their garrison and the Continental troops, encamped with Washington across the Charles River in Cambridge, laid siege to the city. Her visit to Washington's headquarters preceded by a few days the British evacuation of Boston on March 17, 1776, and by this time the Wheatley refuge had shifted to Chelsea. As the British troops left Boston, the Wheatley household returned, but some years later, in 1778, the British came back and the poet fled once more, now as a freed woman, to nearby Wilmington.

Her church was a casualty. In the early fame of her adolescent years the Old South Meeting House invited her baptism there, not being so carried away, however, as to permit the mark of servitude to be washed off in the sacramental ablution. She was christened simply as "Phillis, servant to Mr. Wheatley." By the time of her baptism the ritual admission of black slaves into the churches of their white masters was no novelty. Indeed, the practice is said to have dated back to 1641 when the first black, a woman, was baptized in Massachusetts. Cotton Mather, among others, encouraged the enlightenment and salvation of blacks; his evangelical fervor was joined with the practical consideration that it would be of some value to the masters to persuade the slaves that their condition was divinely ordained. An indispensable prerequisite, of course, was conversion of the slaves to a faith in the divinity. In the houses of the Lord arrangements were created in the image of the presumed divine order. Blacks were generally consigned to an "African corner" in the rear of the church, where they either stood or sat on hard benches. Sometimes they sat on the stairs, and in churches that boasted a gallery a remote section of it, commonly called "Nigger Pew" or "Nigger Heaven," was reserved for them. Phillis Wheatley and other black communicants of the Old South church sat in a gallery. Between her baptismal ceremony and the outbreak of the war the famous church served as a "sanctuary of freedom," Revolutionary colonists assembling in it to urge independence from Britain and to pray for victory of their cause. In the distemper of war British troops sacked the church. The notes of a contemporary describe the scene:

> The spacious *Old South Meeting House,* taken possession of by the Light Horse 17th Regiment of Dragoons commanded by Lieut. Col. Samuel Birch. The Pulpit, pews & seats, all cut to pieces & carried off in the most savage manner as can be expressed & destined for a riding school. The beautiful carved pew with the silk furniture of Deacon Hubbard's was taken down and carried to [blank space]'s house by an officer & made a hog stye.

(Directly following, but in a different hand, was this notation: "The above was effected by the solicitation of General Burgoyne.")

Even the Countess of Huntingdon, the London patron with whom the poet maintained a correspondence, ran afoul of the times, although her difficulties related, at most, only indirectly to the war in the Colonies, as it affected the internal politics of Britain and its established church. In 1779 an ecclesiastical court found that Lady Huntingdon's private episcopate, with its platoon of chaplains deployed and supported by her, was too unorthodox a venture to be countenanced within the confines of the Anglican communion. As a result she had to declare herself a dissenter. The incident was remote from the immediate world inhabited by Phillis Wheatley, but it fitted into the uncertain, crumbling texture of that world.

The poet's correspondence with her black friend Obour Tanner lapsed for four years. Between May 6, 1774 (when she reported the arrival of her 300 volumes from England) and May 29, 1778, there are no letters. Practical considerations, as well as psychological blocks, may have accounted for the long lapse: warring armies crisscrossed the postal routes, rendering the mails uncertain. After the long silence, in the first letter, with her typically cryptic reticence, the poet indicates the mood of the intervening years.

> The vast variety of scenes that have pass'd before us these 3 years past will to a reasonable mind serve to convince us of the uncertain duration of all things temporal, and the proper result of such a consideration is an ardent desire of, & preparation for, a state and enjoyments which are more suitable to the immortal mind.

This philosophical observation constituted almost all the letter. She apologized "for this hasty scrawl," pleading she had "but half an hour's notice" to get the letter to its carrier. Even making allowance for her haste and recognizing that she never was a chatty letter writer, the failure to mention two events in the preceding three months that had transformed her life seems incredible. She had just become a freedwoman and a wife. Although she had now acquired the name of Peters, the signature, in her clear hand, remained "Phillis Wheatley." It is not simply the omission of the facts that seems incredible; it is also the tone of sad reverie, unrelieved by any hint of animation, let alone joy, at being free and being a bride. But then she was poorly prepared for either freedom or matrimony, and neither was to turn out well for her. She might have already sensed this.

Her freedom was a consequence of a chain of events that could have entered into her contemplation of the transitory nature of all temporal

Dr Obour

By this opportunity I have the pleasure to inform you that I am well and hope you are so; tho' I have been silent, I have not been unmindful of you but a variety of hindrances was the cause of my not writing to you — But in time to Come I hope our correspondence will revive — and revive in better times. — pray write me soon for I long to hear from you — you may depend on constant replies — I wish you much happiness and am

D.r Obour your friend & sister
Phillis Peters

Boston May 10. 1779

Pr. Pap. VII. 278.

things. This chain was the mortality of the Wheatley household. In March, 1778, John Wheatley followed his wife to the grave. That same year Mary Wheatley Lathrop, the poet's childhood instructor, passed away. Nathaniel Wheatley, apparently siding with the Loyalists, had earlier moved to England, where he died in 1783.

The poet ceased to be a slave with the deaths of the elder Wheatley and his daughter in 1778, the year midway between the shot at Lexington and the surrender of Lord Cornwallis at Yorktown. Times were hard that year, hard enough for ordinary whites, and immeasurably harder for a newly freed black woman proficient only in intellectual pursuits and lacking any marketable skill other than the writing of poetry. It was a poor market for poetry, but even if it had been better, she was now a free woman of twenty-five, no longer the exotic African child prodigy, favored no more by influential white patrons whose own vanity was served by her success. The elements of patronizing curiosity and condescending sponsorship that entered into her earlier success in the white world no longer obtained. She was on her own with her blackness, and her formerly sheltered existence—the warm fire in her bedroom of a winter night, the lamp and pen at hand—was a poor apprenticeship for being cast adrift on the inflation-ridden, disordered economic waters of a country three years at war.

7
Marriage

Freed amid the chaotic uncertainties of war, and possibly oppressed by her unpreparedness to cope with life as she now faced it, was the marriage of Phillis Wheatley to John Peters on April 1, 1778, her first self-determined act as a freedwoman, a bid for security or an affirmation of defiant rebellion? In motivation it might have been either; in its practical effect the costs of defiance were far more tangible than any rewards of security.

Her closest (and probably only) black friend Obour Tanner, disapproved of the marriage. Indeed, sensitivity to this disapproval was curiously manifested in Phillis' letter of May 29, 1778. This is the letter, the first after a long hiatus, that omitted direct mention of the marriage, but contained an oblique reference to it in this sentence: "You will do me a great favour if you'll write me by every opp'ty— Direct your letter under cover to Mr. John Peters in Queen Street."

Both women had been acquainted with Peters for at least four years, for a reference to him cropped up in their correspondence four years earlier, the poet describing him as "a complaisant and agreeable young man." ("Complaisance" was also a word she used to describe her reception by the British nobility and gentry. Manifestly, she put great stock in the quality of courteous disposition to be obliging, agreeable, and compliant.)

The friend had other opinions of Peters. These were recorded many years later in a letter from Mrs. William Beecher to the Reverend Edward D. Hale (October 23, 1863). Mrs. Beecher, who secured the Wheatley letters from Miss Tanner, reported, "Obour informed me, pious soul that she was, with more than a gleam of that aristocracy of feeling, if not hauteur, which sits so curiously on those full-blooded creatures, that 'poor Phillis let herself down by marrying: yes, ma'am.'" Mrs. Beecher appended a qualification, which she tended to discount. "It is just possible, however," she wrote, "that this opinion might have originated in her own condition of single blessedness. but not probably so, as I heard the same thing expressed frequently by old people in Newport who remembered the circumstances."

Of the poet's friend Mrs. Beecher also wrote: "She died in an odor of sanctity, sometime in 1833 or '4, an uncommonly pious, sensible, and intelligent woman, respected and visited by every person in Newport who could appreciate excellence."

The descriptive phrases are apt for the Wheatley–Tanner correspondence; the seven Wheatley letters preserved are "uncommonly pious" and permeated with an "odor of sanctity," especially the first three letters, which are the longest, their quality being conveyed in the following passages:

> Inexpressibly happy should we be could we have a due sense of the beauties and excellence of the crucified Saviour. In his Crucifixion may be seen marvellous displays of Grace and Love, sufficient to draw and invite us to the rich and endless treasures of his mercy; let us rejoice in and adore the wonders of God's infinite Love in bringing us from a land semblant of darkness itself. . . . [May 19, 1772]

> Let us be mindful of our high calling, continually on our guard, lest our treacherous hearts should give the adversary an advantage over us. O! who can think without horror of the snares of the Devil. . . . [July 19, 1772]

The poet was eighteen when those letters were written. The letters become progressively briefer and less effusive in their religiosity, so that the final two, written after her marriage when she was past twenty-five, are devoid of any explicit reference to either God or the Devil.

How the two friends first met is not known, and there is no reference to their initial meeting in the extant correspondence. However, opportunities for encounter were readily present. Both were domestic slaves, and the Wheatleys, sufficiently affluent to vacation in Newport, even then a fashionable resort, would have brought their prize intellectual possession with them and would have mingled with such resident families as were sufficiently wealthy to own slaves. Once met, the shared distinctions and interests of the two slaves made for friendship. Both could read and write, both were deeply devout. The resultant friendship, as reflected in the correspondence, was flavored with the shared piety of Puritan church sisters. Indeed, the salutation in the first letter is "Dear Sister" and the signature in the last is of "your friend and sister."

In her alliance with Peters, the poet not only risked straining or rupturing her one enduring black friendship, she also transgressed against the values that informed that friendship. And since these values—such as Christian piety and Puritan propriety—were inculcated by white society and definitely approved by it, particularly for blacks, she also risked the alienation of white patronage. This is evidenced by Mrs. Beecher's observation that among the older residents of Newport the marriage was considered a letdown for the poet. More tangible evidence is offered by the poet's biographer, who conceded that the bridegroom was handsome and talented, but described him as "disagreeable," adding that "on account of his improper conduct, Phillis became entirely estranged from the immediate family of her mistress."

Free, black, and twenty-five, the poet hazarded or sacrificed much on the wedding altar: friendship, values, patronage. All that for this man named Peters, an elusive figure, a shadowy reflection mirrored in the disapproval of a sancitified black spinster and white Puritan gentility. If it is very difficult to reconstruct a credible image of Phillis Wheatley, it is impossible to do so with John Peters. She, a writer, left some traces of herself in her literary legacy, and subsequently, Abolitionists and literary historians, each for their own reasons, hunted for clues to her life and character. Peters left no written record and no one saw any reason to search for traces of his life.*

Aside from the poet's own fleeting reference to him as "complaisant and agreeable" and the intangible distaste conveyed by Obour Tanner, there are only the chance impressions of whites, most of these secondhand. What allowances for white prejudice are to be made in assessing the dominant image of him that endures after almost two centuries?

In the archives of the Massachusetts Historical Society Peters is described as "shiftless." There now is a familiar adjective, threadbare from excessive use, worn out in the constant pleading of the white man's burden; all those whites, foolish or noble, expending treasure and energy to scour the coasts of Africa for shiftless blacks, bringing them across the ocean to America's shores where, in their indolence, they could live off the bounty of their generous masters. In the record of the Historical Society's *Proceedings*, the same in which Peters is

---

* Henri Grégoire did search for traces of his death, however. He writes that Peters survived his wife by only three years and gives as his authority a letter from M. Giraud, consul of France in Boston, dated October 8, 1805; he further says that Giraud had known Peters (*De la Littérature des Nègres*, p. 262, n.).

dubbed shiftless by an apparent consensus, it is also reported that a Mr. Quincy "remarked that he well remembered the man . . . that he, at one time, practiced law, or professed to; and Mr. Quincy had met him in the courtroom."

"Practiced law, or professed to . . ." What a nice disdain. The white barrister perceiving presumption or impertinence in the black freedman, lacking the proper academic trappings, attempting the practice of law, this refined ritual of the Judeo-Christian ethic and Anglo-Saxon rationality. In other Colonies the appearance of a black legal practitioner, professed or not, would likely have aroused a more emotional hostility than disdain. In Massachusetts and her New England neighbors, as distinct from Colonies farther south, slaves had been only slightly (if significantly) less equal than freemen before the law. They could appear as plaintiffs against white defendants, even their masters; they could testify for either side in litigation that involved whites only; and one authority has found "much evidence" that in criminal prosecutions they were granted the same safeguards of due process as were whites. But, the same authority found, "Neither slaves nor free Negroes appear to have served as jurors in New England." If they could not be jurors, it is hardly likely that they served as lawyers.

In Massachusetts slavery was abolished in 1780, and it may be assumed that although the newly freed blacks had some experience as litigants and witnesses, there was no surfeit of black advocates, if there were any at all, to represent them before the tribunals of the state. In these circumstances Peters' venture into the breach, with whatever handicaps, may be interpreted as an example of admirable enterprise and initiative. It is not novel, of course, that what might seem like enterprise and initiative from the black viewpoint could appear as presumption and impertinence from the prevailing white vantage point.

A similar contradiction invests the reaction to Peters' many vocations. He is reported variously to have been a grocer, baker, barber, lawyer, and even a doctor (with respect to the last, it is said in the annals of the Massachusetts Historical Society that he "finally imposed upon the credulous by pretending to be a physician"). One chronicler reports that he wore a wig, sported a cane, "and in general felt himself superior to labor."

To a white society that was inclined to apply literally to blacks the biblical curse of Canaan ("Cursed be Canaan; a servant of servants shall he be unto his brethren"), the wig and cane and superior attitude toward menial labor were sufficient to brand Peters "disagreeable," as Mrs. Wheatley's kin found him to be. No more agreeable was his choice of vocations and their multiplicity. In another context such vocation-hopping might have been taken as a sign of brilliant versatility. In Peters, according to the prevailing judgments, it denoted an instability bordering on the shiftless (although, in a literal sense, an excess of shift is signified, rather than a lack of it).

Actually, Peters' vocational pattern might not have been due to any inherent character trait, either shiftlessness or versatility, but to practical circumstance. His marriage to the poet traversed the last years of the Revolutionary War and the first years of the peace that followed, an era of economic dislocation and inflation. The ailing economy worked its greatest cruelty upon blacks. They suffered not only from the general condition but also from the immediate economic consequences of the passage from bondage to freedom. As slaves they had been employed or hired out by their masters; as freemen they had to sell their own labor, a transaction in which they had no practiced skill, and they had to compete with white labor in a very tight job market. They had to do it, on occasion, in the face of insults, threats, and violence by white mobs in the streets of Boston. Economic hardship bred widespread discontent among ordinary whites, driving some to armed rebellion. If poor whites were driven to the breaking point of civil order, the economic situation must have been catastrophic for freed blacks, especially one who sought an alternative to menial labor. Frustrated in one venture, Peters might have been driven to another in an upward—or downward—spiral of desperation (depending upon one's view of his reputed venture into medicine).

One commentator describes him as a "fluent writer, a ready speaker, and an intelligent man" who "pleaded the cause of his brethren, the Africans, before the tribunals of the State." Surely such a description may be inferred from the circumstantial evidence of the very sparse record, more reasonably inferred than the stereotyped label "shiftless." The description can account for the poet's attraction to him and her apparent rashness in marrying him. In her particular condition of slavery she could not have been exposed to many black suitors, and most likely to none with his talents and intellectual achievements.

What might have been good about the marriage is buried. The only certainties that endure are its poverty and tragedy. She bore three children, and all died in infancy.

8

Tragedy and Death

Her first-born infant was dead and Phillis Wheatley was residing in a shell-wrecked house in Boston, a shelter she found for some six weeks with a niece of Mrs. Wheatley, a widow whose son had been killed in battle.

At this time she wrote to her friend Obour Tanner. The date, May 10, 1779, is about a year after her marriage and also about a year after her previous letter to Miss Tanner. This time the marriage is avowed simply in the signature, "Your friend & Sister, Phillis Peters." But there is no mention of the first-born infant, neither of the birth nor of the death. Nor does she reveal that she is in Boston alone, her husband having remained in Wilmington, where they had fled the year before.

There is only the most reticent allusion to her troubles: " . . . tho' I have been silent, I have not been unmindful of you but a variety of hindrances was the cause of my not writing to you. But in time to come I hope our correspondence will revive—and revive in better times." The correspondence did not revive—the better times did not come.

She tried to improve the times by turning to her one distinctive skill, the writing of poetry. A notice published in several editions of Boston's *Evening Post and General Advertiser* (October 30; November 6, 27; December 4, 11, and 18, 1779) read:

> Proposals, for printing by subscription a volume
> of Poems & Letters on various subjects, dedicated
> to the Right Hon. Benjamin Franklin Esq: One of
> the Ambassadors of the United States at the Court
> of France, By Phillis Peters.

The name Wheatley was dropped, but the image associated with it was retained in a description of the author as "a *female African*, whose lot it was to fall into the hands of a *generous* master and *great*

Tragedy and Death / 49

benefactor." The advertisement promised a volume of 300 pages, listing the titles of 33 poems, only one of which (that addressed to Washington) had been published before. Also promised were 13 letters, three of them to the Countess of Huntingdon and one to Dr. Benjamin Rush.*

The last several of the notices appeared during the Christmas season, but they tapped no springs of generosity. The project never came to fruition, presumably for lack of response. For one thing, the subscription price, twelve pounds ("neatly Bound & Lettered") and nine pounds ("sew'd in blue paper"), was inordinately high even in those inflationary times. Another factor is underscored by the poet's biographer. "It must be remembered," she wrote, "that this was a season of general poverty. Phillis's friends of former days were scattered far and wide. Many of them, attached to the royal interest, had left the country."

The notice attests that the poet continued to write, just as its failure attests that she could not make a living at it, or even supplement the family income. Despite this rejection, despite the void in the preserved record that shows nothing of hers in print between 1776 and the war's formal end in 1783, the poet continued to write.† Finally in 1784 three poems were published. The first was an elegy for the Reverend Dr. Samuel Cooper, one of the eighteen Bostonians of substance who had vouched for the authenticity of her published volume eleven years earlier. The second also was on a post-mortem theme, although this one could have touched a tender area of intimate experience; it was

---

* The three letters to the Countess of Huntingdon could well have been the three that were brought to light in 1972 (see Notes, p. 73). Two of these three letters have been cited on pages 32 and 33.

† Even as nothing of hers was being published, on August 4, 1778, a broadside appeared at Hartford, Connecticut, with "An Address to Miss Phillis Wheatly [*sic*], Ethiopian Poetess, in Boston, who came from Africa at eight years of age, and soon became acquainted with the Gospel of Jesus Christ." Consisting of twenty-one quatrains, each accompanied by a precise scriptural reference, the address was "composed by Jupiter Hammon, a Negro Man belonging to Mr. Joseph Lloyd, of Queen's Village on Long Island, now in Hartford." If the message ever reached its addressee, she might have derived some solace from these representative stanzas:

> Come, dear Phillis, be advis'd,
>   To drink Samaria's flood;
> There nothing that shall suffice
>   But Christ's redeeming blood.
>
> While thousands muse with earthly toys;
>   And range beyond the street,
> Dear Phillis, seek for heaven's joys,
>   Where we do hope to meet.

addressed to two parents on the loss of their infant son. By then her second child had died in infancy. There is no reference in the poem to her personal loss, and it is not possible to discern in the lines any special measure of emotion that is traceable to her own ordeal.

Perhaps the publication of the two poems on conventional themes (even the second appeared so to a general public that did not know and might not have cared about the element of personal tragedy suggested by it) was symptomatic of a return to a semblance of "normalcy" after the peace treaty of 1783. Indeed, the third poem celebrates the war's end. Running sixty-four lines, it speaks of British tyranny, of the foreign allies of the Revolutionary Army ("Gallia's power espous'd Columbia's Cause"), and of the destruction visited on the Colonies, but its ultimate note is struck in the following lines:

> Descending *Peace* and Power of War confounds;
> From every Tongue celestial *Peace* resounds:
> As for the east th' illustrious King of Day,
> With rising Radiance drives the Shades away,
> So Freedom comes array'd with Charms divine,
> And in her Train Commerce and Plenty shine.

By the time those lines appeared in print she had been dead for several days, dead in circumstances that mocked the poem's tranquil optimism.

Because of the family's poverty, because she could realize no income from her poetry, by then, as recorded in the Massachusetts Historical Society's annals, "she, poor Phillis, was obliged to earn her own subsistence in a common negro boarding-house." It was menial work, the kind of hard drudgery she had been spared in the Wheatley household, and now there was no dispensation to drop the broom or dustcloth when she was struck by a poetic line or image. Her physical frailty, noted by her purchaser when she stood in the slave market on a Boston dock at the age of seven, was a constant companion throughout her life, and now it was put to the test of hard labor, to which she was unaccustomed. There is no testimony of the toll taken by her labor, neither her own nor any by her contemporaries. There is only the mute testimony of her death at age thirty-one.

The lodgings at this "common boarding-house" for blacks and the other physical appointments were not embellished with the privileged comforts she had known in the Wheatley household, or as the London guest of Lady Huntingdon. All this belonged to another world. In her present world it mattered little that Washington, now retired to his Virginia plantation as the most celebrated citizen of the newborn

Tragedy and Death / 51

country, had once paid tribute to her genius, had said he would be happy "to see a person so favored by the Muses, and to whom nature has been so liberal and beneficent in her dispensations."

All this was of the past, and beneficent nature had turned cruel. As she lay dying in her squalid lodgings, her one intimate companion was her third-born infant, also mortally ill. The child died a few hours after the mother. Her husband was not at her side. The only clue as to his possible whereabouts when his wife and child were on their deathbed appears in the records of the Massachusetts Historical Society: ". . . in 1784 . . . he was forced to relieve himself of debt by an imprisonment in the county jail."

The time of Peters' imprisonment for debt is given with no more precision than that. The date of her death is pinpointed, December 5, 1784, and so is the utter solitude of it. It is not possible to ascertain with certainty whether he was in jail when she died; however, in the scant notices of her death and burial there is no hint of his presence.

She had written much about death, performing the office of professional mourner with her many elegies to famous white men of her day. Now an "Elegy on the Death of a Late Celebrated Poetess" appeared in the *Boston Magazine* in December, 1784, and it was signed "Horatio." Some of the lines read:

> . . . PHILLIS tun'd her sweet mellifluous lyre;
> (Harmonious numbers bid the soul aspire)
> While AFRIC'S untaught race with transport heard,
> They lov'd the poet, and the muse rever'd.
>   What tho' her outward form did ne'er disclose
> The lilly's white, or blushes of the rose;
> Shall sensibility regard the skin,
> If all be calm, serene, and pure within? . . .
>
> Free'd from a world of wo, and scene of cares,
> A lyre of gold she tunes, a crown of glory wears.
>   Seated with angels in that blissful place,
> Where she now joins in her Creator's praise . . .

A prosaic notice appeared in the *Independent Chronicle* on the Thursday after her death:

> Last Lord's Day, died Mrs. Phillis Peters (formerly Phillis Wheatley), aged thirty-one, known to the world by her celebrated miscellaneous poems. Her funeral is to be this afternoon, at four o'clock, from the house lately improved by Mr. Todd, nearly opposite Dr. Bulfinch's at West Boston, where her friends and acquaintances are desired to attend.

If all this indicated some interest in her passing, a later chronicler was to record that she "was carried to her last earthly resting-place, without one of her friends of her prosperity to follow her, and without a stone to mark her grave." Her child was buried beside her. No gravestone has ever been found.

A memento of her one-time glory and of her tragic end cropped up some forty years later. It was a copy of Milton's *Paradise Lost*, bearing on its flyleaf the inscription "Mr. Brook Watson to Phillis Wheatley, London, July–1773." This is in Phillis Wheatley's hand. Following, in another hand, is this inscription:

> This Book was given by Brook Watson, formerly Lord Mayor of London, to Phillis Wheatley—after her death was sold in payment of her Husband's debts.—It is now presented to the Library of Harvard University at Cambridge, by Dudley L. Pickman of Salem, March, 1824.

From an unmarked village in Africa she finally arrived at an unmarked grave in America. All that remains now is her literary work, an indistinct image of her, and a poor legacy of critical appraisals.

9
The Critics

Most illustrious of Phillis Wheatley's contemporary critics was Thomas Jefferson, part revolutionary and part Virginia patrician, offering his judgment of the poet in his latter guise.

"Religion indeed has produced a Phyllis Whately [sic]; but it could not produce a poet," Jefferson wrote in his *Notes on the State of Virginia* (1781–82). "The compositions published under her name are below the dignity of criticism." (Note the gratuitous skepticism even about the authenticity of her authorship in the phrase "published under her name.")

One reply to Jefferson came from Samuel Stanhope Smith, president of the College of New Jersey and a member of the American Philosophical Society. In "An Essay on the Causes of the Variety of Complexion and Figure in the Human Species" (1810), Dr. Smith wrote: "The poems of Phillis Whately, a poor African slave, taught to read by the indulgent piety of her master are spoken of with infinite contempt. But I will demand of Mr. Jefferson, or of any other man who is acquainted with American planters, how many of those masters could have written poems equal to those of Phillis Whately?"

In one sense, Dr. Smith's challenge begs the question. To say that Phillis Wheatley wrote better verse than American planters is not yet to say she was a poet. It is on the anthropological or sociological plane, rather than the literary, that Dr. Smith scores a point in contesting Jefferson's belief in the inherent inferiority of blacks.

A similar thrust came from a distinguished French contemporary, Henri Grégoire, prominent abbé in the French Revolutionary era and later a bishop. Among Grégoire's labors was a pioneer treatise, *De la Littérature des Nègres* (1808), in which he reproaches the American President. "Jefferson," he wrote, "appears unwilling to acknowledge the talents of Negroes, even those of Phillis Wheatley. . . ." To refute this prejudice, Grégoire cites the public response to the Wheatley volume of 1773 and offers selections from that volume. Among the first French responses to the volume of 1773 was one from Voltaire, who on occasion expressed no high regard for blacks. But in 1774 he wrote to Baron Constant de Rebecq: "Fontenelle was wrong in saying that there were never any poets among the Negroes; there is in fact one Negress who writes very good English verse."

As in the United States and France, so in the Germanic states there was a dissent from Jefferson's judgment among his scholarly contemporaries. Johann Friedrich Blumenbach, often referred to as the father of anthropology and an original investigator of ethnic categories, described the Wheatley volume as "a collection which scarcely anyone who has any taste for poetry could read without pleasure" (*Anthropological Treatises*, 1865).

In Britain, where her volume was comprehensively reviewed in major periodicals upon its publication in 1773 and where she was, at the time, the best known Colonial poet, the tide of opinion was stronger and more widespread. Not that there was an excessive praise for the poems (they "display no astonishing powers of genius," said one review, and another found them "merely imitative"), but sufficient merit was discerned in them to arouse concern "that this ingenious young woman is yet a slave."

Later, in 1788, Thomas Clarkson, a tireless antislavery agitator and leader in the successful campaign to halt British participation in the slave trade, protested, "if the authoress *was designed for slavery* . . . the greater part of the inhabitants of Britain must lose their claim to freedom."

This again is Abolitionist argument rather than literary criticism, but only a mindless literary purist would exclude it from an ultimate assessment of Phillis Wheatley. It was no small achievement for the African child to have become a modest standard in the conflict that dominated the first nine decades of this country's history and in a different form continues to this day. She did not aspire to become an Abolitionist symbol, but the role was thrust upon her just the same because she absorbed the New England culture so swiftly and so well as to be the peer of any white contemporary in its poetic expression.

The poetic world of Phillis Wheatley was circumscribed by rigid boundaries: by the decasyllabic line in the heroic couplet, by the ornate diction of neoclassicism and the ritualistic obeisances it prescribed. Within these boundaries of meter and language other narrowing constrictions defined the thoughts and emotions that inhabited her poetic world.

Conforming to neoclassical ritual, she constantly addressed the Muses, singly or collectively, in such terms as these: Celestial Muse, heavenly Muse, Muse divine, sacred Nine, indulgent Muse, gentle Muse, tuneful Nine, tuneful goddess, sacred choir, blooming graces.

Among representative invocations to the Muses were these: inspire my song; aid my high design . . . assist my strains . . . my arduous flight sustain—raise my mind to a seraphic strain . . . assist my labors —my strains refine . . . inspire—fill my bosom with celestial fire . . . lend thine aid, nor let me sue in vain.

In the effulgent imagery of neoclassicism the sky became ethereal space, ethereal train, starry train, heavenly plains, Phoebe's realms, orient realms, azure plain, empyreal skies. The earth appeared as this vast machine, rolling globe, dusty plain, dark, terrestrial ball.

The verse is peopled with figures from the Greek and Roman classics, literary and mythological; Homer and Virgil and Terence are here, as are gods and goddesses in profusion, and such place names as Helicon, Olympus, and Parnassus. Niobe appears much more often than any other figure from the Greco-Roman classics. Indeed, the tragedy of Niobe, as taken from Ovid's *Metamorphoses*, inspired her longest poem, running to 224 lines. Only one other is so ambitious, containing 2 lines less, and it, too, is derivative, transmuting into heroic couplets the biblical narrative of David and Goliath. These choices, Ovid and Samuel, attest to the primacy of the classics and the Bible in forming her poetical mind. The coincident and related influence of Puritanism probably accounts for a suggestive omission in her recital of David's conquest. She discreetly ignores the two biblical references to Goliath as an "uncircumcised Philistine."

Something of her style may be gleaned by juxtaposing a biblical passage and her rendition of it.

> And David spake to the men that stood by him, saying, What shall be done to the man that killeth this Philistine, and taketh away the reproach from Israel? for who *is* this uncircumcised Philistine that he should defy the armies of the living God?
> —I Samuel, 17:26

> Then Jesse's youngest hope:—"My brethern, say,
> "What shall be done for him who takes away
> "Reproach from Jacob, who destroys the chief,
> "And puts a period to his country's grief?
> "He vaunts the honours of his arms abroad,
> "And scorns the armies of the living God."
> —Phillis Wheatley

The biblical prose gains nothing in felicity or clarity by this rearrangement into neat columns, each line dressed, as it were, to the rhyming word on the right, and each marching to the beat of ten syllables. Only on rare occasions, as in the poems to her mistress, did she depart from this rigid form. In discussing Pope, the master of the form, George Saintsbury remarked that "artificiality . . . is the curse of the couplet," but in the same sentence he reiterated an admission that the curse "can be vanquished." Such conquest of artificiality depends not only upon prosodic skills in fashioning the mold, but even more upon the poetic sensibility that is poured into it. The more limited the sensibility, the more protrudent the artificiality. Phillis Wheatley's sensibility was indeed limited (although, as has often been repeated, hers was at least as fine as that of any Colonial poet). She was totally incapable, for example, of the playful sophistication in Pope's celebrated couplet:

> Nature and Nature's Laws, lay hid in Night:
> GOD said, *Let Newton be!* and all was Light.

More is contained here, however, than playful sophistication; there is not only an awareness of Newton but also a conception of his junior partnership with God. In some critical analysis, the decasyllabic couplet, which attained its apogee with Pope, is perceived as an appropriate reflection of a harmonious confluence between science and religion in the early eighteenth century. Newton's discovery of natural laws, the argument goes, was greeted by contemporaries as illumination of God's infinite wisdom in designing the universe; thus, scientific discernment of order in the apparent chaos of nature reinforced the faith in divine order. In turn, the mathematical precision of Pope's couplets was attuned to the discipline of science and the vision of a larger divine order to which it bore witness.*

Whatever the merit of such interpretive speculation in relationship to Pope, its applicability to Phillis Wheatley is somewhat vitiated because she was imitative. Certainly her own work does not reflect a comparable familiarity with the science of the age. Yet imitation also

---

* Of the many lines by Pope that celebrate the synthesis of nature and God the following may be cited:

> All are but parts of one stupendous whole,
> Whose body Nature is, and God the soul;

> All Nature is but Art, unknown to thee;
> All Chance, Direction which thou canst not see;
> All Discord, Harmony not understood;
> All partial Evil, universal Good.

All of this is encompassed in a climactic line:

> One truth is clear, WHATEVER IS, IS RIGHT.

involves an element of choice. That she chose Pope as her model is readily explicable by his fashionable pre-eminence at the time and the Colonial cultural dependence on England, but the New England ambience must also enter into the explanation. There was a manifest affinity between the Puritan culture, with its admixture of practicality and faith, and the conception of a universal order, created by God and corroborated by science.

Wheatley's vision of the universe was etched most explicitly in "Thoughts on the Works of Providence":

> ARISE, my soul; on wings enraptured, rise,
> To praise the Monarch of the earth and skies,
> Whose goodness and beneficence appear,
> As round its centre moves the rolling year . . .
>
> Adored forever be the God unseen,
> Which round the sun revolves this vast machine . . .
>
> Almighty, in these wondrous works of thine,
> What Power, what Wisdom, and what Goodness shine!
> And are thy wonders, Lord, by men explored,
> And yet creating glory unadored?

In Wheatley's verse there is, indeed, a harmony between the symmetrical pattern and the apprehension of a well-ordered universe. There is a third part in this harmony: the human condition. In her view, despite the oh-so-slight reproach in the final lines cited above, there is no serious discord between man and the divinely enacted laws of nature. Nor is there much concern with the contradictions in man. She definitely does not imitate Pope's notorious flights into misogyny, and for her man was not, as he was for Pope, "The glory, jest, and riddle of the world . . . Born but to die, and reas'ning but to err . . . Created half to rise, and half to fall." With her benign disposition she does not divide man into such equal parts; her emphasis is on human redemption, not on wickedness and folly.

Even in her rare venture into polemic, the adolescent "Address to the Atheist," sin and its wages are couched in the gentlest terms:

> Muse! where shall I begin the spacious field
> To tell what curses unbelief doth yield?
>
> If there's no heav'n, ah! whither wilt thou go
> Make thy Ilysium in the shades below?

There are scattered references in her work to divine wrath, and in her rendition of verses from Isaiah these lines appear:

> Great God, what lightning flashes from thine eyes!
> What power withstands if thou indignant rise?

But those are rare exceptions. She heralded God's wisdom and benevolence, not his vengeance. She was more prone to commend the human capacity for virtue than to scorn human susceptibility to vice. In the most personal testament to this credo, "On Being Brought from Africa to America," she wrote:

> 'TWAS mercy brought me from my pagan land,
> Taught my benighted soul to understand
> That there's a God—that there's a Saviour too:
> Once I redemption neither sought nor knew.
> Some view our sable race with scornful eye—
> 'Their color is a diabolic dye.'
> Remember, Christians, Negroes black as Cain
> May be refined, and join the angelic train.

In this striking illustration of the suffusive religiosity in her work, slavery is incidental to salvation, and there is only the mild admonition to Christians that blackness is no bar to the angelic train. In a sense, this is her own adaptation of Pope's ultimate truth: "Whatever is, is right." Given her time and place and her conditioning, there is not much good in reproaching her for an insufficiency of mind and spirit to transcend Pope's dictum.

Nor is there much point in belaboring the contradiction between the depiction of a well-ordered universe in well-ordered verse and the overturn of the established order by revolutionary upheaval. True, the American Revolution was much less convulsive than the French one that followed, but even for the American an approximation of the carmagnole would have been more appropriate than the minuet. That the cadence of her verse more closely resembled the latter, even when she attempted to respond to the times, as in the ode to Washington, is also an explicable fault. Art, and most especially the forms in which it is rendered, often lags behind history, and there is no reason why Wheatley should have been less laggard than others.

So her poetry did not rise to the greatness that truly expresses the spirit of an age, but such poetry is rare, and there was none of it in Colonial times.

Summarizing the initial debate about her more than a century later (1915), Arthur Schomburg, who was devoted to the appreciation and preservation of black culture, offered his own judgment. "There was no great American poetry in the 18th century," Schomburg wrote, "and Phillis Wheatley's poetry was as good as the best American poetry of her age."

There is a depressing element in the literary argument to the degree that it hinges on whether she was a nonpoet or a mediocre one. To be sure, it is relevant to determine what was par for the course in a given time and place, but if this establishes her as the peer of her contemporaries, it also defines a less flattering place in the longer span of literary history. In purely literary terms, viewing her as a poet in the abstract, criticism cannot break out of such narrow confines. But she was a *black* poet, and it is not enough to say that the quality of her verse was as good as that of her best white contemporaries. She also has to be assessed in terms of her own identity.

Not until recently has black scholarship attempted to assess her in explicitly black terms. The more traditional view among black scholars was presented by James Weldon Johnson, who wrote:

> Phillis Wheatley has never been given her rightful place in American literature. By some sort of conspiracy she is kept out of most of the books, especially the text-books on literature used in schools. Of course, she is not a *great* American poet—and in her day there were no great American poets—but she is an important American poet. Her importance, if for no other reason, rests on the fact that, save one, she is the first in order of time of all the women poets of America. And she is among the first of all American poets to issue a volume.

Johnson concluded:

> . . . her work must not be judged by the work and standards of a later day, but by the work and standards of her own day and her own contemporaries. By this method of criticism she stands out as one of the important characters in the making of American literature, without any allowances for her sex or her antecedents.

This does not differ in substance from what has been said in sympathetic white criticism. It is not a matter of making allowances for her antecedents (that is, for her blackness and her slavery), but of taking them properly into account. This is attempted explicitly by the black critic J. Saunders Redding and in a curiously inverse way by the black novelist Richard Wright.

In his lecture on "The Literature of the Negro in the United States,"

Wright read passages from the works of Alexander Pushkin and Alexandre Dumas and made the obvious point that nothing in those passages suggested they were written by Negroes. "The writings I've just read to you," he went on, "were the work of men who were emotionally integrated with their country's culture; no matter what the color of their skins, they were not really Negroes. One was a Russian, the other a Frenchman."

Then he posed the question: has any American Negro ever written like the Russian poet and the French novelist? And he replied that one, only one, had done so—Phillis Wheatley. "Before the webs of slavery had so tightened as to snare nearly all Negroes in our land," he elaborated, "one was freed by accident to give in clear, bell-like, limpid cadence the hope of freedom in the New World."

Wright sketched an idyllic picture of her condition—she "was accepted into the Wheatley home as one of the family, enjoying all the rights of the other Wheatley children. . . . she got the kind of education that the white girls of her time received." As a consequence of her integration, he argued, she was able to articulate a "universal note" that was in total harmony with the Colonial culture. Only later on, he said, did a distinct "Negro literature" take form as "a reservoir of bitterness and despair and infrequent hope . . . a welter of crude patterns of surging hate and rebellion." This literature was the product of slavery, of its oppressions, lacerations, and humiliations, but since Wheatley did not experience these, and indeed antedated them, she "was at one with her colonial New England culture," just as Pushkin and Dumas were with theirs.

But was she? Is the comparison with Pushkin and Dumas valid? She was born an African; the two men were born Russian and French. She entered her incarnation as Phillis Wheatley a naked child, a slave, forcibly abducted and cruelly transported. They were born into social status and moderate means. Pushkin, the son of landed gentry and a reluctant attendant at the czar's court, was three generations removed from the black slave who was his maternal grandfather. Dumas, the son of a French general, traced his lineage to a black grandmother and a wealthy French colonist in Haiti. Such genealogical traces of blackness in the Russian and the Frenchman had no real bearing on their lives or social status, although Pushkin expressed his awareness of it with a narrative about his great-grandfather. For Wheatley blackness was an ever-present reality that made its heavy imprint on her life.

Wright could say about Pushkin that "he went to the schools of his choice; he served in an army that was not Jim Crow; he worked where he wanted to; he lived where he wanted to. . . ." One may quibble that this last is not altogther true; Pushkin certainly did not live or work where he wanted to during his forced exile because he had displeased the czar but it is sufficiently true to underscore the contrast with Wheatley. (For that matter, Pushkin was punished, not for his great-grandfather's blackness, but for political and literary unorthodoxies that, in a sense, reinforced his oneness with the emergent Russian literature of the early nineteenth century.) Wheatley did not serve in any army, but she did serve a church where she was consigned, according to all the circumstantial evidence, to a "Nigger Pew" or "Nigger Heaven." She did not live or work where she wanted to, not even when she was free. The black lodging house was not her choice, and its designation as black indicates it was not simply a matter of means. Black ghettoes—situated near the docks or riverfronts or in alleys—had already sprouted in the New England of Wheatley's time.

A distinction may be drawn between Wright's general thesis and its specific application to Wheatley. The works of Dumas and Pushkin are impressive evidence to support his general argument that Negro literature is not rooted in some anthropological or biological mystique but is a socially and historically conditioned response to slavery and its legacies. This thesis is stated succinctly in a reference to George Moses Horton's poetry: it "does not stem from racial feeling, but from a social situation." Applying this analysis to Wheatley, the issue is, did Wright accurately comprehend the social situation that enveloped her, and the degree to which her poetic reflection of that situation was artificial or authentic?

Wright's sketch of Wheatley's condition is much too idyllic, and in spots careless. (For example, referring to her trip to England, he adds, "This was, of course, after the Revolutionary War.") To be sure, she was favored by kind and considerate masters, but the question still remains whether benign slavery, with its subtle discriminations, is the same as the freedom that Dumas and Pushkin enjoyed. It isn't, and the distinction makes dubious the identity that Wright discerned. It may be said that in Pushkin and Dumas, the oneness with the respective national culture was a natural extension of their social being. They wrote as a Russian or a Frenchman because this is, in fact, what they were. With respect to Wheatley, there is a nagging sense of contradiction between her cultural assimilation and her social situation, which was, despite its unique, individual features, also related to the general black condition.

It is to this contradiction that critic Redding addresses himself, arriving at a judgment that is the opposite of Wright's. What Wright hails as Wheatley's triumph, Redding deplores as her failure.

"There is no question but that Miss Wheatley considered herself a Negro poet: the question is to what degree she felt the full significance of such a designation," Redding wrote. "Certainly she was not a *slave poet* in any sense in which the term can be applied to many who followed her. She stands far outside the institution that was responsible for her. . . . Not once . . . did she express in either word or action a thought on the enslavement of her race; not once did she utter a straightforward word for the freedom of the Negro."

Redding quotes the lines from the poem to the Earl of Dartmouth:

>   I, young in life, by seeming cruel fate
>   Was snatched from Afric's fancied happy seat.

and comments:

>   "Seeming cruel" and "fancied happy" give her away as not believing either in the cruelty of the fate that had dragged thousands of her race into bondage in America nor in the happiness of their former freedom in Africa. How different the spirit of her work, and how unracial (not to say unnatural) are the stimuli that release her wan creative energies. How different are these from the work of George Horton who twenty-five years [sic] later could cry out with bitterness, without cavil or fear:
>
>   > "Alas! and am I born for this,
>   >   To wear this slavish chain?"
>
>   It is this negative, bloodless, unracial quality in Phillis Wheatley that makes her seem superficial, especially to members of her own race. . . . She is chilly. . . . First and last, she was the fragile product of three related forces—the age, the Wheatley household, and New England America. Her work lacks spontaneity because of the first, enthusiasm because of the second, and because of the third it lacks an unselfish purpose that drives to some ultimate goal of expression.

Harsh as it is, Redding's judgment points to obvious truths, which are insufficient for their very obviousness. It is easy enough to characterize the quality of personality mirrored in the poetry—negative, bloodless, unracial, chilly. The difficult question is what made her so. Redding replies that "she was the fragile product of . . . the age, the

Wheatley household, and New England America." This is not enough, for if you change the name of the household, you can say the same about any *white* product of middle-class or upper-middle-class New England. But Phillis Wheatley was *black* and this is the difference and also the contradiction: the contradiction between her blackness, which she recognized and never was permitted to forget by a thousand humiliations, and white, mercantile New England, whose world was never truly hers but whose values she seemed to accept. The same contradiction is suggested in Redding's remark that "she stands far outside the institution [of slavery] that was responsible for her. . . ." It would be more apt to say she was in the slave world but not truly of it. This is the contradictory reality that shaped the subjective raw material which was processed by the three forces Redding lists—the age, the Wheatley household, New England America. The vital element missing from his critical assessment is just what was fed into the triple-gear machine he specifies.

For this we must revert once more to the frail, near-naked girl of seven displayed for sale on a Boston dock. At that age the native African culture and values are not firmly imbedded, certainly not with the depth and strength needed to withstand the powerful assimilative impact of the new culture into which she is thrust. She has no defenses against Puritan certitude and self-righteousness, no resources for *critical* assimilation. To begin with she does not have a chance, and then two specific factors reinforce the process that is better described as inundation than assimilation.

One is her precocity, and the Wheatley's appreciation and cultivation of it. She is encouraged with patronizing kindness. Privileges and material rewards are compensation for piety and for poetry that respects the prevailing conventions in theme and style. It does no good to reproach an adolescent child for yielding to these attractive influences, especially when within herself there is no strong residue of any other influence or tradition. These are her formative years, and the subsequent years are so disordered and, as it turns out, so brief that they do not modify the initial mold.

This first factor is complemented by the second, her isolation from the society of slaves and its subculture. In this respect, Redding astutely notes the difference between her and George Moses Horton, who came a generation later. Unlike Wheatley, Horton was born a slave on a Southern plantation and there never was any ambiguity about his status or identity. Knowing clearly what he was, it was easier for him to determine what he ought to be.

From suckling infancy he absorbed the slave world subculture and its two interwoven strains: the African origins and the realities of slavery, of the master-slave relationship. Most of the original African slaves were, of course, older than Phillis Wheatley was at the time of her abduction, old enough to retain much of African culture and customs, and this retention, although diffused by time and diluted by the flow of strong stimuli from the immediate environment, remained a pervasive influence, handed down through the generations that shaped the Afro-American community. The more proximate influence was the master-slave relationship with its constant tensions, often bursting into open conflict, along with the contradictory accommodations of expediency. To survive as a human being in the context of slavery is no simple art, one not mastered without some training and without the folk wisdom born of community experience. Horton had such sustenance; Wheatley did not.

Further, as the first significant black writer in North America she faced a problem that her successors were to face. She wrote for a white audience, this being the audience created by the economics of publication and the realities of a market shaped by the affluence to buy and the literacy to consume. For the most part, her successors—even to this day—write for a white audience, but with the consciousness that on the sidelines and behind them black contemporaries are readers and critics. Removed as she was from black society, and possibly also because black reader-critics were so few then, no such critical restraints seemed to affect her.

"There is no question," Redding says, "but that Miss Wheatley considered herself a Negro poet: the question is to what degree she felt the full significance of such a designation." The answer is that all circumstances conspired to diminish, in her own perception, the significance of what she was. Therefore, she was diminished as a poet —and as a human being. For one reading her verse almost two centuries later, the almost reflex reaction is to scorn it and its creator. This response is misconceived and misaddressed. Anger would be more appropriate, and it ought to be addressed against the institution of slavery.

Perhaps the first significance of Phillis Wheatley is as a laboratory, test-tube exemplar of what was done to black identity, to black pride and self-awareness, by the institution of slavery with all its accessories of custom, culture, and ideological rationales. She was, after all, a first-generation African brought to these shores, and because she was articulate and had the opportunity to cultivate this gift, she left a singular record of this initial encounter between slave and master, between black and white, and its consequence in a setting of unusual circumstances.

She experienced this encounter under supposedly ideal conditions—a kind and understanding mistress, physical comforts, an opportunity to develop her talents—and this gives the experience its test-tube quality. It is not the typical experience of the mass of first-generation slaves, destined for hard, menial labor, for physical deprivation and a more oppressive regime. Such lacerations she was spared as long as she remained in her privileged sanctuary, placing in bolder relief the more refined inflictions she was not spared. What emerges most starkly from her poetry and her private correspondence is the near surgical, lobotomy-like excision of a human personality with warmth and blood and the self-assertiveness that is grounded in an awareness of one's self and relationship of this self to contemporary society. The religious moralisms that lard her letters to Obour Tanner are a poor form of sublimation, a substitute for the expression of emotional response to personal experience. The poems are vicarious in theme and imitative in style. In the circumstances it hardly could have been different. She was permitted to cultivate her intelligence, to develop her feeling for language and her facility in its use, but one thing she was not permitted to develop: the sense of her own distinct identity as a black poet. And without this there could be no personal distinction in style or the choice of themes that make for greater poetry. The barter of her soul, as it were, was no conscious contract. Enclosed by a cloying embrace of slavery at a tender age, alternatives did not at first intrude, and later, when she might have chosen one, she was drained of the will and perception to do so.

Involved here is not a condemnation of Puritanism as such, or of its general influence upon American thought and behavior. Such a judgment, sorting and weighing all the sins and virtues, belongs elsewhere. The concern here is more particular: it is the imposition of Puritanism upon a young African whose color and bondage placed her outside of those premises and compensations to which Puritanism appealed for its validity. Property and its acquisition, the temporal rewards of thrift and abstinence, were not for slaves (and this was true despite the rare and paradoxical exceptions in New England's relatively lenient slave regime). Even the restricted personal range of moral and social choice open to white Puritans was foreclosed to blacks. The full measure of self-reliance was a paradox in the essential dependency of slavery. What blacks were offered was the theology, disembodied from its temporal matrix. It is this that makes Phillis Wheatley's piety seem so empty and repellent, so classical an instance of glorifying celestial promise to tolerate terrestrial misery. For her Puritanism entailed a substitution of simulation for reality as in the most ironic of master-servant cliches, "We treated her like a member of the family. . . ." In sum, whatever Puritanism might have done for its white believers, it was grotesque imposition, amputating and mutilating, upon the black poet.

It may be idle to speculate about her true potential, but surely, given the evidence of her intelligence and talent, it is a permissible assumption that it was far greater than the one realized with the oppressive restrictions imposed upon the flowering of her own personality as a black poet. One school of American literary criticism dwells on the aptitude of American society to frustrate its writers and truncate their growth. If this is a great American tradition, then few, if any, writers were so warped by it as was Phillis Wheatley.

In her case, the primary warping influence was slavery. It mutilated her. Having inflicted spiritual mutilation, its aftermath went on to achieve her physical destruction. Sketchy as it is, the preserved record of her final years—the cold neglect, the poverty, the drudgery, the infant deaths, and finally the circumstances of her own death at age thirty-one—is a searing indictment of slavery, of the cruel nexus of the white-black relationship in the evolution of American society.

Phillis Wheatley is not a great figure in American literary history, but she is a tragic one. It is the tragedy rather than the poetry of Phillis Wheatley that has the more enduring relevance for American life. Elements of the tragedy have far more contemporary urgency than is evoked by the echoes of her poetry. To those in the present black generations, who are involved in the assertion and definition of black identity, in the rekindling of black pride, she can represent, with rare purity, the initial deprivation of that which they seek to regain.

To the contemporary black militant, the poetry will indeed seem "superficial" and "chilly," assuming he reads it at all, and there is little reason to believe he will. The tragedy should be more germane. If this is so, then it is conceivable that in striking some militant blow for freedom, in a spirit of retribution and poetic justice, he might say, "This one is for you, baby."

Notes

The source used for most of the biographic facts concerning Phillis Wheatley is *Memoir and Poems of Phillis Wheatley* (Boston: Geo. W. Light, 1834). This *Memoir* by Margaretta Matilda Odell is closest in time and place to the life of Phillis Wheatley and concludes with a statement as to its authenticity:

> They [the facts] were derived from grand-nieces of Phillis's benefactress, who are still living, and have a distinct and vivid remembrance of their excellent relative and her admired protegee.
>
> Their statements are corroborated by a granddaughter of that lady, now residing in Boston; who, though much younger than the individuals alluded to, recollects the circumstances of Phillis's visiting at the house of her father. . . .
>
> Lastly, the author of this Memoir is a collateral descendant of Mrs. Wheatley, and has been familiar with the name and fame of Phillis from her childhood [pp. 28–29].

Vernon Loggins, author of the scholarly and pioneering work *The Negro Author: His Development in America to 1900* (New York: Columbia University Press, 1931, 1959; Port Washington, New York: Kennikat Press, 1964), is of the opinion that "the main source for the great number of biographical sketches of Phillis Wheatley is the 'Memoir' which prefaces the 1834 edition of her Poems, published by George W. Light, Boston" (pp. 369–370, n. 41).

This *Memoir* (hereafter cited as Odell, *Memoir*) first appeared as anonymous. It seems for some time to have been mistakenly attributed to B. B. Thatcher, *Memoir of Phillis Wheatley, A Native African and a Slave* (Boston: Geo. W. Light, 1834), but was finally correctly identified as the work of Margaretta Matilda Odell, the "collateral descendant" mentioned above, by a letter from the publisher, Light, to Charles Deane, the editor of the *Letters of Phillis Wheatley, the Negro-Slave Poet of Boston* (Boston: Privately Printed, 1864), in which the publisher states that he remembers the manuscript for the *Memoir* "as being in Miss Odell's handwriting" (p. 8, n.). Thatcher's *Memoir* is apparently based on that of Odell.

No attempt will be made at this point to list the various biographical sketches; reference to them will appear later under the appropriate chapter notes. None, however, is so complete as the Odell *Memoir*.

Julian D. Mason, Jr., editor, with introduction, *The Poems of Phillis Wheatley* (Chapel Hill: University of North Carolina Press, 1966), has made available all of her poems (save perhaps one), which in their earlier editions are extremely rare, and her extant letters (except for those recently discovered). The bulk of her poetry was published in London "from the original manuscript, by Arch. Bell, Aldgate" in 1773, and subsequently in Boston in 1834, entitled *Poems on Various Subjects, Religious and Moral* (hereafter cited as Wheatley, *Poems*); a third edition was published in Boston in 1838 (this is the edition that contains George Moses Horton's *Hope of Liberty*, the publishers having changed his title to *Poems of A Slave*). In this study references to the poems in the 1773 edition are to Odell, *Memoir*, mentioned above. References to poems outside that volume, and to her letters, appear in the chapter notes.

The stanza quoted from Phillis Wheatley in the Introduction is from "To the Church and Congregation assembling in Brattle-Street, the following Elegy, Sacred to the Memory of their late Reverend and Worthy Pastor, Dr. Samuel Cooper, is, with the greatest Sympathy, most respectfully inscribed by their Obedient, Humble Servant, Phillis Peters. Boston, Jan. 1784." It is a broadside, and may be found in the New-York Historical Society; and in Mason, *Poems,* pp. 90–92.

1. The Poet and the General

The chronicler mentioned in this chapter is Benson J. Lossing, *The Pictorial Field-Book of the Revolution,* 2 vols. (New York: Harper & Bros., 1851), 1:556. Lossing says the poet visited Washington "a few days before the British evacuated Boston" (ibid.). Washington's courteous reception of the poet is also referred to by James Weldon Johnson, editor, *The Book of American Negro Poetry* (New York: Harcourt, Brace & Co., 1922), p. xxiv, and by Mason, *Poems,* p. xv.

A good source for the exchange of correspondence between the poet and Washington is Walter H. Mazyck, *George Washington and the Negro* (Washington: Associated Publishers, 1932), pp. 48–53. He is the historian who comments on the unusual distinction Washington accorded the poet by his invitation (p. 55).

The speculations regarding Washington's awareness or nonawareness of his correspondent's identity arise from the fact that the original of his letter to her has been lost. His file copy is contained in the Varick Transcripts in the Library of Congress. Richard Varick had been given the task of copying into ledgers all of Washington's voluminous correspondence, and Varick's copy is listed under the subject "To Mrs. Phillis Wheatley," and the copy itself is addressed to "Mrs. Phillis." However, most authorities have arrived at agreement that the letter was addressed to "Miss Phillis." Mazyck wonders if Varick made a copying mistake; his inclination is to agree with the majority (ibid., pp. 53–55). See also Jared Sparks, *The Writings of George Washington*, 12 vols. (Boston: Russell, Odiorne & Metcalf, 1834–1837), 3:297–298; and Worthington Chauncey Ford, *The Writings of George Washington*, 14 vols. (New York: G. P. Putnam's Sons, 1889–1893), 3:440–443. The 1835 (Boston: Light & Horton) and the 1838 (Boston: Isaac Knapp) editions of her *Poems* contain the letter, and the salutation is "Miss Phillis," although there are minor differences in wording and punctuation in the body of the letter (pp. 36–37 and p. 37, respectively).

A discussion of whether Phillis Wheatley wrote "first in peace" or "first in place" in her poem to Washington is presented by Mazyck, who finds Charles Frederick Heartman, ed., *Phillis Wheatley (Phillis Peters), Poems and Letters* (New York: Printed for Charles Frederick Heartman, n.d.— Heartman's Historical Series No. 8), in error in ascribing "first in peace" to Phillis Wheatley. Mazyck says he obtained the version in his book ("first in place") from the *Pennsylvania Magazine* in which the poem was first published, and bolsters his argument by noting that a handwritten lower case "L" with a short loop may easily be mistaken for a lower case "e" (*Washington and the Negro*, pp. 49–50). He could have further strengthened his argument had he read Heartman's Historical Series No. 7, entitled *Phillis Wheatley (Phillis Peters): A Critical Attempt and Bibliography of Her Writings* (New York: For the Author, 1915), in which Heartman quotes the poem and uses the phrase "first in place" (pp. 20–21).

On the subject of Lord Dunmore's proclamation, and Washington's changing attitudes toward admitting slaves into the Continental Army, the following sources were used: Mazyck (*Washington and the Negro*, pp. 39–46, 74); Carl Van Doren, *Secret History of the American Revolution* (New York: Viking Press, 1941), p. 24; and Herbert Aptheker, *The Negro in the American Revolution* (New York: International Publishers, 1941), pp. 30–41.

2. From a Fancied Happy Seat

There has been some disagreement among scholars as to whether it was John Wheatley or Susannah Wheatley who personally chose the little girl on the Boston docks.

The Odell *Memoir* states that Mrs. Wheatley "visited the slave market that she might make a personal selection from the group of unfortunates offered for sale" (p. 1). Benjamin Brawley, in *Negro Builders and Heroes* (Chapel Hill: University of North Carolina Press, 1937), writes: "Her bright eyes attracted the attention of Susannah Wheatley, wife of John Wheatley, a tailor, who desired to have a girl who might be trained as her personal attendant. Accordingly, she was purchased, taken home, and given the name of Phillis" (p. 19). He repeats this statement in *The Negro Genius: A New Appraisal of the Achievement of the American Negro in Literature and the Fine Arts* (New York: Dodd, Mead & Co., 1937; New York: Biblo & Tannen, 1966), p. 20.

The above references seem clearly to indicate that although John Wheatley "bought her" in the sense that he paid the bill, it was Mrs. Wheatley who visited the slave sale and made her own selection. Those who differ may well be caught up in semantics, since they repeat what Odell wrote at the beginning of her *Memoir*—"She was purchased by Mr. John Wheatley" (p. 1)—disregarding the remainder of the paragraph that relates Mrs. Wheatley's visit to the slave market and her personal selection. Loggins (*The Negro Author*, p. 17) says she "was bought by Mr. John Wheatley." J. Saunders Redding (*To Make A Poet Black* [Chapel Hill: University of North Carolina Press, 1939], refers to "her purchase by John Wheatley," p. 8). Julian D. Mason, Jr., says she was "bought by John Wheatley" (*Poems*, p. xi).

For a discussion of "refuse" slaves, see Lorenzo Johnston Greene, *The Negro in Colonial New England, 1620–1776* (New York: Columbia University Press, 1942; reissued, Port Washington, N.Y.: Kennikat Press, 1966), p. 35. A footnote to his discussion cites Benjamin Brawley, *Early Negro American Writers* (Chapel Hill: University of North Carolina Press, 1935, p. 31), as saying that Phillis Wheatley was among such "refuse" purchases.

The Odell *Memoir* also contains the reference to the poet's single remembrance of her native land, her mother's daily ritual at sunrise (pp. 10–11).

The conjecture regarding her probable African tribal origins arises from the following: Carter G. Woodson writes that "The colonists imported . . . some Gambia Negroes, prized for their meekness" and describes one "Job . . . a Fula, brought from Futa in what is now French Senegal. He could write Arabic and repeat the whole Koran." He states that the Senegalese were "the most intelligent of the Africans . . . with an infusion of Arabic blood" (*The Negro in Our History*, 6th ed. rev. [Washington: Associated Publishers, 1931], pp. 70, 69). Henri Grégoire mentions the "Foulahs" among whom, he says, "the Islams . . . introduced books . . . mostly concerning religion and jurisprudence" (*De la Littérature des Nègres* [Paris: Chez Maradan, Libraire, 1808], p. 158). Mason cautions against finding a reference in one of her poems ("Phillis's Reply to the Answer in our last by the Gentleman in the Navy") to Gambia as a specific mention of her homeland, regarding it as simply a "poetic pose" (*Poems*, p. 87 and n. 16). Daniel P. Mannix has a good discussion on the various peoples of Senegambia and other regions from which slaves were abducted in *Black Cargoes* (New York: Viking Press, 1962). Although John Wheatley in his letter to the publishers that prefaces the first edition of Wheatley, *Poems*, says merely that she "was brought from Africa to America," most of the biographical sketches state specifically that she was from Senegal; among them are: Benjamin Brawley (*Early Negro Writers*, p. 31); Sterling A. Brown, Arthur P. Davis, Ulysses Lee, editors (*The Negro Caravan* [New York: Dryden Press, 1941], p. 283); Mason, however, says that although reference has been made to Senegal as her native land, this cannot be substantiated (*Poems*, p. xii, n. 2).

Her own assumption that she was kidnapped is contained in her poem addressed to the Earl of Dartmouth, in which she writes that she "was snatched from Afric's fancied happy seat," and in the title, but not the body, of another poem, "On Being Brought from Africa to America." Other biographers vary between "kidnapped" and "brought."

Benjamin Brawley quotes from Gustavus Vassa's *The Interesting Narrative of the Life of Oloudah Equiano, or Gustavus Vassa* (*The Negro Genius: A New Appraisal of the Achievement of the American Negro in Literature and the Fine Arts* [New York: Biblo & Tannen, 1966], pp. 29–30).

A description of the slave pens in Africa and a discussion of the "tight" and "loose" pack theories are found in Mannix (*Black Cargoes*, pp. 76, 106).

The conclusion as to the child's age is quoted from Odell (*Memoir*, pp. 9–10).

3. A Child Prodigy

All the quotations, the biographic facts (save one), and the estimate of Boston society in the poet's time are contained in the Odell *Memoir* (pp. 10–26, *passim*). Although most authorities agree she had developed her poetic talent by the time she was fourteen, there is some disagreement as to her age when she first began composition in that form. Odell says she commenced her career as soon as she could write a legible hand (p. 16); J. Saunders Redding has her writing her first poems at the age of about ten and a half years (*To Make a Poet Black*, p. 8); "We hear that she wrote her first poem at the age of thirteen, according to some even earlier" (Heartman, *Wheatley: A Critical Attempt*, p. 10); Mason estimates "It is generally supposed that Phillis was about thirteen years old when she began to try her hand at poetry" (*Poems*, p. xiii).

Anne Bradstreet—The Tenth Muse, by Elizabeth Wade White (New York: Oxford University Press, 1971), is the principal source for the remarks about that poet.

Lorenzo Johnston Greene provides the facts relating to Lucy Terry (*The Negro in Colonial New England*, pp. 242–243, 248, 314).

Benjamin Brawley's *Negro Builders and Heroes* is the main reference for the discussion of Benjamin Banneker (pp. 25–29).

The critic who referred to Pope's "viperish disposition" is George Saintsbury, *A History of English Prosody, From the Twelfth Century to the Present Day*, 3 vols. (New York: Russell & Russell, 1961), 2:48.

"An Address to an Atheist" is not included in Wheatley, *Poems;* it is very likely one of her many fugitive poems circulated privately. The manuscript bears on its face, in handwriting distinct from hers, "by P. Wheatley at the Age of 14 Years—1767." It is to be found in the Warren File, Robie-Sewall Papers, 1611–1789, at the Massachusetts Historical Society.

4. Poetry and Fame

The full title of her elegy to the Rev. George Whitefield appeared in various broadsides; in the first edition of her *Poems* the title was simply "On the Death of the Rev'd Mr. George Whitefield.—1770." Both Mason and Loggins give October 11, 1770, as the first extant announced publication date of the elegy (Whitefield's death occurred September 30, 1770), for the *Massachusetts Spy* advertised it as "this day . . . published." Mason's opinion is that it may have been published prior to the newspaper's announcement; he further states it was republished as a broadside "once in Newport, four more times in Boston, once in New York, and once in Philadelphia" (*Poems*, pp. 66, no. 4, 67). Loggins' conclusion is that the elegy was published in Boston, Philadelphia, and New York in six different editions within a few months (*The Negro Author*, pp. 16, 369, n. 40). Loggins is the authority that the elegy was published in London in two editions (ibid., p. 18).

In Wheatley, *Poems*, a footnote to the elegy refers to the Countess of Huntingdon "to whom Mr. Whitefield was chaplain." Brawley devotes a paragraph to the patron-chaplain relationship in *Negro Builders and Heroes* (p. 20), and mentions it again in *The Negro Genius* (p. 21); Loggins refers to it also (*The Negro Author*, pp. 18–19).

Samuel Johnson's estimation of George Whitefield is quoted from George Birbeck Hill, *Boswell's Life of Johnson*, 6 vols. (New York: Bigelow, Brown & Co., n.d.), 2:91. The characterization by Pope of Whitefield is in *The Dunciad*, Book the Second, lines 253–258. Benjamin Franklin's story appears in his *Autobiography* (Garden City, N.Y.: Doubleday, Page & Co., 1922), pp. 152–153. Loggins quotes Gustavus Vassa (*Interesting Narrative*, p. 4).

The testimony taken in connection with the Boston Massacre is from *Transcript, The Trial of the British Soldiers of the 29th Regiment on Foot, for the Murder of Crispus Attucks, Samuel Gray, Samuel Maverick, James Caldwell, and Patrick Carr* (Boston: Wm. Emmons, 1824), pp. 9–10, 15. This interesting document is lodged at the Massachusetts Historical Society. The inquest referred to bears the title *Inquest on Michael Johnson alias Crispus Attucks,* and is a reprint from the New England Historical and

Geneological Register, October, 1890, to be found in the Thomas Collection, Massachusetts Historical Society.

The letter from the poet to the Earl of Dartmouth is in the Wetmore Collection on Rhode Island Commerce, 1771–1772, Massachusetts Historical Society; it may also be found in Mason (*Poems*, pp. 110–111).

The references here made to Lord Dartmouth's relation to the colonies are in B. D. Bargar, *Lord Dartmouth and the American Revolution* (Columbia, S.C.: University of South Carolina Press, 1965), pp. 43, 57–58, 69.

Phillis Wheatley's poem to King George contains a footnote that her reference is to the repeal of the Stamp Act.

It was Sir Nathaniel William Wrazell who called Dartmouth the "Psalm-Singer" (Barger, ibid., p. 10, n. 4; Bargar is also the authority for Whitefield's characterization of Dartmouth, ibid., p. 13, n. 23).

That a slave poet should have addressed such a poem to Lord Dartmouth contains a certain irony since, in 1775, commenting on the opposition by the North American colonists to the growing slave trade, he said: "We cannot allow the Colonies to check or to discourage in any degree a traffic so beneficial to the nation" (E. D. Morel, *The Black Man's Burden* [New York: Monthly Review Press, 1969], p. 21). The quoted phrases following the poem are from Redding (*To Make a Poet Black*, p. 10). The other poet of African origin referred to is Pushkin.

5. Triumph in London

The subject of Phillis Wheatley's ill health that resulted in her trip to England is discussed in Odell, *Memoir* (p. 17); and in most of the subsequent biographical sketches, among them Mason (*Poems*, p. xiv); Loggins (*The Negro Author*, p. 18); and Brawley (*The Negro Genius*, p. 21).

The letter from Susannah Wheatley and the two letters from Phillis Wheatley to the Countess of Huntingdon are to be found in the *Journal of Negro History*, Vol. LVII, No. 2, April, 1972, pp. 212–215. In a preface to these letters Sara Dunlap Jackson wrote they were "recently discovered" among the papers of the Countess in the custody of the archivist at Churchill College, Cambridge, England.

There are seven other letters extant from the poet; these are to Obour Tanner (the first two addressed as "Arbour Tanner"); they may also be found in the printed *Proceedings of the Massachusetts Historical Society*, vol. 7, 1863, pp. 273–278 (hereafter cited as *Proceedings;* the other references to the *Proceedings* appear at pp. 267–279, *passim*). Mason contains the Tanner letters (*Poems*, pp. 103–109), as do Deane (*Letters*) and Heartman (*Wheatley, Poems and Letters*).

The attestation addressed "To the Public" contains a footnote: "The words 'following page,' allude to the contents of the Manuscript copy, which are wrote at the Back of the above Attestation." Evidently the signatories were taking no chances that an unauthorized poem would be slipped in.

John Wheatley's letter to the publisher is dated "Boston, November 14th, 1772," an indication that the volume was in preparation before the poet's visit to England.

The exclamation attributed to Mrs. Wheatley's reaction to the "elegant engraving" is in the Odell *Memoir* (p. 18).

The letter asking Obour Tanner to get subscriptions is dated "Boston, Oct. 30, 1773."

Nathaniel B. Shurtleff published a short biography of the poet, "Phillis Wheatley, The Negro-Slave Poet," in the *Boston Daily Advertiser* for December 21, 1863, in which he says that Mrs. Wheatley died at age sixty-five on March 3, 1774; Mr. Wheatley, at age seventy-two, on March 12, 1778; Mary Wheatley Lathrop, at age thirty-five, on September 24, 1778; and Nathaniel Wheatley, at age forty, in the summer of 1783 in England. This biography was reprinted in the *Proceedings* (pp. 270–272, n.).

The poet's letter informing Obour Tanner of Mrs. Wheatley's death was dated March 21, 1774, eighteen days after the event.

6. War, Revolution, Freedom

Wheatley's poem on General Lee "seems to have remained in manuscript form until it was printed in the *Proceedings of the Massachusetts Historical Society*, 1863–64" (Loggins, *The Negro Author*, p. 21); "The Massachusetts Historical Society reports that it does not have the manuscript of this poem" (Mason, *Poems*, p. 97, n. 22). Mason reprints the poem in full (ibid., p. 97). There is an interesting discussion of Lee's treachery in Van Doren (*Secret History*, pp. 28–36).

That the poet was a freedwoman by the time she went to Wilmington with her husband in 1778 is evidenced by her marriage license, which, on April 1, 1778, describes her as a "free negro" (Loggins, *The Negro Author*, pp. 19, 371, n. 53). However, there is disagreement as to when she received her freedom. Benjamin Rush, *An Address to the Inhabitants of the British Settlements in America, Upon Slave-Keeping* (Boston, 1773), p. 2, n., wrote: "There is now in the town of Boston, a Free Negro Girl about 18 years of age . . ." (quoted in Mason, *Poems*, pp. xlii–xliii); Odell, *Memoir*, says, "We cannot ascertain that she ever received any formal manumission" (p. 12); Loggins says "she was still regarded as a slave" when she left for England, but concludes that upon the death of John Wheatley (March 12, 1778) "she had undoubtedly by this time received her manumission (*The Negro Author*, pp. 18–19); Brawley says, "Mrs. Wheatley, not willing to have her go [to England] as a slave, saw to it that she was manumitted before she sailed" (*Negro Builders*, p. 20); Mason provides further evidence that she was not yet freed when she went to England, for he quotes from *The Monthly Review* of London, December, 1773, "The people of Boston boast themselves chiefly on their principles of liberty. One such act as the purchase of her freedom, would, in our opinion, have done them more honor than hanging a thousand trees with ribbons and emblems" (*Poems*, xxxvii). The matter seems definitely to be settled by the internal evidence (John Wheatley's letter to the publisher dated November 14, 1772, in which he said, "This Relation is given by her Master, who bought her, and with whom she now lives" [Odell, *Memoir*]), and by the Attestation to the public with its eighteen signatories, among them "Mr. John Wheatley, (the Master)," which states she had been brought "an uncultivated barbarian from Africa, and has ever since been, and now is, under the disadvantage of serving as a slave in a Family in this Town." If further evidence is needed, there are her letters to the Countess of Huntingdon, in which the poet refers to her arrival in London "with my young master" (June 27, 1773). Shurtleff gives still another version of the circumstances of her freedom, saying, ". . . it is supposed that Mrs. Lathrop, who became her owner at the decease of her father, gave Phillis her freedom" (*Proceedings*, p. 272, n.).

Authorities agree as to the date (August 18, 1771) and the name and designation by which the poet was received as a communicant in the Old South Meeting House, then under the stewardship of the Reverend Doctor Joseph Sewall; some point to the fact that she represented an exception to the rule that slaves were not to be baptized there, Brawley, for instance, writing that it was "said later that 'her membership in the Old South was an exception to the rule that slaves were not baptized into the church'" (*Early Negro Writers*, p. 32). Others omit reference to this fact when describing her baptism (Odell, *Memoir*, p. 13; Shurtleff, *Proceedings*, p. 271, n.; Loggins, *The Negro Author*, pp. 18, 370, n. 45; Mason, *Poems*, p. xiv). However, Lorenzo Johnston Greene makes the definite finding that the admission of slaves to white churches began as far back as 1641 and was no novelty in the New England communities (*The Negro in Colonial New England*, pp. 257, 268). He is also the authority for the statement regarding segregation in the churches (ibid., p. 283) and for the fact that the Old South church had a gallery for black converts (ibid., p. 284).

The quotation describing the depredation of the Old South Meeting House is in the Miscellaneous Collection, 1775, Massachusetts Historical Society.

Bargar discusses the circumstances leading to the Countess of Huntingdon's becoming a dissenter (*Lord Dartmouth*, p. 9).

7. Marriage

Odell tries to remove "unworthy or mercenary motive" behind the marriage with a somewhat more flattering picture of Peters than appeared in the earlier pages (*Memoir*, pp. 28–29).

The letter from Mrs. Beecher to the Rev. Hale appears in the *Proceedings* (pp. 267–269, n.).

Heartman speculates on the acquaintance of the poet and Obour Tanner when he describes the latter as "a colored lady friend who was a servant in

Newport and who probably had much the same fate, perhaps had even been transported on the same ship" (*Wheatley: A Critical Attempt*, p. 12).

Most of the characterizations of John Peters are from Odell, *Memoir*, which others have followed; one exception is that of Arthur A. Schomburg, who found him to have considerable intellectual accomplishments (introduction, "Appreciation" to Heartman, *Wheatley, Poems and Letters*, p. 12). The various references to Peters in the Massachusetts Historical Society are to be found in the *Proceedings*.

For a discussion of the legal aspect of slaves vis-à-vis the courts, see Lorenzo Johnston Greene (*The Negro in Colonial New England*, pp. 179–186). He is also the source for the difficulties of black freedmen in securing work (ibid., p. 304).

Henri Grégoire has some interesting comments about Peters. He wrote: ". . . nobody was astonished to see her husband, who was a grocer, become a lawyer under the name of Dr. Peter, and plead cases on behalf of Negroes in the tribunals. The reputation he had led him to fortune." Grégoire also offers his own concept of their married life: "The sensitive Phillis, who had been brought up . . . as a spoiled child, understood nothing about running a household, and her husband wanted her to occupy herself with that task; he began with reproaches, after which followed ill treatment which was so constant that his wife died of grief" (*De la Littérature des Nègres*, pp. 260–261). Perhaps Grégoire knew something that Odell did not, for she writes: "We know little of Phillis in her relations of wife and mother" (*Memoir*, p. 21). But Grégoire errs when he says that they had but one child (p. 262). Mr. Quincy's remark concludes the meeting of the Massachusetts Historical Society that was devoted to the subject of Phillis Wheatley (*Proceedings*, p. 279).

8. Tragedy and Death

The account of the poet's return to Boston after the British evacuated it, and the description of the economic scene in that city at the time are in Odell (*Memoir*, p. 22).

That she continued to write after the Revolution is evidenced by three poems: an elegy on the death of the Reverend Samuel Cooper, published as a pamphlet in January, 1784; one on the death of an infant, published in *The Boston Magazine*, September, 1784; and "Liberty and Peace," published posthumously as a pamphlet in 1784, the only poem of this period that suggests a warlike theme. The text of these three poems is printed in Mason (*Poems*, pp. 93, 90, 95, respectively). That she had been writing during this period is indicated by the "Proposals" advertised in 1779 (Loggins, *The Negro Author*, pp. 21, 372, n. 61; Mason, *Poems*, pp. 111–113, 111, n. 4).

Jupiter Hammon's poem to Phillis Wheatley may be found in *America's*

First Negro Poet: The Complete Works of Jupiter Hammon of Long Island, editor with introduction by Stanley Austin Ransom, Jr.; biographic sketch of Jupiter Hammon by Oscar Wegelin; critical analysis of Jupiter Hammon by Vernon Loggins.

Odell says that the poet's last days were spent in "extreme misery" in a "filthy apartment" in an "obscure part of the metropolis" (*Memoir*, p. 23), but she does not mention that she ended her days working in a "common negro boarding-house." That was a statement by Shurtleff which has been picked up by several of her other biographers (Shurtleff, *Proceedings,* p. 272, n.; Brawley uses the phrase, "a cheap boarding house," (*Negro Builders and Heroes,* p. 23; see also Mason, *Poems,* p. xvi).

For the poem signed "Horatio," see Mason (ibid., pp. xvii–xviii).

Shurtleff is the source for the statement that Peters was imprisoned for debt in 1784 (no more precise date given), and he adds that "soon after his liberation from jail, Peters worked as a journeyman baker. Subsequently he attempted to practice law, and finally, imposed upon the credulous by pretending to be a physician" (*Proceedings,* p. 272, n.). Odell makes no mention of imprisonment, saying only that Peters did not "see fit to acquaint them [the poet's former friends] with the event [her death], or to notify them of her interment." As a final note she adds, "After her death, these [the poet's] papers were demanded by Peters, as the property of his deceased wife, and were, of course, yielded to his importunity. Some years after, he went to the South, and we have been unable to ascertain what eventually became of the manuscripts" (*Memoir,* pp. 24, 29).

9. The Critics

James Weldon Johnson quotes Jefferson as saying "her poems are beneath contempt" (*American Negro Poetry,* p. xxiii). Though not so gentlemanly in expression, Johnson's phrase is no doubt much closer to what Jefferson actually felt than what he wrote.

The remarks of Jefferson, Samuel Stanhope Smith, Henri Grégoire, Johann Friedrich Blumenbach, and Thomas Clarkson are referred to by Arthur A. Schomburg (introduction, "Appreciation," Heartman, *Wheatley, Poems and Letters,* pp. 14–15). Edward D. Seeber quotes Voltaire's remark ("Phillis Wheatley," *Journal of Negro History,* Vol. 24, no. 3, July, 1939, pp. 259–262); see also Mason (*Poems,* pp. xlvi–xlvii).

Mason is the source for the reviews of her poems in English periodicals (ibid., pp. xxxvi–xxxvii).

Thomas Clarkson's remark is in *An Essay on the Slavery and Commerce of the Human Species* (Philadelphia: Cruikshank, 1786), p. 122; see also Mason (*Poems,* p. xlvi).

George Saintsbury's discussion of Pope and the heroic couplet is to be found in *English Prosody,* 2:454.

There is an interesting presentation of the relation between science and poetry in *Science and English Poetry, A Historical Sketch, 1590–1950*, by Douglas Bush (New York: Oxford University Press, 1950).

The two lines on Newton are quoted from Pope's "Epitaph Intended for Sir Isaac Newton." The quotations from Pope contained in the footnote on page 56 are from his *Essay on Man*, Epistle I, lines 267–268, 289–294. The subsequent quotations from Pope are in his *Essay on Man*, Epistle II, lines (variously) 10–17.

James Weldon Johnson's assessment of her poetry is contained in his *American Negro Poetry* (pp. xxii–xxiv). His estimation of the time span between Anne Bradstreet and Phillis Wheatley ("Anne Bradstreet preceded Phillis Wheatley by a little over twenty years. She published her volume of poems, 'The Tenth Muse,' in 1750" [ibid., p. xxiii] is off by about a century. Bradstreet's collected works were first published in England in 1650; the second edition was published in 1678, and the third in 1758, the latter two in Boston (see Elizabeth Wade White, *Anne Bradstreet*). The critical comparison of Bradstreet and Wheatley made by Johnson appears on page xxiii. The quote from Arthur Schomburg is in his introduction to *Poems and Letters* by Phillis Wheatley (Phillis Peters) (New York: C. F. Heartman's Historical Series #8).

Richard Wright's discussion of Phillis Wheatley is in *White Man, Listen* (New York: Doubleday & Co., 1964), pp. 74–79.

For Redding's quotation see *To Make a Poet Black*, pp. 8–11. (He is the victim of either a mathematical or typographical error when he says that twenty-five years after Phillis Wheatley's poem to the Earl of Dartmouth [1772], Horton wrote the lines he quotes. The year of Horton's birth is usually estimated as 1797.) Loggins also advances the theme Redding develops, that ". . . she neglected almost entirely her own state of slavery and the miserable oppression of thousands of her race." He finds that "In all of her writings she only once referred in strong terms to the wrongs of the Negro in America." That once is her poem addressed to Lord Dartmouth (*The Negro Author*, pp. 24–25).

George Moses Horton

1

A Natural Poet

Among Southern white scholars and critics, who are not predisposed to put black before white, this black man has been called "quite the most remarkable literary figure ever born in North Carolina" and that state's "most amazing natural poet."

"A forest-born poet, who learned his letters while turning his plow at the end of a furrow"—having been so described, it was inevitable that he would be called "another Burns." In a different context he has been compared with Lord Byron and Edgar Allan Poe, as well as Robert Burns. Like them, says a Southern white historian, "he has often quenched the divine spark with unpoetic whisky." To a lady novelist from the North, who knew him well, he evoked an altogether different image unsuggestive of the volatile mixture of verse and spirits. "He has," she recalled, "the mild gravity of a Grecian philosopher."

If these judgments and tantalizing impressions of him make one wonder why George Moses Horton remains virtually unknown to his countrymen, the wonder grows with the list of his distinctions, with the account of things he did that no man similarly situated had ever done before. He was the first slave poet of the South, the first Southern black man to have his poetry published, not only in one volume, but in three that have been preserved and quite likely in more that have been lost. He was the country's first black professional man of letters who earned most of his living from writing. His was the first clear black outcry in poetic form against slavery.

With the lines

> Alas! and am I born for this,
> To wear this slavish chain?

he first struck the chord that has ever since dominated Afro-American poetry. A pioneer in black protest, he was also a pioneer in black pride. "He himself, Othello like, boasted of the purity of his black blood," says a Southern white scholar.

In some of his verse he invites comparison with the great slave of antiquity, Aesop, but his fables bear the imprint of his life's first setting, the early American frontier, and they are flavored with the frontier idiom, with its humor and folk wisdom. In this, too, he was among the pioneers along a trail that many were to follow.

Such heights as he attained seem the more towering for the burdens and obstacles on his ascent. Nothing came easy. Born a slave on a barren plantation in rural North Carolina and bound by slavery for the first sixty-eight years of his life, the mere mastery of reading was an exercise in human ingenuity and tenacity, for literacy among Southern slaves was first discouraged by custom and then prohibited by law. Poetic compositions began to form in his mind before he knew how to set them down on paper. To find an audience for his verse in these circumstances, to gain access to a knowledge of language and form for the perfection of his work, and finally to secure its publication and sale in a Southern state—each of these successive strides was for a rustic slave a miracle of mind and spirit.

Confronted with such pertinacity, one seeks for a passion that could have motivated it. Horton was possessed by such a passion. It was a passion for poetry—and freedom. Poetry, a lonely pursuit he attained by his own incredible effort. Freedom was something else. In his own way he tried to secure his liberation from slavery by purchase, but ultimately it was purchased with much blood in four years of civil war.

"I have," Horton wrote in a brief autobiographic sketch, "composed love pieces in verse . . . and acrostics on the names of many of the tip-top belles of Virginia, South Carolina and Georgia."

This was a bold thing for him to say in public print in North Carolina in 1845. He was a black slave, then about forty-eight years of age, and the belles were white, presumably maidens, and courted with varying degrees of intensity by junior-grade Southern aristocrats attending the University of North Carolina.

By the standards of the time (and not only of that time) a black man might have been lynched for composing love pieces to white belles. Instead, Horton was paid for them. He wrote the verses to order for university students, who sent them in their own names to excite the favor of young ladies. If the lyrics evoked a romantic sigh or flutter, these being the proper response by belles of the ante-bellum South, this was innocent of the knowledge that the poetic ardor was a gift purchased from a black man. Had some belle learned the secret would she have screamed, "I've been raped!"?

All this was in the pre-Freudian era when biblical prophets had greater vogue than Viennese psychiatrists. There was not the same kind of public preoccupation with sexuality as a factor in white-black relations as there is today, although there were brooding daydreams and night dreams that mixed sex, color, and violence, and what white male slaveowners did in private could be read in public in the pigment of their unclaimed offspring. In our time, with its tracts and treatises about white impotence and black virility (and/or emasculation), about white fear and black aggression, about the sexual polarization of the races with its attractions and repellences, the story of a black man supplying the language of passion for the courtship of white young ladies by white young gentlemen is enough to trigger a mind-blowing Freudian excursion.

In his own time it was an audacious thing for Horton to do, and to keep on doing for almost a half-century. He must have composed hundreds of love poems, love letters, and romantic acrostics for his white patrons, making him one of the most prolific romantic ghost-writers in our history.

But this poet's heart was elsewhere, and he displays the greatest originality in the poems where he speaks for himself, in the outcry against slavery, in his self-portrayals as an artist, and in the humorous wisdom of his folk idiom.

These, particularly the antislavery poems, also required audacity, and since even a little of it could get a slave killed, is it too much to assume that the poet, with his quick wit, sensed that audacity had to be employed with skill and tempered with discretion, accompanied by occasional resort to the common devices of feigned ignorance and the jester's mask? If slaveowners were ready to believe anything about slaves, it was that they were ignorant. The masters were not as certain about the slaves' good humor, but it pleased them to profess a belief in it even as their precautionary and repressive measures belied what they professed.

If Horton did indeed resort to the slaves' discretions, then he did so with consummate skill. He had need for skill; the more audacity the more tempering it required, and for a field slave to become a poet was in itself incredibly audacious. Did he keep them guessing: is this slave being bold or is he just naive? This question is posed repeatedly by his acts at critical junctures of his life, to such a point that reconstruction of his life is a constant challenge to discern between reality and the put-on.

2

The Slave and the Citadel

Sometime in 1817 or thereabouts, among the slaves who came from the surrounding countryside on Sunday to sell their masters' fruit and produce at the University of North Carolina campus in Chapel Hill, a new man appeared.

Students sized up the newcomer for such sport as they might have with him, for making sport of the slave peddlers was a student amusement. Chapel Hill offered few diversions on Sunday, or any other day for that matter. The university "was still the primeval grove so appealing to the founding fathers," according to one loving historian, and Chapel Hill boasted only one street, Franklin, crossed by the Raleigh and Hillsboro roads, and inhabited by "a blacksmith shop, one hotel, two stores, two boarding houses and about twelve residences." Cows and pigs wandered through the forest-ringed town and, in their innocence, sometimes ventured onto the campus with its two plain redbrick buildings at right angles.

There was little to do in Chapel Hill, and on occasion students relieved their extracurricular boredom by getting drunk, then wandering and shouting through the town and even assaulting black men for the fun of it. On a Sabbath morning, however, sobriety was the rule and fun with the black visitors was nonviolent. In surveying the newcomer for the fun he might provide, students saw a handsome black youth of approximately their age. He seemed to be about twenty, slender, and of medium height. What else they perceived, things not evident to the naked eye, and what followed from their perception was recalled by George Moses Horton almost three decades later.

"Having got in the way of carrying fruit to the college at Chapel Hill on the Sabbath the collegians who, for their diversion, were fond of pranking with the country servants who resorted there for the same purpose that I did, began also to prank with me. But somehow or other they discovered a spark of genius in me, either by discourse or other means, which excited their curiosity, and they often eagerly insisted on me to spout, as they called it. This inspired in me a kind of enthusiastic pride. I was indeed too full of vain egotism, which always discovers the gloom of ignorance or dims the lustre of popular distinction. I would stand forth and address myself extempore before them, as an orator of inspired promptitude. But I soon found it an object of aversion, and considered myself nothing but a public ignoramus."

The initial encounter between the rustic slave and a citadel of Southern white culture thus ended in his humiliation. He had been put upon, cast as something of a buffoon, but he had the sense to recognize it and the resources to recover.

"I abandoned my foolish harangues," he later wrote, "and began to speak of poetry, which lifted them [the students] still higher on the wings of astonishment. All eyes were upon me, and all ears were open. Many were at first incredulous; but the experiment of acrostics established it as an incontestable fact. Hence my fame soon circulated like a stream throughout the college."

The slave claimed he could compose poetry, and the skeptical collegians put him to the test by insisting that he compose an acrostic. He passed the test and with the resultant fame came a demand for more such compositions.

"Many of these acrostics," Horton recalled, "I composed at the handle of the plough, retained them in my head (being unable to write), until an opportunity offered, when I dictated whilst one of the gentlemen would serve as my amanuensis."

He composed hundreds of acrostics in his long subsequent association with the university, and later still he composed many more for Union soldiers, but only one has been preserved:

> *J*oy like the morning breaks from one divine
> *U*nveiling streams which cannot fail to shine
> *L*ong have I strove to magnify her name
> *I*mperial floating on the breeze of fame.
>
> *A*ttracting beauty must delight afford,
> *S*ought of the world and of the Bards adord
> *H*er grace of form and heart alluring powers
> *E*xpress her more than fair, the queen of flowers.
>
> *P*leasure fond nature's stream from beauty sprung
> *A*nd was the softest strain the Muses sung
> *R*everting sorrows into speechless Joys
> *D*ispelling gloom which human peace destroys—

Presumably, this verse, with the first letter of each line spelling out the name of a Julia Shepard, is an example of his best work in this form and not one of his earlier efforts. Still the first efforts were good enough to create a campus mystery: where and how did the country slave learn to read and to compose poetry, even though he did not know as yet how to set it down on paper? And since the meeting between the slave and the campus began a relationship that was to endure for almost half a century it is well to introduce them properly by sketching their respective histories prior to their first encounter.

"I was born . . . the property of William Horton, senior, who also owned my mother, and the whole stock of her children, which were five before me, all girls, but not of one father," the poet wrote. "I am the oldest child that my mother had by her second husband, and she had four younger than myself, one boy and three girls. But to account for my age is beyond my power."

The best estimate is that the unrecorded date of his birth fell some time in 1797. Equally hazy is the identity of the father. He does not appear in any of the biographies, and the poet's own account contains only two passing references to an off-stage figure. Since there is no record of an adult male slave on the Horton plantation, it may be assumed the father was the property of a nearby planter. Thus, the poet was born into a matriarchal family as fashioned by slavery. He may have been more fortunate than others, however, in that the one family represented all the slaves on the plantation, and in the beginning, at least, this made for a close-knit unit.

The plantation was situated in Northampton County, within four miles of the Roanoke River, not far from where the river dips from Virginia into North Carolina on its course to the sea a hundred miles away. William Horton was a small operator, recording only eight slaves in the 1800 census (the three youngest members of the poet's family were still unborn), when the successful planters in the region, mostly settlers from nearby Virginia, owned anywhere between fifty and one hundred. It was a domain of women over which the elder Horton reigned. His sons having left the declining plantation to make their own way, he was its sole male inhabitant until the boy slave was born. Young Horton's mother and sisters slaved in the fields, ministering to tobacco, a voracious plant as demanding of human sweat as of the soil's nutriment. The elder Horton women folk—apparently five of them were on the plantation—operated a small wayside tavern.

By 1800 William Horton decided to abandon the plantation, its soil depleted by tobacco, and to push along some hundred miles westward, purchasing land in the northern section of Chatham County, "a more fertile and fresh part of the country . . . whose waters were far more healthy and agreeable," as the poet later described it.

For the child slave another aspect of the new locale was to prove more important than its soil and climate. In 1792 a site for the University of North Carolina was chosen at Chapel Hill, only eight miles from the new Horton plantation. If this chance circumstance had a decisive bearing on the poet's life, so did another occurrence a year later. In 1793, in nearby Georgia, necessity and Eli Whitney conceived the cotton gin. The first event was to influence Horton's aspiration as a poet; the second was to shape his condition as slave. The poet came to know the university intimately; the slave never knew the gin firsthand, but just the same his fate—like the fate of millions of blacks—was sealed by it as it laid to rest earlier Southern uncertainty about the economic utility of slavery. During his childhood cotton culture flourished, and as the gin separated the seed from the fiber so did it solidify the system of slavery.

On Master Horton's plantation in Chatham County the crop was not cotton. Nor was it any longer the tobacco of the uplands that framed the Roanoke River. Corn and wheat were Master Horton's staples, and these were supplemented by cows, which became the charges of the boy slave.

"I here became a cow-boy, which I followed for perhaps ten years in succession or more," he later recalled. Except to call it "this disagreeable occupation," he said no more about driving the cows to and from pasture, although this is how he spent most of his waking day well into adolescence. Instead, in his brief autobiographic sketch, he quickly turned to the intrusion of the printed word into his pastoral world. He tended cows—and thought about the alphabet.

The sources of this curious interest are only sketchily presented by him, and quite likely he could be no more definite or precise about them. Unlike Phillis Wheatley, he was not a domestic slave residing in a home where books were much in evidence. Nor was he subjected to middle-class Puritan pressures for the improvement of his mind and morals, and if he exhibited intellectual precocity, it evoked no patronage or encouragement from a benevolent master.

Horton lamented the fact that "the planters' comfortable homes dotting the countryside were centers of political movements, sporting events, and social activities, but hardly of literature." "My old master," he wrote "being an eminent farmer who had acquired a competent stock of living through his own prudence and industry, did not descend to the particularity of schooling for [his] children at any high rate; hence it is clear that he cared less for the improvement of the mind of his servants."

From somewhere, and apparently not from the mores of the masters, a literary interest was kindled. It was foreshadowed (and later accompanied) by an earlier interest in a more elemental art form. "I was early fond of music with an extraordinary appetite for singing lively tunes, for which I was a little remarkable."

From this immodest recollection he leaped to his years as a "cowboy." "In the course of this disagreeable occupation, I became fond of hearing people read; but being nothing but a poor cow-boy, I had but little or no thought of ever being able to read or spell one word or sentence in any book whatever." Where did he hear people read? He does not answer directly, but later on indicates that the first books of his acquaintance were the Bible and the Wesley hymnal, and it may be assumed that the reading he heard was at religious camp meetings, the only kind of gatherings permitted to slaves, their only institutionalized exposure to culture, such as it was.

Although at first the conquest of reading seemed remote and even impossible for him, his interest was stimulated by members of his immediate family. "My mother," he wrote, "discovered my anxiety for books and strove to encourage my plan; but she, having left her husband behind, was so hard run to make a little shift for herself that she could give me no assistance in this case."

The phrasing "having left her husband behind" was over-delicate. The choice was not hers. When William Horton moved his household and his chattel to Chatham County, the slave husband and father, being the property of another planter, remained in the Roanoke River country. The ties of family, made tenuous by the impositons of slavery, were now totally severed by it. For the boy, only three years old at the time, the part-time father became a fact for incidental reference, acknowledged but not truly known.

His hard-pressed mother could give the poet no tangible assistance with books and reading, but her encouragement may have been a spur, for he goes on: "At length I took a resolution to learn the alphabet at all events; and lighting by chance at times with some opportunities of being in the presence of school children, I learnt the letters by heart, and fortunately afterwards got hold of some old parts of spelling books abounding with these elements, which I learnt with but little difficulty."

At this juncture maternal encouragement was reinforced by fraternal competition. Excited by the future poet's venture, his younger brother entered the literary lists, egged on by his own ego and "some of his partial friends" (in the poet's phrase) to outdo the older brother. In the poet's account the younger brother emerges as something of a dandy: "an ostentatious youth . . . of a far more attractive person than myself, more forward in manly show . . . fond of popularity to an astonishing degree for one of his age and capacity . . . much too full of vain longing among the fair sex."

Part acid, part envy, still the portrait is credible, made so by what is known about the subject. Handsome and bright, he was also the younger of only two boys in a matriarchal family with eight sisters, and surely such a combination of circumstances may be conducive to the vanities sketched in the poet's portrait of him. For the poet, not without vanity himself, there was nettle in the challenge. Seeing himself as second in looks and social accomplishment, he now faced competition in his quixotic intellectual pursuit. Both brothers must have been in their teens then, adding the fervor of adolescence to their contest, but even many years later, in writing of it, the poet recaptured some of the excitement.

"He strove hard on the wing of ambition to soar above me," the poet recalled, conceding that in one skill the brother was quicker and more facile: "[He] could write a respectable fist before I could form the first letter with a pen or barely knew the use of goose-quill." This is the only concession. "My brother never could keep time with me. . . . through blundering I became a far better reader than he . . ."—at this point competition yields to fraternal solidarity—"but we were indeed both remarkable for boys of color and hard raising." (They would have been remarkable even among boys of no color but hard raising, for a Southern scholar has lamented, "The United States Census of 1840 revealed to the world the humiliating fact that, after more than sixty years of independence, one-third of the adult white population of North Carolina could neither read nor write.")

Horton, having won the contest, magnanimously attributed his victory to "blundering," which sacrificed precision for modesty. Blundering there must have been as the boy slave grappled, alone and unaided, with the mystery of the printed word, but there was also a single-minded, ascetic concentration, which the younger brother, with so many other things on his mind, was not disposed to match.

According to some biographic sketches, the key to the poet's progress from a knowledge of the alphabet to a mastery of reading was the Wesley hymnal. Having often sung the words at camp meetings, "the melodies were in his heart and the forms of the corresponding words became fixed in his brain," says one biographer. Once he knew the alphabet, he matched the words he had learned by hearing them sung with the printed words in the hymn book—"a practical evolution of the word-method," this same biographer notes, "by a man who was innocent of pedagogy."

In his autobiography he does not pinpoint his method of learning or self-teaching, and it is not clear whether he mastered the printed words in their entirety before breaking them down into their component parts, or whether he followed the more traditional course of assembling the alphabetical particles into the wholeness of a word. From his own testimony, the latter method seems more likely, but not certainly so. He was, as the biographer said, innocent of pedagogy, and in his remembrance the sheer strains of his effort eclipsed the niceties of pedagogic technique.

He could pursue his self-education only in the time free from his slave chores. The plantation slave's work day being "from day clean to first dark," this left the evening, and the masters did not provide facilities, either light or space, for nocturnal study by their slaves. Then there was the Sabbath, the only day of rest, when other pleasures beckoned to a boy.

"On well nigh every Sabbath," he recalled, "did I retire away in the summer season to some shady and lonely recess, where I could stammer over the dim and promiscuous syllables in my old black and tattered spelling book, sometimes a piece of one and then of another; nor would I scarcely spare the time to return to my ordinary meals, being so truly engaged with my book. And by close application to my book at night, my visage became considerably emaciated by extreme perspiration, having no lucubratory apparatus, no candle, no lamp, nor even lightwood, being chiefly raised in oaky woods. Hence I had to sit sweating and smoking over my incompetent bark and brush light, almost suffocated with smoke; consequently from Monday morning I anticipated with joy the approach of the next Sabbath, that I might retire to the pleasant umbrage of the woods, whither I was used to dwell or spend the most of the day with ceaseless investigation over my book."

To such physical hardships were added social pressures. Poring over a spelling book on the Sabbath, when there were more entertaining things to be done, seemed like madness to his contemporaries.

"A number," he wrote, "strove to dissuade me from my plan and had the presumption to tell me that I was a vain fool to attempt learning to read with as little chance as I had. Play boys importunately insisted on my abandoning my foolish theory, and go with them on streams, disport, and sacrifice the day in athletic folly, or alibatic levity. Nevertheless did I persevere with an indefatigable resolution, at the risk of success."

So he learned to read, and soon displayed yet another remarkable inclination. In the limited reading matter available to him he early developed a marked preference for poetry:

> I became very fond of reading parts of the New Testament, such as I could pick up as they lay about at random; but I soon became more fond of reading verses, Wesley's old hymns, and other pieces of poetry from various authors.
>
> I became fond of it to that degree that whenever I chanced to light on a piece of paper, so common to be lying about, I would pick it up in order to examine it whether it was written in that curious style or not. If it was not, unless some remarkable prose, I threw it aside; and if it was, I as carefully preserved it as I would a piece of money.

There is no disputing taste, the Romans said, and there is no true accounting for the first origins of some tastes. Horton's earlier attraction to song may have foreshadowed his preference for poetry. His inclination may have been influenced by the rhythmical rituals at the camp meetings, his sole encounter with communal culture. These meetings were religious, but they were different from the services at the Old South Meeting House in Boston, where Phillis Wheatley was a communicant. They were all black, and although the texts were derived from the Old and New Testaments, these were infused with cadences traceable to the African origin and modified by the experience of slavery. Songs and camp meetings may have nurtured an inclination to poetic form, but the inclination had to be there, for millions of blacks were exposed to the same influences, and even among those who attained literacy very few exhibited Horton's predilection.

From an appreciation of poetry he proceeded to attempts at its creation, wondering, as he said, "whether it was possible that I ever could be so fortunate as to compose in that manner." He could not write and the lines had to be formed and retained in his mind. Writing of it some thirty years later, he still remembered two stanzas of his first composition and two more of his earliest poems, setting these down and adding: "Many other pieces did I compose, which have long since slipped my recollection, and some perhaps better than those before you."

The first was composed on a Sunday morning, "a while before the time of preaching," and took the form of a divine hymn:

> Rise up, my soul, and let us go
> Up to the gospel feast;

> Gird on the garment white as snow,
>   To join and be a guest.
>
> Dost thou not hear the trumpet call
>   For thee, my soul, for thee?
> Not only thee, my soul, but all
>   May rise and enter free.

Another poem was inspired by the biblical story of Israel's exodus from Egypt and the crossing of the Red Sea:

> Sing, O ye ransomed, shout and tell
>   What God has done for ye;
> The horses and their riders fell
>   And perished in the sea.
>
> Look back, the vain Egyptian dies
>   Whilst plunging from the shore;
> He groans, he sinks, but not to rise:
>   King Pharaoh is no more.

As in Wheatley's first poems the inspiration is religious, or at least biblical, and yet the contrast between his and hers is striking. His are not missionary sermons for the conversion of doubters or nonbelievers. They already contain the antislavery nuances of the spirituals, most obviously in the symbolism of Israel's deliverance from the Pharaoh's bondage ("O ye ransomed"), but also in the trumpet call that "all may rise and enter free." Her more polished verse was imitative not only in style but in the Puritan themes of white New England; his reflects the black camp meeting with its subtle assertions of the aspirations to freedom within the religious wrapping. Hers was black poetry only in the sense that it was written by a black poet, conscious of her blackness; his was black in the more profound sense of reflecting the black experience and the distinctive culture being fashioned by it.

He had come upon his life's work, almost certainly ignorant then of his older contemporary, Goethe, but like the privileged German the untutored black might have written: "And thus began that bent of mind from which I could not deviate my whole life through; namely, that of turning into an image, into a poem, everything that delighted or troubled me, or otherwise occupied my attention. . . ."

The slave poet later did write: "At any critical juncture, when anything momentous transpired, such as death, misfortune, disappointment, and the like, it generally passed off from my mind like the chanting of birds after a storm, for my mind was then more deeply inspired than at other periods."

Later yet, in a poem, "George Moses Horton, Myself," he wrote:

> My genius from a boy
>   Has fluttered like a bird within my heart

When he first discovered his genius (he used the word in the sense of innate ability and inclination) and began to articulate it, the nascent poet was ready for the university. Not in the conventional sense, of course. It would be many decades and four historical eras before the university would be ready to open its doors to any black student. He was ready for this proximate center of culture, which could provide an audience for poetry and intellectual resources for cultivation of his genius, although neither he nor anyone else could have foretold the precise terms on which a black slave might establish such a relationship with a white Southern institution of higher education. There were no precedents, and the only blacks on white campuses were there as menials, not as poets.

Just then, capricious chance, or more accurately, a slaveowner's caprice, which could determine the fate of a slave, snatched him from the university's environs. In 1814 William Horton, well along in age, decided to distribute some of his slaves among his sons. Lots were drawn and son James "won" slave George. Fourteen years earlier, while still an infant, the slave had been taken from the neighborhood of his father, and now at seventeen he was torn from his family.

This experience was reflected in a poem published some three decades later, "Division of an Estate":

> . . . but O, the state,
> The dark suspense in which poor vassals stand,
> Each mind upon the spire of chance hangs, fluctuate,
> The day of separation is at hand . . .

By the luck of the draw the poet was hurtled back to the Roanoke River country, a hundred miles away from his family and the university, for the new owner, James, had remained in Northampton County when his father moved westward. Had the poet stayed here his poetic gift might have been wasted, as so much else was wasted, in the fields of tobacco, but once again a master's misfortune was a slave's good luck. This time the misfortune was more general and struck at a good many slaves as well; in 1815 an outbreak of "Camp Plague" took a heavy toll in the region of James Horton's plantation, inducing him to follow his father's trail to Chatham County.

Back in the vicinity of Chapel Hill, the poet soon found his way to the university. Just what prompted him to go and how he managed to get there is somewhat obscure. According to some biographers, one day he overheard someone in his master's house reading a poem in the *North Carolina University Magazine*. This fired his imagination, and he begged leave of his owner to visit the place where young men composed poetry. In his autobiography the poet records no such incident, and indeed does not describe his first visit to the university or the events leading up to it. His first mention of the campus is most casual: "Having got in the way of carrying fruit to the college at Chapel Hill on the Sabbath . . ."

By the time the poet wrote his autobiographic sketch, he had much reason beyond the ordinary owner-slave relationship to despise James Horton, and was not disposed, perhaps, to record that anything good happened in his household or to impute to him the generosity of indulging a slave's whimsical request for permission to visit Chapel Hill. Maybe the poetry-reading story is true, but its embellishments invite skepticism. One biographic essayist, for example, wrote: "This was probably the very first time he had ever heard poetry read. It was the divining rod that touched the buried treasure of his undeveloped muse. Thrilling with the melody of a well-turned verse, he besought his master to permit him to visit Chapel Hill, to get acquainted with some of the professors and students who were also interested in poetry."

The quest for poetry lends itself to more romantic prose than the sale of fruit. However, it was the custom among planters in the vicinity to dispatch slaves to sell their produce in the university town, and whatever private ambitions the poet had, his public purpose was to sell fruit. His own account of how he progressed from the sale of fruit to the discussion of poetry is so ingenuous as to suggest no prior design.

Indeed, Horton might have been too ingenuous, for once again it needs to be remembered that he was a slave, writing for white publishers in a Southern state in 1845. Neither time, place, nor circumstance made it prudent for a slave to suggest any guile in dealing with whites. His appearance at the university could have been fortuitous, simply the result of his arbitrary selection by his owner to peddle fruit; yet, his poetic bent and his fascination with learning, along with his purposeful ingenuity, suggest both an attraction to the university and some design on his part to get there. What is implausible is his discovery of the university as an apocalyptic revelation triggered by a poetry reading.

Whether it was chance or design that first brought him to the campus, he was there, and what he made of his presence depended in

The Slave and the Citadel / 95

the first instance on his talent and charm. The university he encountered was a bigger and more sophisticated world than he had ever known, although it was still primitive and a long way from what it was to become.

Presently, the University of North Carolina at Chapel Hill accommodates a co-educational student body of some sixteen thousand, including a few blacks. When Horton first visited it, the student body numbered about one hundred, all of them male and, of course, all of them white. The class of 1818, for instance, graduated only fourteen, among them James Knox Polk, who was to become the eleventh President of the United States twenty-seven years after his graduation with highest honors. Legend has it that Polk was among the students who helped the poet by lending him books, but there is no evidence of it, although there is ample evidence of assistance by others.

Despite its rustic quality and modest dimensions in the early 1800's, the university was a source of pride for the North Carolina Establishment. Chartered in 1789, only Georgia, among the Southern states, could boast of an older state university charter. However, North Carolina was the first state university in the South to open its doors to students, which may be a bit grandiloquent, for the doors were opened January 15, 1795, and no student walked through them. It was not until February 12, that one student finally appeared. The faculty then consisted of one "Professor of Humanity," who was also called the presiding professor, occupying in this last capacity the president's house and performing the duties of his office. For all this he received a salary of $300 a year and two-thirds of the tuition money. Luckily for him, the original student body of one grew to forty-one by the end of the first term. In the second term nearly one hundred students enrolled, and the faculty was doubled with the employment of a tutor in mathematics.

Still, it was the oldest functioning state university in the South, and being wedged between Virginia, which already was the Mother of Presidents, and South Carolina, which then was becoming the ideological leader of the slave states, North Carolina cherished its lesser distinctions. When Horton came to the Chapel Hill campus the chartering of the University of Virginia, under Thomas Jefferson's sponsorship, was still two years off, and this institution, which Jefferson claimed as his greatest single accomplishment, was not to open until 1825.

Balm to the state's ego, the university also performed the utilitarian function of social refuge for rich planters' sons who could not make it to the more prestigious universities in the North. A later campus memoir recalled that at the time the university was "held to be something respectable, which it was proper the State should have—every rich man must send his son to college, of course. In order to be a gentleman it was necessary that he should forget a little Latin, Greek and Mathematics. That accomplished, the ex-student proceeded also to forget the University, till he in his turn had a son to be 'educated.' Then Chapel Hill occurred to his mind as a safe and good place to send a boy to, and the process was renewed."

A university rule prescribed "plainness of dress and manners" for the would-be gentlemen, presumably because this Spartan mode was good for character. However, the rule was waived for ceremonial occasions when the sons of the Southern aristocracy blossomed in sartorial splendor. Of his costume at the Commencement Ball of 1818, one student wrote:

> ... my coat was broadcloth, of sea-green, high velvet collar to match, swallow-tail, pockets outside with lapels, and large silver-plated buttons; white satin damask vest, showing the edge of a blue undervest; a wide opening for bosom ruffles, and no shirt collar. The neck was dressed with a layer of four or five three-cornered cravats, artistically laid and surmounted with a cambric stock, pleated and buckled behind. My pantaloons were white canton crepe, lined with a pink muslin, and showed a peach-blossom tint. They were rather short in order to display flesh-colored silk stockings, and this exposure was increased by very low cut pumps with shiny buckles.

The young man had a feel for cloth, an eye for color, and a taste for elegance. Perhaps his olfactory sense was lacking, for he mentions no perfume or any other scent. His detailed and knowledgeable description of what he wore is not simply a divertissement, even if it suggests no more than the thought that these students came by their letters with far less effort and hardship than did the young slave. This is important, because he was to match wits with forty-three classes of them, and they were to serve as patrons, clients, and auditors. In the beginning they were pranksters making sport of a country slave.

3

Poet Laureate

The acrostic is a trick, a *tour de force* in rhyme; only a formal solicitation would be content with its restrictions. Greater passion needed freer form. Soon Horton was commissioned to compose verse that spelled ardor without having to spell out a name. And at some point he began to be paid for what he did initially just to prove that he could do it.

"Mr. Augustus Alton," he wrote, "first laid the low price of 25¢ on my compositions each, which was unanimously established and has been kept up ever since; but some gentlemen, extremely generous, have given me from 50¢ to 75¢, besides many decent and respectable suits of clothes, professing that they would not suffer me to pass otherwise and write for them."

Alton was a student from Georgia, who attended the university in the early 1820's. This would indicate that Horton's progression from fruit peddler to orator to amateur versifier to professional poet consumed some four years, although it is possible that he received compensation for his verses before Alton set the prevailing rate.

Some biographers assert that payments in excess of the standard twenty-five cent price were not a matter of generosity, but of value received. For an ordinary expression of affection, it is said, the poet charged twenty-five cents, but when greater passion was requested the price went up. The price schedule was attuned to an emotional scale, and there was a surcharge for letters to accompany the verse.

The poet as businessman was shrewd enough to judge which items pleased his patrons, and according to one biographer, if an item moved, as they say in the world of commerce, it was duplicated to be sold again and again. A staple poem in his repertoire, which was sold many times, was entitled "Love." It reads:

> While tracing thy visage I sing in emotion
> For no other damsel so wondrous I see;

> Thy looks are so pleasing, thy charms so amazing,
>   I think of no other, my true-love, but thee.
>
> With heart-burning rapture I gaze on thy beauty
>   And fly like a bird to the boughs of a tree;
> Thy looks are so pleasing, thy charms so amazing,
>   I fancy no other, my true-love, but thee.
>
> Thus oft in the valley I think and I wonder:
>   Why cannot a maid and her lover agree?
> Thy looks are so pleasing, thy charms so amazing,
>   I pine for no other, my true-love, but thee.
>
> I'd fly from thy frowns with a heart full of sorrow—
>   Return, pretty damsel, and smile thou on me.
> By every endeavor, I'll try thee forever
>   And languish until I am fancied by thee.

It was reputed, according to one Southern scholar, that Horton's literary efforts often "not only touched but captured the fair hearts for which they pleaded." One can only guess at how many hearts, encased in privileged, white, feminine flesh, fell to the poem "Love." Its commercial success suggests that it must have been in the fifty-cent price bracket.

In the early years of his professional career, Horton still could not write, and the lyrics formed in his mind behind the plow had to be dictated to their purchaser. Despite this handicap his poetry business flourished, and still more so later on, when he learned to write and production was not limited by what he could commit to memory. One student recalled the scene when the poet came to town, bearing fruit and poems: "On Saturday evening he came to the college from the country with his week's poetical work in manuscript which was ordered by the boys the Saturday before. When he came he was a lion. . . . His average budget of lyrics was about a dozen in number. They were mostly in the love line, and addressed to the girl at home. We usually invested a quarter a week. . . ."

If this recollection is accurate, then Horton's weekly income from his poetry ran somewhere between three and five dollars, and this in a time when wheat sold for about $2.50 a bushel and a university student's spending money allowance ran as low as a dollar a month. More pertinent, it was also a time when, according to one authority, "the yearly charge for the support of an adult slave seldom exceeded $35 and was often considerably less than this," and white laborers in the North received between fifty cents and eighty-seven cents a day for man-killing construction work on canals and turnpikes. In all probability the student's recollection, recorded many years after the event, tended to exaggerate as aged memory is prone to do in the remembrance of youth. A dozen poems a week, making allowances for quality and reuse, still seems like a prodigious output, even if he did little else, and he was doing much more, enough to occupy three men. He was performing the chores of a field slave, composing more serious verse, and continuing his self-education to perfect his craft and enlarge his knowledge.

For him the university was more than a marketplace; it was also an access to culture. In one hectic day on campus each week he sold fruit and poems, secured commissions for more poems, and cultivated those in the student body and faculty community who would assist him in his further education.

In his autobiography he listed twenty-two students who gave him books, adding that there were "several more whose names have slipped my memory, all of whom were equally liberal to me, and to whom I ascribe my lean grammatical studies."

"Among the books given me were Murray's English Grammar and its accordant branches; Johnson's Dictionary in miniature, also Walker's and Sheridan's, and parts of others. And other books of use they gave me, which I had no chance to peruse minutely. Milton's Paradise Lost, Thomson's Seasons, parts of Homer's Iliad and Vergil's Aeneid, Beauties of Shakespeare, Beauties of Byron, part of Plutarch, Morse's Geography, the Columbian Orator, Snowden's History of the Revolution, Young's Night Thoughts, and some others, which my concentration of business did not suffer me to pursue with any scientific regularity."

Students come and go, of course, and the twenty-two he listed spanned a ten-year period at the university, beginning in 1817. The faculty stays on, and the more sustained, perhaps wiser, help and counsel came from this quarter. The university's president and the guiding spirit of its formative years, Dr. Joseph Caldwell, took an interest in the young slave. In campus tradition Dr. Caldwell is acclaimed as the educator who placed the university on the "highest table-land of Southern institutions" and as "a man incapable of a mean action or even of a tortuous line of policy." From all accounts he was a scholar, whose passion for scholarship was not extinguished by the bureaucratic demands of administration. This may account for his interest in the slave with the poetic gift, with the phenomenal zeal and capacity for learning, who must have provided a measure of relief from the academic routine of adding some intellectual gloss to the social polish of Southern white gentlemen-to-be.

Neither man has left any record of their relationship, nor has anyone else. All that remains is a general impression, flavored by Southern white bias. "It was a common saying in Chapel Hill," wrote one Southern scholar, "that Poet Horton . . . all but owned the president of the University." It is as if the Southern white imagination could not conceive of a black-white relationship at the time that was not rooted in possession, and since Caldwell did not own Horton, then Horton must have owned Caldwell. The possibility of an attraction of minds is excluded.

Caldwell's reticence to write anything about his relationship with the slave poet is readily understandable. He was, after all, the president of a Southern university, a state institution at that, and the more vulnerable to all the crossfires of Southern politics. Awareness of such considerations might have restrained Horton. To list twenty-two students does not entail the same political hazards as to list one university president.

Horton was unrestrained, however, in acknowledging his debt to another teacher. This was Caroline Lee Hentz, a poet and novelist from Massachusetts, who came to Chapel Hill in 1826 with her husband, Nicholas Hentz, a Frenchman who taught modern languages. To the cosmopolitan Mrs. Hentz, who had known the intellectual environment of New England, Chapel Hill was provincial and backward. There were no novelists or poets there, nor any serious literary critics. Her excitement at discovering the slave poet in these unpromising surroundings is reflected in her novel *Lovell's Folly*. In this novel she wrote:

> I have never told you of the black poet we have on our plantation,—another Burns, who sings the requiem of the wild violet, that he turns up ruthlessly with his ploughshare. He taught himself to read when a little boy, and after mastering the spelling book and Testament, petitioned for admission to my grandfather's library. Poems, romances, dramas, mythological works he devoured as eagerly as the famished child the cakes and sweetmeats within his reach. I never shall forget the astonishment I felt when he first asked me to write down a piece of poetry, which he dictated; nor the inspired expression of his sable countenance, as he repeated the really melodious numbers. . . . The lips of George have been bathed with pure Castilian dew. He is a legitimate child of the muses, as you would not hesitate to acknowledge, if you could read some of his genuine inspirations. . . . he *has* panted for liberty and his prayers have been granted.

To the above passage the novelist appended a footnote: "The black poet mentioned here, is not an imaginary character. The author has only changed the place of his birth, and given him the reversion of a freedom he has little hope of enjoying. He is now of Orange County, N.C., and resides in the vicinity of Chapel Hill. . . . The author has often transcribed stanzas, which he would dictate with quite an air of inspiration; and has marvelled at the readiness with which he would change a verse or sentiment, which was objected to, as erroneous in expression or deficient in poetical harmony. Though familiar with the best classic works belonging to the fine libraries of the university, he has not been taught to write a legible hand, and was obliged to be indebted to others for embodying the dreams of his muse. He labored hard on his master's plantation, and it was only during the evening, and on Sunday—the holiday of the slaves—he found leisure to study the authors he loved."

Horton, in turn, climaxed his autobiography with a poetic tribute to "this celebrated lady." Entitled "Eulogy," the poem's opening lines are:

> Deep on thy pillar, thou immortal dame,
> Trace the inscription of eternal fame;
> For bards unborn must yet thy works adore
> And bid thee live when others are no more . . .

Of her, he wrote, "I owe much for the correction of many poetical errors. Being a professional poetess herself and a lover of genius, she discovered my little uncultivated talent and was moved to uncover to me the beauties of correctness, together with the true importance of the object to which I aspired."

He recalled a poem he had composed on the death of her first-born child and the circumstances of its delivery to her. "Not being able to write myself, I dictated while she wrote: and while thus engaged she strove in vain to avert the inevitable tear slow trickling down her ringlet-shaded cheek."

From his account and hers, it is plain she was a sympathetic teacher and critic, and he responded to her criticism and instruction. He spoke of "her aid, which I shall never forget in life." The aid extended beyond the literary style and theme; he mentions "a handsome reward" for the elegy on the infant's death, and also this: "She was indeed unequivocally anxious to announce the birth of my recent and astonishing fame, and sent its blast on the gale of passage back to the frozen plains of Massachusetts."

Dr. Caldwell performed a similar office closer to home. Barely a decade had passed since the poet transcended the rural plantation; now he transcended the university campus, his poetry and his name reaching out to nearby Raleigh and faraway New England.

Meanwhile, he remained a slave, confined to the plantation except for the weekly Sabbath excursions to Chapel Hill, an eight-mile hike each way. He no longer was a boy tending cows, but a man behind the plow or with a hoe, performing the physically more taxing chores of a field hand.

The plantation's slave complement was increased when old William Horton died. To divide the estate among several heirs, its effects—including slaves—were sold. Son James bought three of the slaves at auction for $282.50, which sum was itemized as follows: Judy, $220; Ben, $50; Lucy, $12.50. The prices indicate that Ben and Lucy were either not of prime age, much too young or much too old, or in very poor physical condition. All three or any one of them might have been of the poet's family, but there is no record of it, for the records of such transactions, meticulous as to price, were unconcerned with genealogy. Almost certainly, if all of old Horton's slaves were placed on the auction block, families were broken up. This practice, the North Carolina Supreme Court once ruled, may be "harsh," yet "it must be done, if the executor discovers that the interest of the estate requires it; for he is not to indulge his charities at the expense of others."

The poet could well have had this auction in mind when he wrote "A Slave's Reflection the Eve Before His Sale":

> O, comrades! tomorrow we try,
>   The fate of an exit unknowing—
> Tears trickled from every eye—
>   'Tis going, 'tis going, 'tis going!

James Horton apparently exhibited no direct interest in his slave's unique talent, and he professed that "he knew nothing of his poetry except as he heard of it from others." This fitted the poet's assessment of the masters he knew; men more taken with alcohol, he said, than with culture. "On friendly wilderness farms," he wrote, "such a proclivity as drinking was not only tolerated but encouraged. Poetry was neither expected nor required." His most bitter complaint was specifically directed at James Horton—"a man who had no regard for liberty, science or genius."

The slave poet had scorn for the master class as he encountered it, and his judgment of the masters was, on its face, a repudiation of their superiority and the implicit affirmation of a sense of his own worth. He was most outspoken about the Hortons and their peers, men with small slave holdings, whose sons worked in the fields alongside their slaves, whose eyes were so fixed on the earth they furrowed as to exclude any broader intellectual vision. For them, for their narrow horizons, for their intellectual standards and moral values, the slave-intellectual had disdain, made more bitter because they were the masters who, exercising the powers of property, could dispose of him as they saw fit.

In all the accounts, including his own, there is no hint that these were excessively cruel, driving masters. As a rule the extremes of cruelty and exploitation were more likely to occur on the large plantations where overseers commanded platoons of slaves in the staple crops of the slave system, notably in cotton, sugar, and rice, but also in hemp and tobacco. Smaller landholders, who relied as much or more on the labor of their own families as on that of the slaves to work such crops as corn and wheat, had no comparable incentive to terrorize and drive their slaves. The Hortons apparently conformed to this general rule. It was not then the excesses of slavery that lacerated the poet, but slavery itself. So he wrote:

> Oh, Heaven! and is there no relief
> This side the silent grave—
> To soothe the pain—to quell the grief
> And anguish of a slave?

His own intellectual attainments and his passionate commitment to poetry made the bondage more galling, for on this plateau of knowledge and creativity he could easily see that his immediate masters were beneath him in perception and aspiration. What of the young gentry at the university who had greater intellectual pretensions than the master Hortons? Here the relationship was more subtle. These were his patrons; the university was a refuge from the plantation, and if it first served as a beachhead for his poetry, he also hoped it would open the way to his freedom. He could not jeopardize this position by giving overt offense to those who could so swiftly drive him from it. Still, as their romantic ghostwriter and later yet as the ghostwriter of verse that appeared in the university magazine over student signatures, he must inwardly have savored the irony of an arrangement in which the hand was the hand of the master but the voice was the voice of the slave. Whatever he felt about it had to be expressed with discretion, which he later stretched to its limits with the boast that he had composed romantic verses to the tip-top belles of the South.

Neither campus nor plantation offered anything to reconcile him to his bondage, most certainly not on the slaveowner's premise that he was inherently inferior. On the contrary, the campus experience, giving him a small taste of relative freedom, stimulated his longing for release from slavery. In the late 1820's he had good reason to hope that this goal was within his reach.

4

Hope of Liberty

George Moses Horton's verse and something of his life story began to appear in periodicals of his native state and the distant North. Not widely, to be sure, and not often, but it was enough to inspire efforts to secure the poet's freedom by purchase.

Participants in these efforts were of the most diverse political hues, ranging from militant black Abolitionists to moderate white apologists for slavery, and this diversity was reflected in the geographic spread from North Carolina to New York and New England. Involved were a governor of North Carolina—and a black man, born in North Carolina and, for a time, the black man most feared by the Southern slavocracy. White advocates of selective black colonization in Africa sought Horton's purchase—and so did black free men, who vehemently opposed the colonization plan.

No coherent account exists of the extraordinary endeavor to buy Horton's freedom. There are only fragments and missing pieces, so that any outline of the story is broken by gaps and unresolved mysteries.

A part of the story was told in *Freedom's Journal,* an antislavery weekly published by blacks in New York, which in August and September of 1828 conducted a sustained campaign for Horton's emancipation. The campaign was opened in the August 8 edition with a front-page story about Horton, "an extraordinary young slave . . . who has astonished all who have witnessed his poetic talent." The story related sketchily how Horton had learned to read and how he had embarked upon his career as poet. This was all.

Three weeks later, on August 29, an announcement on an inside page read: "It is with pleasure we inform our readers that measures are about to be taken to effect the emancipation of this interesting young man." This announcement preceded a dispatch from an anonymous North Carolina correspondent, who reported that "a philanthropic gentleman of this country being on a visit to Chapel Hill as one of the Members of the Board for the annual visitation at the college" came upon Horton's poetry and was so impressed by it that "since that time he has undertaken the unpopular task of casting about to see if George's liberation can be effected." The name of the would-be emancipator was not divulged, but from the description he may be identified as a Southerner (being "of this country") and a white man of influence (being a gentleman, a philanthropist, and a member of a ceremonial delegation to the college).

Horton's master was written to, presumably by the mysterious "philanthropic gentleman" or an agent of his, "and has replied that he is not in the circumstances to do without the manual labor of the young man, as he is no less a farmer than a poet, but that towards the close of the year he might be induced to take a fair price for him." This seemed reasonable; it was then near the end of summer, when a healthy field hand was most needed on a farm, but later on, in the slack of the winter months, the owner would entertain a bid for the purchase of his slave.

The correspondent estimated a fair price for the slave at $400 to $500, and he appealed to readers of *Freedom's Journal* to contribute toward this sum. He did so apologetically, "Situated as you are, at a distance from our scenes of action," he wrote, "you might suppose in such an extent of territory as is embraced in N. Carolina, a sum like 4 or $500 might soon be gathered—and so it might, but for any other purpose sooner than the emancipation of a fellow human being—it is contrary to the policy of this country, and the few philanthropists whose hands act with their hearts, must despair of effecting this desirable object, without such auxiliaries as we fancy your caste to be."

In its September 5 edition *Freedom's Journal* sustained the campaign on a low key with a poem by Horton, entitled "Gratitude" and "dictated to the Gentleman who takes so kind an interest in his behalf." Two of its nine stanzas read:

>Philanthropy, thou feeling dove,
>Whose voice can sound the vassal free,
>Upon thy wings of humane love
>I'll fly to liberty.
>
>Thus may the feeling heart rejoice,
>And cause me to rejoice with thee,
>And triumph with a cheerful voice,
>The voice of liberty.

Hope of Liberty / 107

In the next edition (September 12) the campaign was continued on a higher pitch with a direct, urgent appeal. "*Something must be done—George M. Horton must be liberated from a state of bondage*," said the paper, underscoring these lines. "Were each person of colour in this city to give but one penny, there would be no danger about obtaining his liberty."

Then, after a lapse of three weeks, this appeared on October 3: "We feel proud in announcing the name of *David C. Walker* of Boston, Mass., as a subscriber to the fund to be raised for the purchase of George M. Horton, of North Carolina. . . ." Walker's was the only name announced during the campaign for the free-Horton fund. Walker, like Horton, was a black native of North Carolina, but he was born free; although his father was a slave his mother was free, and according to the law at the time his mother's status determined his. Free to move, he later did so, from North Carolina to New England, where he made his living by selling old clothes and made his reputation by fiery antislavery agitation. In 1828 he was listed in *Freedom's Journal* as among its "authorized agents in Massachusetts"; a year later he was to publish his impassioned appeal for revolt against slavery, which secured for him an eminent place in the history of the long battle for black freedom.

From the *Freedom's Journal* item that used Walker's name in Horton's behalf it seemed that funds were slow in coming and that time was running out. "Appeals to the humane and charitable have become we are well aware, so frequent of late, that many persons whose means are small, are at a stand to know which are the most deserving of their charity," the paper said. "As the time is drawing near when efforts will be made by the gentleman who has benevolently come forward to purchase him, we hope all who feel disposed to assist in this case of Christian philanthropy, will send us their names, in order that the expectations which have been raised by our correspondent of North Carolina, may not be disappointed."

This was the last mention in *Freedom's Journal* of Horton and the efforts to free him. Without any explanation the paper's readers were left with unanswered questions. Was enough money raised? Was Horton freed? If not, why not? The readers could have inferred that this was an instance when no news is bad news and the silence signified failure. This still would leave the related questions unanswered.

About twenty-five years later, in an address to students at Chapel Hill, Horton supplied some answers. He revealed that more than enough money was raised and that no less a personage than Governor John Owen of North Carolina undertook to negotiate the purchase of the poet from his slave master. "He [the Governor] made an extraordinary proposition which was refused with a frown of disdain," Horton recalled. "The proposition was to pay $100 more than any person of sound judgment should say I was worth. To this my master would not accede. Such was the miscarriage of the proposition from the feeling Governor to a man who had no regard for liberty, science or genius. Not even a spark of generosity then pervaded his iron heart."

In all the record of what Horton said and wrote there is no passage of greater anger and reproach; that he said it a quarter-century after the event suggests the enduring bitterness of his disappointment. At the time of the frustrated transaction, however, in 1828, he was not crushed by it, for he promptly tried another tack to secure his freedom. He planned to publish a volume of poetry and with the receipts from its sale and the sympathetic donations it elicited to realize a sum sufficient to purchase his release from bondage.

A baffling question attends this new venture. If Master James Horton declined to sell his slave into freedom when asked to do so by the governor of the state and when offered $100 more than the slave's fair market price, what grounds were there for believing that, in effect, he would permit the slave to buy himself? No answer is contained in the available record, and one can only speculate about the poet's calculation. Perhaps the calculation was related to one condition that was made explicit and public in the freedom-through-poetry undertaking: once freed, the poet would promptly sail for Liberia.

Because the prior negotiations, initiated by the "philanthropic gentleman" and conducted in their final phase by Governor Owen, were shrouded in secrecy, it is not known whether they entailed the poet's self-exile to Liberia. But there is firm ground for doubting that *Freedom's Journal* and, most certainly, David Walker would have associated themselves with the venture if migration to Africa was a condition. Both the paper and its Massachusetts agent were opposed to the African colonization scheme. Both argued that the country's black inhabitants were Americans, having validated their claim to a share of the land and its wealth through their sweat and suffering.

"We are Americans," said *Freedom's Journal*. "Many would rob us of the endeared name of 'Americans,' a description more emphatically belonging to us, than to five-sixths of this nation, and one that we will never yield."

With more forceful eloquence, Walker was to write later: "Let no man budge one step, and let slaveholders come to beat us from our country. America is more our country, than it is the whites—we have enriched it with our *blood and tears*:—and will they drive us from

Hope of Liberty / 109

property and homes, which we have earned with our *blood?* They must look sharp or this very thing will bring swift destruction upon them."

Walker was a principled man, and feeling this strongly about the proposed transplantation of troublesome blacks to Africa, it is hardly plausible that he would have participated in the free-Horton campaign if he knew it was contingent upon the poet's expatriation to Liberia. It might be, of course, that an expatriation proviso was involved in the secret diplomacy pursued by the "philanthropic gentleman" and his North Carolina associates on the scene and neither Walker nor *Freedom's Journal* ever knew of it. If this was so, then the subsequent publishing venture was different and no secret was made of exile as a condition for the poet's freedom.

Associated with Horton in producing his volume of poems *The Hope of Liberty* were the publishers, Gales & Son of Raleigh, North Carolina. Joseph Gales was the editor of the Raleigh *Register*, the paper that already had published some of Horton's verse. Gales was also the regional secretary of the American Colonization Society, which promoted emigration of Afro-Americans to Liberia. His son, Weston R. Gales, was entrusted with the funds realized from the book, either through subscriptions or donations, promising to return any donation if the total receipts were not enough to purchase the author's freedom. All this was conditional, as explained in the introduction to the poetic volume:

> Many persons . . . are solicitous that efforts at length be made to obtain by subscription, a sum sufficient for his [Horton's] emancipation, upon the condition of his going in the vessel which shall first afterwards sail for Liberia.

Consistent with the emigration proviso and the opinion of the publishers, the introduction is carefully attuned to the peculiar sentiment of white moderates in a Southern environment that was dominated by "the peculiar institution." The author is referred to as "George," no other name being appended and certainly no title such as Mister. Indeed, the introduction itself is not so labeled, but is called instead "Explanation." It begins: "George, who is the author of the following poetic effusions, is a Slave, the property of Mr. James Horton, of Chatham County, North Carolina. . . ."

The publishers conclude "this account of George" with "an assurance that he has been ever a faithful, honest, and industrious slave." They also assure the reader that "it is his earnest and only wish to become a member of that Colony [Liberia], to enjoy its privileges, and apply his industry, and mental abilities to the promotion of its prospects and his own."

Having portrayed him as the very model of a slave, the publishers faced the problem of explaining why anyone should part with money to help his release from a condition to which he was so well adapted. If they sensed any contradiction, they did not show it. They simply asserted: "That his heart has felt deeply and sensitively in this lowest possible condition of human nature, will easily be believed, and is impressively confirmed by one of his stanzas:

> Come, melting Pity, from afar,
> And break this vast enormous bar
>   Between a wretch and thee;
> Purchase a few short days of time,
> And bid a vassal soar sublime,
>   On wings of liberty.

It is a curious wringer of contradiction through which the mental and emotional processes of Southern white moderates passed. They described slavery as "this lowest possible condition of human nature," but deemed it a virtue to submit to slavery with faithfulness, honesty, and industry. They thought it admirable of a man to feel "deeply and sensitively" about this condition, but attached the penalty of self-exile from his native land to release from that condition. Still the most amazing contradiction of all was that a volume of verse by a slave, called *The Hope of Liberty*, was published in the capital of a slave state, and its publication, as one historian said, "was aided and abetted by some of the best men in the state."

The volume itself ran a modest twenty-two pages with twenty-one poems, three of them explicit protests against slavery. The most celebrated of these, "On Liberty and Slavery," reads:

> Alas! and am I born for this,
>   To wear this slavish chain?
> Deprived of all created bliss,
>   Through hardship, toil and pain.
>
> How long have I in bondage lain,
>   And languished to be free!
> Alas! and must I still complain—
>   Deprived of liberty.
>
> Oh, Heaven! and is there no relief
>   This side the silent grave—

Hope of Liberty / 111

> To soothe the pain—to quell the grief
>   And anguish of a slave?
>
> Come Liberty, thou cheerful sound,
>   Toll through my ravished ears!
> Come, let my grief in joys be drowned,
>   And drive away my fears.
>
> Say unto foul oppression, Cease:
>   Ye tyrants rage no more,
> And let the joyful trump of peace,
>   Now bid the vassal soar.
>
> Soar on the pinions of that dove
>   Which long has cooed for thee,
> And breathed her notes from Afric's grove,
>   The sound of Liberty.
>
> Oh, Liberty! thou golden prize,
>   So often sought by blood—
> We crave thy sacred sun to rise,
>   The gift of nature's God!
>
> Bid Slavery hide her haggard face,
>   And barbarism fly:
> I scorn to see the sad disgrace
>   In which enslaved I lie.
>
> Dear Liberty! upon thy breast,
>   I languish to respire;
> And like the Swan unto her nest,
>   I'd to thy smiles retire.
>
> Oh, blest asylum—heavenly balm!
>   Unto thy boughs I flee—
> And in thy shades the storm shall calm,
>   With songs of Liberty!

The poem was more an outcry of personal anguish than a militant clarion call, and even if Horton had been inclined to the latter, he would have been restrained by the auspices, circumstances, and purpose of the publication. At that he stretched discretion to its limits with those lines in the seventh stanza—"Oh, Liberty! thou golden prize,/So often sought by blood." To apprehensive slaveowners the conjunction of liberty and blood might have suggested more than poetic license, especially in the light of events that soon were to unfold.

More muted was "On Hearing of the Intention of a Gentleman to Purchase the Poet's Freedom." Inspired by the poet's recent experience and possibly intended to stimulate the generosity of the reader, typical lines were:

> The silent harp which on the osiers hung,
> Was then attuned, and manumission sung;
> Away by hope the clouds of fear were driven,
> And music breathed my gratitude to Heaven.

The third of the slave poems acquired a drumbeat from the repetition of a one-word line, imparting a marching militance to the rhythmical form, although the content is mostly plaintive, as expressed in the title, "The Slave's Complaint." The flavor of the poem is conveyed by these stanzas:

> Am I sadly cast aside,
> On misfortune's ragged tide?
> Will the world my pains deride
>   Forever?
>
> Must I dwell in slavery's night,
> And all pleasure take its flight,
> Far beyond my feeble sight,
>   Forever?
>
> Worst of all, must hope grow dim,
> And withhold her cheering beam?
> Rather let me sleep and dream
>   Forever!
>
> Something still my heart surveys,
> Groping through this dreary maze;
> Is it Hope?—then burn and blaze
>   Forever!

Aside from the three on slavery, the other poems in the volume were on more conventional themes—some romantic, some religious, some on death and some on nature. Included was "Love," that durable item in his on-campus business. Another that had seen prior service, having first appeared as a ghostwritten contribution to the university magazine and later in the Raleigh *Register* under Horton's by-line, was "On the Evening and Morning." One stanza reads:

> At length the silver queen begins to rise,
> And spread her glowing mantle in the skies,
> And from the smiling chambers of the east,
> Invites the eye to her resplendent feast.

The poem "To Eliza" was noteworthy for borrowing whole its last two lines from Byron:

Hope of Liberty / 113

>Eliza, I shall think of thee—
>My heart shall ever twine about thee;
>Fare thee well—but think of me,
>Compell'd to live and die without thee.
>"Fare thee well! and if forever,
>Still forever fare thee well!"*

The range of theme is further displayed in "On Death," with its felicitous final line:

>Methinks I hear the doleful midnight knell—
>Some parting spirit bids the world farewell;
>The taper burns as conscious of distress,
>And seems to show the living number less.

Modest as the volume was, it was the first by an Afro-American poet to be published since Phillis Wheatley's had appeared fifty-six years earlier. It was the first poetic volume ever by a black man in the South, slave or free. And it was the first, of course, by a black slave to cry out against his enslavement. A slave had published a book, prompting one Southern historian to remark, "How many university professors could boast as much?"

The volume was a literary milestone and for Horton an enormous personal achievement, but it did not realize his hope of liberty. One Southern commentator wrote, "whether from inadequate distribution, unsuitable promotion, public indifference, or racial opposition, the little booklet was ignored. The publisher later reported that not much profit was derived from it." A Northern editor, who brought out another edition of *The Hope of Liberty* in Philadelphia in 1837, hinted that Weston Gales retained the money realized from the first Raleigh edition.

There being no record of the financial arrangements and accounting, there is no evidence to sustain the Southern assumption of financial failure or the Northern insinuation of financial irregularity. Presumably, the money that Governor Owen commanded the previous year was re-

---

* The indebtedness to Byron is explicitly acknowledged by clothing the borrowed lines in quotation marks. Is there also an unacknowledged debt to Burns? The Scotch poet wrote in "From Thee Eliza," "Farewell, farewell, Eliza dear,/The maid that I adore!" Horton has been likened to Burns, and some of his verse has an affinity with the Scotsman's, but in listing poets he had read, he never mentioned Burns. Considering Burns's popularity in the United States and all the manifest reasons for his relevance to Horton, one would think that Mrs. Hentz or Dr. Caldwell brought him to Horton's attention, but there is no hard evidence of it.

turned to contributors when Master James Horton refused to accept it as payment for the poet. (It would be antic historical humor if Governor Owen returned any money to David Walker, for cash was to figure in later events that linked their names; it was cash that Owen offered as a price on Walker's head.) The volume of poetry, then, was intended to accumulate a new fund, and if it realized "not much profit," what exactly did this mean and what happened to it? Did Gales keep it, or did he give it to Horton, who spent it, once it proved insufficient for its intended purpose? In one respect Gales and Horton were brothers under their different-colored skins; both were inclined to "convivial excess," as one North Carolina chronicler said of Gales.

What happened to the money, if any, is a mystery that is not likely to be solved, but about one thing there is no mystery. It is the timing of Horton's volume, which could well have capsized the hopes that rode on the publishing venture. The poet's slender booklet coincided with the end of an era in the South, and now, portentous events signaled a new era that was destined toward the bloody climax of civil war.

5
Years of Reaction

The introduction to *The Hope of Liberty* was dated at Raleigh, July 2, 1829. A few months later David Walker's *Appeal* struck the South like a thunderbolt. The first of the three editions of Walker's tract was dated at Boston, September 29, 1829, and copies of it filtered into the South before October was out. Horton was lucky to get his volume off the press when he did; had publication been delayed until late autumn, it most likely would not have seen the light of day, not at that time, not after the shock of Walker's *Appeal to the Colored Citizens of the World, But in Particular, and Very Expressly, to Those of the United States of America.*

Like Nat Turner and John Brown, Walker was possessed by religious zeal in his assault upon slavery, not only as an injury to man, but as a blasphemous affront to God. His angry passion occasionally broke out of the bounds of sentence structure and grammatical form. But to Southern slaveowners ideological structures and social forms, far more vital than the grammatical, were threatened by his torrential eloquence.

Walker was the militant prophet, not the lyric poet; his seventy-six page pamphlet was the trumpet call for war against slavery that Horton's verse was not. Horton's poetry, addressed essentially to a white audience, could be tolerated and patronized in the South, but not Walker's prose, which was an impassioned appeal for revolt by the slaves, containing such passages as these:

> The whites want slaves, and want us for their
> slaves, but some of them will curse the day they ever
> saw us. As true as the sun ever shone in its meridian
> splendor, my colour will root some of them out of
> the very face of the earth. . . .
>
> Remember Americans, that we must and shall be
> free and enlightened as you are, will you wait until

we shall, under God, obtain our liberty under the
crushing arm of power? Will it not be dreadful for
you? I speak Americans for your own good. . . .

Symptomatic of the sickly fear with which the Southern Establishment ruled over its slave empire was the reaction to Walker's *Appeal,* the initial hysteria being fanned as copies of that "diabolical Boston pamphlet" cropped up among blacks and whites in scattered Southern locales, from Virginia to Louisiana.

A slave was caught with one in Savannah, Georgia, and sixty copies were found in the possession of a black preacher. In New Orleans four blacks were arrested on the charge of circulating the *Appeal.* In Richmond, Virginia, a copy was found among the effects of a free Negro, recently deceased, and later thirty copies were discovered in the possession of a live one. Two missionaries to the Cherokee Indians in Georgia—the Reverends Worcester and Butler—were arrested for owning a copy. A printshop in Milledgeville, Georgia, was raided after authorities came into possession of an alleged letter from Walker to its white proprietor, Elijah H. Burritt. Twenty pamphlets were found. Burritt was forced to flee when a hostile mob attacked his dwelling in the middle of the night.

When a black man in Walker's native town of Wilmington, purportedly an agent for the pamphlet's distribution in North Carolina, "was arrested with the vile goods upon him," says Horton's principal Southern biographer, the "state was shaken with horror." In Wilmington and the vicinity, along the Atlantic seaboard in the southeastern corner of the state where it adjoins South Carolina, slave patrols were reorganized, security watches were doubled. The tremor of horror spread as copies were reported not only up the coast at New Bern but also in Fayetteville, Chapel Hill, and Hillsborough, towns that dot a long line stretching inland to the northwest from Wilmington.

In Raleigh, Governor Owen, who had tried to purchase Horton's freedom less than a year earlier, now demanded legislative action against Walker, his distant and fortuitous associate in those manumission efforts. The governor sent copies of the *Appeal* to the legislators along with his opinion that it was part of a gigantic conspiracy by Northern Abolitionists. The legislature responded by placing a price on Walker's head: $1,000 dead, $10,000 alive. The reward was a brief temptation. Walker died in 1830 at age forty-four, and although his black compatriots in Boston suspected murder ("I expect some will try to put me to death, to strike terror to others," he had written in the *Appeal*), his body was not for bounty hunters.

The reward was a demonstration of official temper, which soon

Years of Reaction / 117

produced other legislative enactments, stamped with the logic of practical men concerned with the perils of the printed word. The first law provided that any person found guilty of writing or circulating publications that might "excite insurrection, conspiracy, or resistance in the slaves or free Negroes" was to be "imprisoned for not less than a year and be put in the pillory and whipped at the discretion of the court." For a second offense the penalty was "death without benefit of clergy."

Severe as this was, it was deemed not enough. By December, 1830, North Carolina's legislators concluded that the danger lay not simply in the nature of written material directed to blacks but in the very capacity of slaves to read or write. Such knowledge, the legislators decreed, afforded slaves with "facilities of intelligence and communication, inconsistent with their condition, destructive of their contentment and happiness, and dangerous to the community." They passed a law "to prevent these evils," reiterating in the preamble, "Whereas the teaching of slaves to read and write has a tendency to excite dissatisfaction in their minds and to produce insurrection and rebellion. . . ."

The law provided three gradations of penalty for three grades of humanity. For teaching or attempting to teach any slave to read or write ("the use of figures excepted"), or for giving or selling any book or pamphlet to a slave, the penalty was:

For a white person, a fine of not less than $100 and not more than $200, or imprisonment (the period being left to the discretion of the court).

For a free black person, a fine, imprisonment, or whipping, "at the discretion of the court," this discretion being circumscribed only in the case of whipping: no more than thirty-nine lashes and no less than twenty.

A slave who attempted to teach another slave to read or write, again excepting the use of figures, was "to receive thirty-nine lashes on his or her bare back."

Much more barbarous laws than this were enacted in other Southern states to keep the knowledge of reading and writing from slaves. However, even the North Carolina law hardly improved the market for a slave's literary efforts, for now his attainments were explicitly branded by public policy as an evil that ought to be stamped out. Nor were matters helped by the antislavery protest in those efforts. Not much elasticity or imagination was required in the prosecuting or judicial mind to discern "a tendency to excite dissatisfaction" in some of Horton's verse.

After white North Carolina was shaken with horror by Walker's *Ap-*

peal, a venture to purchase a slave's freedom was not the same thing as it was before. Moreover, if James Horton was unwilling to sell the poet in calmer times, he was even less likely to do so now when prevailing public opinion was so inflamed against any suggestion that it was proper for a slave to be freed. Whether *The Hope of Liberty* might have generated sufficient momentum to achieve its purpose is idle speculation; once Walker's *Appeal* fevered the Southern white imagination, with its deep fears and dark guilts, the hope may not have been totally extinguished, but any prospect for its imminent realization was gone.

The question was, for how long? As it turned out, it was for a long time in a man's life span. Before the furor over Walker's *Appeal* had run its course the flames of Nat Turner's insurrection of 1831 streaked across the Southern sky like an earnest of Walker's prophecy. It was late August and the summer's heat lay heavy on tidewater Virginia when the small band of slave rebels, no more than seventy at the peak, struck with the vengeful fury of the long-oppressed, knowing that for them liberty-or-death was not just the rhetoric of a bygone Virginian, and between those alternatives being far more familiar with death than with the other. The revolt was as brief as it was sudden; within ten days, overwhelmed by superior force, all but Turner were captured, and two months later he too was taken. They were crushed and killed, but not before they had underlined in blood the question that Walker had asked of Americans: "Will it not be dreadful for you?"

The panic at words and exhortations turned into frenzy at the sight of blood and weapons, mostly farm implements and wooden staves with a few firearms. For the fifty-seven white lives taken by Turner and his insurrectionaries, many more black lives were exacted in retribution and fear, some far from tidewater Virginia and for no more reason than suspicion or apprehension. In eastern North Carolina scores of slaves were arrested and more than a dozen were executed. Arrests and executions were reported in other parts of the South, and throughout the region there were counterinsurgency measures that approximated martial law.

Still more restrictive laws were enacted. A North Carolina historian observed, "The period around 1830 is a turning point in the history of Negro slavery in the United States. Prior to that date the South had more or less apologized for its 'peculiar institution.' After that date it defended slavery as a 'positive good.' . . . Laws pertaining to slaves became more severe." Among the laws were those imposing new restrictions and conditions on manumission. By the mid-1830's North Carolina required a $1,000 surety before manumission to guarantee the freed slave's good behavior, and the freed slave had to leave the state within ninety days, never to return.

It was a watershed year, 1830, and for Horton in a personal vein as well. Up until 1829 his life described an ascending curve: the mastery of reading followed by the conquest of poetry; his unique professional status, mostly as a ghostwriter, climaxed with the publication of a volume. With this progression in his chosen lifework freedom seemed a realizable goal. Then came 1830, sandwiched in between Walker's *Appeal* and Turner's insurrection and the reaction of the slavocracy. In the decade that followed there were no efforts to purchase his freedom, and there is no record that his own endeavors aimed at anything more than a relaxation of slavery's restrictions upon his person. No new volume of his was published in the 1830's, although at least two editions of *The Hope of Liberty* were published in the North and individual poems cropped up in the Abolitionist press.

In 1830 Horton reached the age of thirty-three, and this at a time when life expectancy was less than what it is today, when slaves (and most free workmen as well) began their labors in childhood and, ready or not, soon bore the cares and burdens of maturity. At thirty-three a man was likely to become anxious about the passage of time, to wonder whether what was left of it for him was as much as the portion he had already consumed, especially if at the moment time was shadowed by adversity.

In the preceding two years Horton's hope of liberty had been twice dashed. The political and social climate afforded scant ground for anticipating an early and realistic revival of such hope, and even if he were only vaguely aware of the larger political and social currents in the wake of Walker's *Appeal* and Turner's insurrection, his manifest intelligence and the particular social sensitivity acquired by slaves as a survival mechanism should have sufficed to inform him that it was a poor time for freedom. The general adversity of the times was soon compounded by two intimate, personal blows. He lost his two most helpful patrons and counselors. Caroline Lee Hentz left Chapel Hill in 1831; university president Caldwell died in 1835.

More than ever Horton was thrown back upon his own resources. These were not now directed toward emancipation, but to making life as tolerable as possible within the bonds of slavery. Poetry was his principal resource, and he continued to write and to preserve his unique place at the university even after the departure of Mrs. Hentz and the death of Caldwell. He sought solace in whisky. He married. He also achieved the maximum "freedom" possible for a slave by hiring out his time.

Hiring out was an arrangement whereby a slave was required to pay his master a specified sum, and in return was free to seek such work as he could find and support himself as best he could. Frederick Douglass, before his escape from slavery, was permitted to hire out his time to work as a caulker in Baltimore shipyards, and later described his arrangement: "I was allowed all my time; to make all bargains for work; to find my own employment, and to collect my own wages; and, in return for this liberty, I was required, or obliged, to pay . . . three dollars at the end of each week, and to board and clothe myself and buy my own calking tools. A failure in any of these particulars would put an end to my privilege. This was a hard bargain."

In short, a slave was permitted to support himself, providing he contributed to the support of his master. Presumably Douglass' labors as a caulker also produced a profit for the shipyard owner. He was thus privileged to contribute toward the support of two masters, instead of just one. In Douglass' case, the $156 a year he was obliged to pay his slavemaster may be compared with the estimated annual cost of $25 to $35 for the total upkeep of a slave on a Southern plantation. As hard as the hiring out bargain was, it was considered a privilege among slaves, whereas most slaveowners regarded it as a dangerous practice because it permitted slaves too much freedom and was apt to stimulate an appetite for more. Indeed, in the post-1830 period North Carolina was among the Southern states to prohibit the practice by law, but as with other slave laws its enforcement was sufficiently flexible to suit the convenience (or the profit) of the slaveowner.

Just when Horton began to hire out is obscure; so is the frequency and consistency with which he did it. The publisher's introduction to *The Hope of Liberty* still had the poet working full-time on his master's plantation in 1829. This may have been so, but even if it were not so and Horton already was hiring out, it is unlikely that the publishers would have revealed it, for they were aware of the prevailing disapproval of the practice and were anxious to present Horton as an industrious slave worthy of Southern philanthropy.

Also uncertain are the precise terms of the arrangement, but they changed for the worse after the poet's second master, James Horton, died in 1843. The plantation passed to Hall Horton, James's son, and the movable appurtenances and chattel, including the poet, were placed on the auction block to pay off accumulated debts. Many years later the poet is said to have recalled that his purchaser "reckoned his age by looking into his mouth, judged the state of his health by whipping him, and determined the condition of his immortal soul by damning him to hell." This, at least, is the story told by one historian, although it may be assumed that the successful buyer had some prior knowledge of the poet's age and health, if not of his immortal soul which was not a tangible asset. The purchaser was Hall Horton, a practical man who must have taken the trouble to become acquainted with the estate he was to inherit.

A tanner by trade, Hall Horton had the reputation of being a "hard master," who worked his slaves hard and punished them well. Exhibiting confidence in his methods, he concluded he could exact more from the poet by working him on the plantation than his father had by permitting him to hire out. The poet, understandably, disapproved of any such arrangement. Wise, resourceful, and forty-six, he resorted to a "slowdown," the most common form of passive resistance among slaves. In conception the stratagem was simple enough, but it required subtlety in execution; the slowdown could not be so conspicuous as to invite punishment and yet had to be effective enough to persuade Hall Horton that it would be more profitable for him to permit his slave to hire out. It was a battle of wills and the poet finally prevailed, but it was a costly victory. Hall Horton was still the master with the power to set the terms for the hard bargain of the hiring-out contract. He doubled the price, demanding payment of fifty cents per day, instead of the twenty-five cents his father took. For the price of letting one poet go, he could hire two good field hands, either one of whom, as one historian observed, would be more productive on the plantation.

At fifty cents a day the conditional ransom approximated that exacted from Douglass, but Horton was more fortunate because he derived his primary earnings from the sale of his poems, and being a familiar figure on campus he could supplement this income with odd jobs. Just where or how he lived as poetic entrepreneur and occasional wage earner is a matter that Horton kept private, and no one else thought it of sufficient moment to ascertain and record it. It must have been a spare existence, but it gave him a sense of relative freedom and more time for poetry. And for whisky.

Much about his life between publication of *The Hope of Liberty* in 1829 and the appearance of his next preserved volume in 1845 can only be inferred from the content of the latter. It reveals an intimate and excessive acquaintance with the bottle.

In the autobiographic sketch appended to the 1845 volume he wrote: "One thing is to be lamented much; that is, that ever I was raised in a family or neighborhood inclined to dissipation . . . Drinking . . . was a catholic toleration. . . . Hence it was inevitably my misfortune to become a votary of that growing evil."

Having made the acquaintance of alcohol on the plantation, he met it once again on campus, for he wrote: "There is one thing with which I am sorry to charge many of these [student] gentlemen. Before the moral evil of excessive drinking had been impressed upon my mind, they flattered me into the belief that it would hang me on the wings of new inspiration, which would waft me into the regions of poetical perfection. And I am not a little astonished that nature and reason had not taught me better before. . . ."

He turned to the same theme in a poem, "The Tippler to His Bottle":

> Often have I thy stream admired,
>   Thou nothing hast availed me ever,
> Vain have I thought myself inspired;
> Say have I else but pain acquired?
>   Not ever! No, never!

The self-reproach, the recrimination, the reference to pain, the resort to exclamation points, the familiarity of the address—all of these denote more than a casual companionship with the bottle. Much alcohol must have flowed between 1829 and 1845 to have produced those lines. Those sixteen years covered the span between his early thirties and late forties. He no longer was the contemporary in age of the university students, and although they encouraged him to drink, they did so as pranksters and not as boon drinking companions. The barriers of color and condition of servitude were formidable enough, and now there was also the age gap. It is also hardly likely that he found drinking partners among the blacks, for none shared his unique status. Either they were tied to the plantations in the vicinity, or if in town they were likely to be household servants who had to be discreet in the protection of their preferred position. In any event, from all the available accounts Horton did not particularly seek out the company of blacks. Apparently he drank alone, and unlike other drinking poets, none of his references to the pastime is buoyed by any sense of conviviality or companionship.

Still, he wrote about his drinking. But he did not write about his marriage. Not even the name of his wife has been preserved. All that is known about her is that she was the slave of a man named Franklin Snipes, and gave birth to two children, a son and a daughter, in her marriage with the poet. The son was known as Free Snipes (deriving his surname from the slave master, and not the father) and he died in Durham, North Carolina, in 1896. The daughter, Rhody, married a man named Van Buren Byrum and was reported to be still living in 1897, then residing in Raleigh.

This is all, absolutely all, that is known about the poet's marriage

Years of Reaction / 123

and his family. At best the marriage was a part-time liaison, for the wife belonged to one slaveowner and he to another, and even when the poet enjoyed the relative freedom of movement in hiring out, the time and place of sojourns with his wife were subject to the convenience of her owner. These hardly were the circumstances for a happy marriage, and there may have been other barriers that can only be surmised. What sense did his consuming interest in poetry make to her, or what effort did he make to excite her interest? Aside from their physical union, was there anything between the center of his universe in Chapel Hill and hers in Snipes' slave domain? It has been said that only Franklin Snipes profited from the marriage. He at least secured two more slaves from this union.

One wonders if the poet read to his matrimonial partner an earlier poem that was published in his 1829 volume, entitled "On the Consequence of Happy Marriages," containing such stanzas as these:

> Their peaceful life is all content and ease,
> They with delight each other strive to please;
> Each other's charms, *they* only can admire,
> Whose bosoms burn with pure connubial fire.
>
> Th' indelible vestige of unblemished love,
> Must hence a guide to generations prove:
> Though virtuous partners moulder in the tomb,
> Their light may shine on ages yet to come.

If he did read these lines was he sober? And what did she make of them? For that matter, when he wrote the lines was the feeling authentic, expressing a slave's romanticized dream of what might be, in contrast to the humiliating reality of mutilated marriage under the slave system, or were these lines a mere extension of his romanticized ghostwriting, which supplied conventional verse forms to articulate what others were supposed to feel? He wrote no such verse during his marriage or after.

A chronic drinker burdened with an unhappy marriage—it is a stereotype of a pathetic figure, and if this were all there was to the poet, he soon would have been crushed. But he was not crushed. There was more to the man, and one wellspring of strength marked a vein of his poetry that was not included in *The Hope of Liberty*, possibly for fear that it might offend Christian philanthropists and their sense of propriety, most particularly their feeling for what is virtue in a slave. There is irony in this vein, and earthy humor, a subtly mocking irreverence mixed with folk wisdom. The poems written in this vein are his most original and more revealing of a human personality than all but a very few of the verses in a more conventional cast. An exemplar of this is "The Fate of an Innocent Dog":

> When Tiger left his native yard,
> He did not many ills regard,
>   A fleet and harmless cur;
> Indeed, he was a trusty dog,
> And did not through the pastures prog,
> The grazing flocks to stir, poor dog,
>   The grazing flocks to stir.
>
> He through a field by chance was led,
> In quest of game not far ahead,
>   And made one active leap;
> When all at once, alarm'd, he spied,
> A deadly wounded sheep, alas!
>   A deadly wounded sheep.
>
> He there was fill'd with sudden fear,
> Apprized of lurking danger near,
>   And there he left his trail;
> Indeed, he was afraid to yelp,
> Nor could he grant the creature help,
> But wheel'd and drop'd his tail, poor dog,
>   But wheel'd and drop'd his tail.
>
> It was his pass-time, pride and fun,
> At morn the nimble hare to run,
>   When frost was on the grass;
> Returning home who should he meet?
> The weather's owner, coming fleet,
> Who scorn'd to let him pass, alas!
>   Who scorn'd to let him pass.
>
> Tiger could but his bristles raise,
> A surly compliment he pays,
>   Insulted was his wrath;
> Returns a just defensive growl,
> And does not turn aside to prowl,
> But onward keeps the path, poor dog,
>   But onward keeps the path.
>
> The raging owner found the brute,
> But could afford it no recruit,
>   Nor raise it up to stand;
> 'Twas mangled by some other dogs,
> A set of detrimental rogues,
> Raised up at no command, alas!
>   Raised up at no command.

> Sagacious Tiger left his bogs,
> But bore the blame of other dogs,
>   With powder, fire and ball;
> They kill'd the poor, unlawful game,
> And then came back and eat the same;
> But Tiger paid for all, poor dog,
>   But Tiger paid for all.
>
> Let ev'ry harmless dog beware,
> Lest he be taken in the snare,
>   And scorn such fields to roam;
> A creature may be fraught with grace,
> And suffer for the vile and base,
> By straggling off from home, alas!
>   By straggling off from home.
>
> The blood of creatures oft is split,
> Who die without a shade of guilt;
>   Look out, or cease to roam;
> Whilst up and down the world he plays
> For pleasure, man in danger strays
> Without a friend from home, alas!
>   Without a friend from home.

More than a commentary on the ways of the world is suggested in the above fable or parable in verse; there is also the pleasure of irony in observing them. The poet savored life, and he must have relished much in his struggle for self-assertion or survival, recognizing the definite limits imposed upon him by circumstance, and yet, short of breaking out of these limits, achieving victories and triumphs of varying proportion. Above all, he remained a poet.

6

Poetical Works

Everything seemed to change for George Moses Horton, the temper of the times and the contours of his private life, but one thing remained constant. He continued to write poetry. And he continued to cast about for the publication of what he wrote.

In the early 1840's he assembled at least two volumes of verse, possibly more, only one of which has been preserved. References crop up in existing records to a missing volume entitled *The Museum*. It is mentioned in a communication to the *Southern Literary Messenger* in early 1843 from Professor William Mercer Green, who enclosed two selections from what he described as a collection in manuscript form. In 1845 there is another reference to *The Museum*, and this time the implication that it had been available to the general public suggests that it was published. This last reference was contained in the introduction to the volume of Horton's works in this period that has been preserved.

Seed money for the 1845 volume, published in Hillsborough, North Carolina, by Dennis Heartt, editor of the Hillsborough *Recorder*, was secured through advance subscription lists, according to one Southern historian. In the unsigned introduction the contents are described as "miscellaneous effusions" that "are original, and recently written" and, in their sum, "entirely different from his other work entitled The Museum." Since *The Museum* proved to be more ephemeral than its name, the difference alleged cannot be explored, but the contrasts with *The Hope of Liberty* can be noted and they are significant.

The 1845 volume was more ambitious—ninety-six pages bound in blue paper (compared with twenty-two pages in 1829). The title, more ornate, was also more muted. It read:

THE POETICAL WORKS
of
GEORGE M. HORTON

The colored Bard of North-Carolina

To Which is Prefixed
The Life of the Author
Written by Himself

Nothing so subversive as liberty in this title, and nothing so dangerous as hope, and in the introduction there is no direct mention of slavery, only allusions to it. There is no implicit condemnation of it, no reference to the poet's feelings about it, and certainly no hint that he might desire freedom. None of these ingredients of the 1829 introduction is now present. Now there is self-abnegation:

> The author is far from flattering himself with an idea of superiority, or even equality with ancient or other modern poets. He is deeply conscious of his own inferiority from the narrowness of the scope in which he has lived during the course of his past life. . . .
> He was actuated merely by pleasure and curiousity, as a call to some literary task, or as an example to remove the doubts of cavilists with regard to African genius.

After this single affirmative note the introduction goes on: "His birth was low, and in a neighborhood by no means populous; his raising was rude and laborious; his exertions were cramped, and his progress obstructed from start to goal; having been ever deprived of the free use of books and other advantages to which he aspired. Hence his genius is but an unpolished diamond, and can never shine forth to the world."

Although the 1845 volume contained twice as many poems as its 1829 predecessor, only one bears directly on slavery, and even this one treats with but a facet of bondage, avoiding any protest so explicit as that voiced in the famous lines of 1829:

> Alas! and am I born for this,
> To wear this slavish chain?

Now, in 1845, the one slave poem is entitled "Division of an Estate" and might have been inspired by his own memories of the several personal encounters with this procedure. Lines from this poem read:

> . . . but O, the state,
> The dark suspense in which poor vassals stand,
> Each mind upon the spire of chance hangs, fluctuate,

> The day of separation is at hand.
> Imagination lifts her gloomy curtain
> Like evening's mantle at the flight of day,
> Through which the trembling pinnacle we spy,
> On which we soon must stand with hopeful smiles,
> On apprehending frowns to tumble on
> The right or left forever.

Avoidance of slavery or liberty as subject matter was conspicuous also in the autobiography. Rambling and repetitive, studded with moralisms, especially about the evils of dissipation, it ran for twenty printed pages, but there was not one reference or allusion to the efforts of 1828–29 to secure his freedom, although, as disclosed a decade later, these events, with their disappointment, were deeply inscribed on his memory. This was another decade in 1845, another era, and prudent recognition of it did not permit the poet at forty-eight to recollect his hopes at thirty-two, and the hope of liberty having been banked, he settled for poetry.

The staple themes of 1829—nature, love, mortality, religion—were staple once again, but there also were new themes: poems about famous contemporaries (a eulogy to Andrew Jackson and two poems about Henry Clay, one in praise and one in detraction) and, more important, verses in the humorous folk vein. "The Fate of an Innocent Dog" was joined in the volume with "The Woodman and the Money Hunter," "The Creditor to His Proud Debtor," and "Troubled with the Itch and Rubbing with Sulphur." This last poem, with its free indulgence in personal experience and physical sensation, reads:

> 'Tis bitter, yet 'tis sweet,
>   Scratching effects but transient ease;
> Pleasure and pain together meet,
>   And vanish as they please.
>
> My nails, the only balm,
>   To ev'ry bump are oft applied,
> And thus the rage will sweetly calm
>   Which aggravates my hide.
>
> It soon returns again;
>   A frown succeeds to ev'ry smile;
> Grinning I scratch and curse the pain,
>   But grieve to be so vile.
>
> In fine, I know not which
>   Can play the most deceitful game,
> The devil, sulphur, or the itch;
>   The three are but the same.

> The devil sows the itch,
> > And sulphur has a loathesome smell,
> And with my clothes as black as pitch,
> > I stink where'er I dwell.
>
> Excoriated deep,
> > By friction play'd on ev'ry part,
> It oft deprives me of my sleep,
> > And plagues me to my heart.

Two other facets of personal experience lace the volume. As noted before, bouts with the bottle are recorded in the autobiography and a poem, and there is also the reflection of difficulties with money. Presumably, such difficulties were among his privileges in hiring out and fending for himself, not only having to provide his own food, clothes, and possibly shelter, but also compelled to make the weekly payments to his master on pain of forfeiting his limited freedom.

Just how cruel the necessity for money became at times is indicated by one money-raising venture he contrived. He would pen a verse sorrowing over mythical sickness and distress in his family. Then, fortified with alcohol, he made the rounds of student dormitories, reading the verse aloud in tearful tones, pleading that the students "lend a hand to the unfortunate old bard." Without resorting to such dissembling pathos in the volume his chronic money problem was conveyed in "The Woodman and the Money Hunter":

> Throughout our rambles much we find;
> > The bee trees burst with honey;
> Wild birds we tame of every kind,
> At once they seem to be resign'd;
> I know but one that lags behind,
> > There's nothing lags but money.
>
> The woods afford us much supply,
> > The opposum, coon, and coney;
> They all are tame and venture nigh,
> Regardless of the public eye,
> I know but one among them shy,
> > There's nothing shy but money.

His maturity as a poet, in verse pattern, in originality and humor, is displayed in "The Creditor to His Proud Debtor":

> Ha! tott'ring Johnny strut and boast,
> But think of what your feathers cost;
> Your crowing days are short at most,
> > Your bloom but soon to fade.

Surely you could not stand so wide,
If strictly to the bottom tried,
The wind would blow your plumes aside,
    If half your debts were paid.
        Then boast and bear the crack,
        With the sheriff at your back,
        Huzza for dandy Jack,
        My jolly fop, my Jo.

The blue smoke from your segar flies,
Offensive to my nose and eyes;
The most of people would be wise
    Your presence to evade.
Your pockets jingle loud with cash,
And thus you cut a foppish dash,
But alas! dear boy, you would be trash
    If your accounts were paid.
        Then boast and bear the crack.
        With the sheriff at your back,
        Huzza for dandy Jack,
        My jolly fop, my Jo.

My duck bill boots would look as bright,
Had you in justice served me right;
Like you, I then could step as light,
    Before a flaunting maid.
As nicely could I clear my throat;
And to my tights my eyes devote;
But I'd leave you bare, without the coat
    For which you have not paid.
        Then boast and bear the crack,
        With the sheriff at your back,
        Huzza for dandy Jack,
        My jolly fop, my Jo.

Psychologically, it appears, money was less oppressive than alcohol. He wrote about it more impersonally, with humorous verve.

In the discernment of personal emotion and experience in the volume, still another poem, "The Traveller," is highly suggestive, possibly reflecting his response to schemes for his emigration to Liberia sixteen years earlier. At the time his publishers, Gales & Son, assured readers that in seeking freedom it was Horton's "earnest and only wish to become a member of that Colony [Liberia]," but the poet's own writings never expressed such a sentiment. He wrote then of his hopes and wishes, and if Liberia beckoned to him as a haven or inspired any enthusiasm at all, his expression of such feeling would not have been inhibited by considerations of prudence.

Against this background of 1829 there are these verses in "The Traveller":

> I never shall forget
> The by-gone pleasures of my native shore,
> Until the sun of life forbears to set,
>   And pain is known no more.
>
> When nature seems to weep,
> And life hangs trembling o'er the watery tomb,
> Hope lifts her peaceful sail to brave the deep,
>   And bids me think of home.

Any fancier of poetry circa 1845 would have recognized in the above a meter and rhyme pattern that had been employed by the most celebrated American poet of the age, William Cullen Bryant. But was Horton familiar with Bryant's work? There is no direct testimony, either by him or anyone else, that he was, and yet it seems implausible that he was not. It seems unlikely that Caroline Lee Hentz, and perhaps some others who gave him counsel and help, would not have directed Horton's attention to the contemporary who was widely acclaimed as the country's first poet laureate.

Whatever the merit of such credible speculation, there is a prosodic resemblance between the stanzas above and this from "To a Waterfowl":

> Vainly the fowler's eye
> Might mark thy distant flight to do thee wrong
> As, darkly seen against the crimson sky,
>   Thy figure floats along.

The most striking similarity between the two poets, however, lies not in the use of any particular form but in the diversity of forms. Lacking hard evidence that the Southern slave was directly influenced by the Northern editor, one may also attribute resemblance to the poetic spirit of the times that affected both. Horton was a man of the nineteenth century, when romanticism dethroned neoclassicism in the kingdom of poetry. He was more fortunate than Wheatley, for the change of sovereigns had released poetry from the tyranny of the couplet, from the heavy burden of ornamental rhetoric and ritualistic invocation of muses and the rest of the Greco-Roman panoply. He was not the poet Bryant was, either in prosodic range or craft discipline or in the emotional and intellectual articulation that is poetic essence, but in his poetic freedom he had the discernment and versatility to choose the verse form that suited what he wanted to say. And his forms ranged from the popular ballad, with its refrain, to the decasyllabic couplet, used with discretion, although most of his work was attuned to the lyric strains of romanticism.

In lyric lilt there is a parallel between Bryant's

> I cannot forget with what fervid devotion
> I worshipped the visions of verse and of fame

and Horton's

> While tracing thy visage I sing in emotion
> For no other damsel so wondrous I see . . .

The two poets also shared in a familiar affection for nature, expressing it often without neoclassical flourish. Plantation slavery was, of course, at least as intimate an introduction to nature as childhood in the home of a New England country doctor, and Horton's intimacy was the more enduring as Bryant moved on to an editorial office in New York. A suggestive contrast in their perceptions of nature is afforded in two poems that are otherwise similar in their humorous paradox. In "To the Gad-Fly," the rustic bondsman's accent is on utility:

> Majestic insect! from thy royal hum,
> The flies retreat, or starve before they'll come;
> The obedient plough-horse may, devoid of fear,
> Perform his task with joy when thou art near.

In "To a Mosquito," the urban editor also began with an exclamation, "Fair insect!" but his winged subject is apprehended on a wayward flight into New York:

> Thou'rt welcome to the town; but why come here
> To bleed a brother poet, gaunt like thee?
> Alas! the little blood I have is dear
> And thin will be the banquet drawn from me.
>
> Try some plump alderman, and suck the blood
> Enriched by generous wine and costly meat . . .

For Horton the "pleasures of my native shore" embraced the Carolina countryside, its fields and woods and their inhabitants. How often had he walked alone the eight miles between plantation and campus, through all the seasons and climates of the year, in the several times of day, observing nature in all its moods? This was his home. He knew it with a poet's perception and sensitivity, and in 1845, when his volume was published and he was nearing fifty, he had known no other. So traces of nostalgia appear, and they extend from the countryside to the campus in a poem "On the Pleasures of College Life." This is in praise of learning, filled with great names and academic staples— Homer, Demosthenes, Plato, Ovid, Pope, Addison, Locke, Newton, the Greek and Latin tongues, geography, botany, zoology.

For such themes the texture of "dandy Jack, my jolly fop, my Jo" would not do. His sense of the appropriate called for the couplet:

> Around me spread a vast extensive lawn;
> 'Twas there the most of college life begun,
> Beneath the rays of erudition's sun,
> Where study drew the mystic focus down,
> And lit the lamp of nature with renown;
> There first I heard the epic thunders roll.
> And Homer's light'ning darted through my soul.
> Hard was the task to trace each devious line,
> Though Locke and Newton bade me soar and shine.

Nostalgia tinges the past; death shadows the future. In "Imploring To Be Resigned at Death," he wrote:

> Let me die and not tremble at death,
> But smile at the close of my day,
> And then at the flight of my breath,
> Like a bird of the morning in May,
> Go chanting away.

In the range of mood and theme (except for the dangerous theme of slavery and liberty), in the variety of verse forms and language usage, the volume eclipsed the earlier efforts of 1829. The forms ranged from the blank verse of "Division of an Estate" to the couplet of "On the Pleasures of College Life," from the simple quatrain of "Troubled With the Itch . . ." to the intricate pattern of rhyme and rhythm in the twelve-line stanzas of "The Creditor to His Proud Debtor." In the latter the rhyme pattern—aaabcccbdddd—is given a fillip with the unrhymed last line of the refrain, "My jolly fop, my Jo." There are also five-line and six-line stanzas, different in rhyme and meter.

A similar variety marks the diction; much of it is demotic vernacular —*itch, stink, segar, bump, hide*—but it also encompasses such lines as these:

> Imagination lifts her gloomy curtain
> Like evening's mantle at the flight of day.

> There first I heard the epic thunders roll
> And Homer's light'ning darted through my soul.

In this volume Horton reached his maturity as a poet. But he was no monetary success. The volume was priced at fifty cents (the equivalent then of the price of four pounds of butter or six dozen eggs). "Seven years after publication," one historian reports, "copies were still available, the price down to twenty-five cents."

7
Vain Appeals

Once George Moses Horton began to hire out, more than ever the campus became for him the critical arena, in which he had to maintain his precarious balance in economics and status, walking a tightrope between plantation slavery and the semblance of "free enterprise." And the university was no longer presided over by his counselor and patron, Dr. Caldwell.

With Caldwell's death in 1835 an altogether different sort of man was inaugurated to direct the university. Ex-Governor David L. Swain was a politician, not a scholar, and the contrast between him and his predecessor also extended to physical appearance, personal manner, and style.

"In appearance," wrote one university historian, "he was the very reverse of Dr. Caldwell. Though pleasant and accessible, there was a lack of the old-school air of quiet and dignified courtesy—the old *prestige* of literary association and achievement. . . . He was singularly homely in countenance, awkward in person and careless in manner and dress, and his unusual height and size gave additional emphasis to every *gaucherie*."

More crudely, a university alumnus recalled in his memoirs: "He was a malformation in person, out of proportion in physical conformation, apparently thrown together in haste and manufactured from scattered debris of material that had been used in other work. . . . In addition . . . he was an unlettered man and owed nothing to the primary or higher schools, and so far as scholastic training goes, he was an ignorant man."

Such descriptions of the man may be tainted with the social snobbery of Southern aristocracy and the intellectual snobbery of the academy. This same historian described Swain as "a man who, from a raw mountain lad, with a very modest share of education, had risen with unexampled rapidity to be Legislator, Solicitor, Judge, Congressman, and, finally, Governor of the State, by the time he was 34 years old. . . . He saw clearly, he acted cautiously, he felt kindly. . . . What power he had . . . . was of his own acquisition among men and not among books. He set very little value on the accumulations of books."

A remarkably successful politician, he apparently was an able administrator, remaining as the university's president for thirty-three years, and when he was removed after the Civil War it was not for incompetence but for offending the sensibilities of unreconstructed Confederates.

His rapid rise from "a raw mountain lad" to the governorship of North Carolina might offhand suggest identification with Jacksonian Democracy, but Swain was no Democrat, he was a Whig. In the contradictions of ante-bellum politics, if his Whiggery set him apart from the democratic aspects of the Jacksonian upsurge, it also set him apart from the most intransigent protagonists of slavery, who were centered in the Democratic party. Representing interests that favored a stronger Union, largely for the economic benefits that accrued from such an arrangement, the Whigs in Southern and border states tended to be more moderate than the Democrats on issues related to slavery, although they did not, of course, challenge it where it existed. The biggest Whig of them all, Henry Clay of Kentucky, became known as the Great Compromiser, but this Whig gift for compromise progressively declined in political value and moral weight as the conflict over slavery became ever more irrepressible and efforts to reconcile the irreconcilable became ever more futile. On a modest plane the politics of Whiggery affected the behavior of Swain, the politician turned academic administrator, toward Horton, the plantation slave turned poet.

By the time Swain arrived on the campus scene Horton had been a part of it for eighteen years and was something of a campus institution. His relationship with Caldwell had been founded on shared interests, on the older man's appreciation of the young slave's poetic gift and his thirst for learning. These were not the foundations for an amicable relationship with Swain, and yet such a relationship was of utmost importance to the poet in his chosen universe. What he established was an odd relationship. He clearly gained access to the new president's office and just as clearly he presumed he was in a position to request favors and services from Swain. What he might not have known is that his presumption was ill-founded, that Swain, while not rejecting the requests out of hand, also did not fulfill them. It is also possible that, in one respect, Swain knew more about Horton than Horton knew about himself. Swain might have known more about the

Vain Appeals / 137

poet's reputation beyond the university's boundaries and its broader Southern environs.

The 1830's, which began with the repressive Southern reaction to the Walker *Appeal* and the Turner insurrection, also marked the firm crystallization of the Abolitionist movement. Symptomatic of it was the launching of the *Liberator* by William Lloyd Garrison on January 1, 1831. If in the South the regime was rendered more repressive in a determination to preserve slavery, elsewhere the movement for its abolition became bolder, more assertive, more intransigent. So the gathering, irrepressible conflict took shape. And Horton's work became involved in it.

In 1837 *The Hope of Liberty* was reprinted in Philadelphia by Abolitionists and retitled *Poems of a Slave*. The publisher's preface called attention to the original edition, brought out by Gales & Son in Raleigh in 1829, and the "Explanation" that introduced it; all this to make the following points:

> Observe 1st, That Gales, the printer of the pamphlet, is now one of the firm of Gales & Weston, at Washington—*no abolitionist*. Second, The Publisher admits slavery to be "the lowest possible condition of human nature;" and that the slaves are not all happy, for George "felt deeply and sensitively." Third, The man who could write such poems was kept for 32 years in "the lowest possible condition of human nature," and was to remain there if he would not consent to go to Liberia.
>
> Whether the poems sold for sufficient to buy this man, so dangerous to "Southern institutions," and export him, I have not been able to ascertain. Perhaps George is still a slave!

Appended was a note, which arrived after the preface and poems were set in type and confirmed that the poet was, indeed, still a slave. Dated at Washington, September 12, 1837, and based on information supplied by Mr. Gales, the note said that the poet "is still the slave of James Horton of Chatham County, and is employed as a servant at Chapel Hill, the site of the University of North Carolina."

The following year, in 1838, a third edition of *The Hope of Liberty* was published, this time in Boston and bound together with the poems of Phillis Wheatley and a memoir about her. This edition was produced by Isaac Knapp, publisher of Garrison's *Liberator*.

Wheatley was long since dead and buried as a freed woman by the time she became an emblem of the Abolitionist cause, but Horton was alive and still a slave. Was he aware of the uses to which his name and work were being put? An incident in 1844 suggests that he might have had some awareness of it. With greater certainty it may be assumed that Swain was aware of it, for there was Southern surveillance of Abolitionist agitation, and it is extremely unlikely that someone did not call Swain's attention to Abolitionist publication of his campus poet's work.

All of this makes more intriguing the incident of 1844, which involved Horton, Swain—and William Lloyd Garrison. The Abolitionist editor knew of the slave poet; not only had his associate, Isaac Knapp, published the Wheatley–Horton volume, but Garrison himself had published "On Liberty and Slavery" in the *Liberator* (March 29, 1834), reprinting it from the Lancaster *Gazette*, where it had appeared through the good offices of Caroline Lee Hentz. Garrison presented the poem with this introduction:

> The following lines, from the *Lancaster Gazette*, were written by a Carolinian slave, named George Horton, whose education was attained in hours stolen from sleep. The talents of the degraded race of black people appear better of late as they have been exhibited by the revolution in Hayti, than we have been accustomed to consider them; and from the power with which a few individuals have sprung up amid darkness and misfortunes, it seems probable that good education, would in a few generations give them a high standing among the nations of the earth. Look to it, statesmen!

That the Abolitionist editor, the agitator who was tireless in his search for every bit of information that reinforced his purpose, knew of the slave is not surprising. That the slave poet, isolated in rural North Carolina, learned of the Abolitionist editor is a small surprise at most. More surprising was his resolve in 1844 to venture into direct communication with Garrison. Most surprising of all was his choice of an intermediary in this venture. He chose Swain.

Either the poet was incredibly naive or he was incredibly audacious. By then Garrison was the most feared, most hated, most vilified of men in the slaveowning South. Among slaveowners he was the personification of a malignant threat to their way of life, a deranged exponent of murder, rape, sedition, anarchy. Raleigh, North Carolina, indicted Garrison for inciting slave revolts. The Georgia legislature offered a $5,000 reward to anyone who arrested him and brought him to trial in that state. Press and pulpit vied in denunciation of Garrison and his fellow Abolitionists.

Said the Richmond *Whig*, an influential paper in Virginia:

> Let the hell-hounds of the North beware. Let them not feel too much security in their homes, or imagine that they who throw firebrands, although from, as they think, so safe a distance, will be permitted to escape with impunity. There are thousands now animated with a spirit to brave every danger to bring these felons to justice on the soil of the Southern States, whose women and children they have dared to endanger by their hell-concocted plots. We have *feared* that Southern exasperation would seize some of the prime conspirators in their very beds, and drag them to meet the punishment due their offenses. We fear it no longer. We hope it may be so. . . .

The Reverend William S. Plummer of Richmond preached: "If the Abolitionists will set the country in a blaze, it is but fair that they should receive the first warming of the fire."

Much more in the same vein was directed at Garrison. To ask the former governor of a slave state and the incumbent president of a slave state's university to transmit a slave's message to Garrison was like asking a priest to serve as intermediary in communication between a sinner and the devil. Yet this is what Horton did. He handed Swain a letter for transmittal to Garrison. The letter read:

> September 3d, 1844
> Chapel Hill, N.C.

To Mr. Garrison the Editor of a Boston paper.

> Sir,
> Having of late received information of you from a gentleman with whom you must be somewhat acquainted, to wit, Dr. Worster of Philadelphia, and that you are an Editor and a lover of the genius of every tribe and population of the human race, I am necessarily constrained to apply to your honor for assistance in carrying my original work into publick execution; while I gratify your curiosity in resolving the problem whether a Negro has any genious or not. Sir, I am not alone actuated by pecuniary motives, but upon the whole, to spread the blaze of African

genious, and thus dispel the sceptic gloom so prevalent in many parts of the country. My design is to give you my testimony from the pen of the honorable Mr. David Swain, and President of the university of North Carolina; and who is very well apprised of my condition of life. I was born a slave, the property of Wm. Horton in Northampton County, N.C., near the ronoak river; and never had one days schooling in all the course of my life, from the alphabet to the present circle; I was early fond of hearing people read, and was as early with a ear for music. My letters I learned by heart, and by that means, learned them in a book. I also encountered with some of the most formidable difficulties that ever a poor and rustic boy has in the world; from which I have learned, that resolution effects the conquest in almost every [illegible word] in life. I can not but indifferently read, and can make shift to write an almost ilegible fist.

As to philology, I know but little. I have merly caught a light hint of the elements of english grammar, nor have I ever been so fortunate as to have studied any of the arts and sciences and my intellects have been by rude employment deeply clouded. I faithfully trust, sir, that your examination of the facts of my condition will inspire your pleasure to open to the world a volume which like a wild bird has long been struggling in its shell, impatient to transpire to the eye of a dubious world.

Yours respect.
George M. Horton
Of Colour.

A general acquaintance with Garrison's views is implicit in the letter, and if "Dr. Worster of Philadelphia" was the source of this information, might he not also have informed the poet about the Abolitionist publication of his work? This is a fair question, and at the very least it casts doubt on the bland assumption of one of Horton's Southern biographers that he was totally ignorant of the appearance of his work in the North in the 1830's, either in volume form or in the press.

The letter is of extreme interest on another score. Although addressed to the Abolitionist editor, it does not ask for aid in securing the poet's freedom; in fact, the very idea of freedom is unmentioned. The sole entreaty is for aid in the publication of the poet's work.

Vain Appeals / 141

Garrison did not reply. Nor could he, for he never received the letter. Swain did not send it. To this day it rests among his papers at the University of North Carolina. He did not inform the slave poet of his inaction; nor did he rebuke or admonish him for daring to attempt communication with William Lloyd Garrison; nor did he threaten reprisals. This was Swain's Whig-like compromise.

Horton's attempt to communicate to Garrison is saddest perhaps in what it says about his total isolation from the vital milieu in which the Abolitionist editor was a central figure. By 1844 the body of black literature, associated with antislavery agitation, was beginning to assume the proportions that were to become so impressive within a decade. Frederick Douglass had already made his debut on the public platform, and so had William Wells Brown. In the next several years both fugitive slaves were to publish extensively: autobiographic works (the first version of Douglass' autobiography appeared in 1842, Brown's personal narrative two years later), antislavery tracts, assorted correspondence.

Many other works by black writers appeared, among them *The Life of Josiah Henson* (the presumed prototype of Harriet Beecher Stowe's Uncle Tom), *Narrative of Henry Box Brown*, and *Narrative of Sojourner Truth, Northern Slave*. Possessing great utility in antislave agitation, personal narratives of escaped slaves were most prone to be published, but there were also historical works, foremost among them William C. Nell's studies of the services of "colored patriots" in the American Revolution, and sociopolitical essays, notably Martin R. Delany's book-length *The Condition, Elevation, Emigration, and Destiny of the Colored People of the United States, Politically Considered.**

The most versatile and venturesome writer of the lot, William Wells Brown tried his hand at journalism, memoirs, essays, travel sketches, novels, and drama; with *The Escape, Or a Leap for Freedom* (1858), he became the first Afro-American playwright, having previously won the same distinction of place as a novelist with *Clotel, or the President's Daughter* (1853). Brown ventured into poetry only rarely and not too well. His best lines, which make up the concluding stanza of "Lament of the Fugitive Slave," an elegy on his mother, were:

---

* The outpouring of slave narratives in 1844 to 1854 is indicated in a selective (not exhaustive) bibliography by John W. Blassingame (*Slave Community*, pp. 240–242). He lists fifteen such narratives published in those years.

Be near me, mother, be thy spirit near me,
Wherever thou may'st be;
In hours like this bend near that I may hear thee,
And know that thou art free;
Summoned at length from bondage, toil and pain,
To God's free world, a world without a chain!

In his chosen form Horton was superior to those others, despite their advantages. Some of them were born free, some had escaped from slavery on their own, still others, like Henry Highland Garnet (an accomplished essayist and biographer of David Walker) and Samuel Ringgold Ward (author of *The Autobiography of a Fugitive Slave*), were delivered from bondage by enterprising slave parents, but all had two things in common: they worked in the North and they were associated with the antislavery movement. The catalogue of writers and works is far from complete, and in this context it need not be more comprehensive, nor is there much point here in assaying their literary output. With the focus on Horton the point is something else: the 1840's and 1850's witnessed a surge of black writing and the emergence of a black literary community, but he was remote from all that.

Those others profited from the stimulus of association, sometimes as active collaborators, as Delany and Douglass were for a time on the latter's *North Star*. They met at conventions of colored people (as Brown, Douglass, Garnet, and Nell did, for one instance, at Troy, New York, in October, 1847) and had other opportunities to exchange opinions, to compare or dispute, through private conversation and correspondence or in public utterances, Theirs was not a harmonious fraternity; Brown, for example, was involved in public quarrels with Douglass, Garnet, Delany, and others, but disagreement need not be merely disagreeable, it can also be mind-sharpening. It is not possible to measure the intellectual and spiritual value of such association and intercourse among thinking, articulate persons who had much in common, but whatever the measure, Horton had none of it. Indeed, no evidence exists that he was aware of those others or had ever seen their works. Who can calculate the consequences for a creative spirit of this quarantine from peers and colleagues?

His Northern black contemporaries were acquainted with Garrison, and for some the *Liberator* was a significant outlet despite an appreciable growth of black periodicals in that decade; but Horton's supplication was addressed to a stranger and directed across an uncertain void, so that the whim of one man could thwart its passage.

Unaware of the fate of his letter to Garrison, eight years later Horton tried again. Once more his appeal was directed to a celebrated editor in the North, Horace Greeley of the New York *Tribune*. Once more he entrusted his communication to Governor Swain for transmittal. The text of the letter read:

> Sept. 11, 1852
> Chapel Hill, N.C.
>
> To Mr. Greeley
>
> Sir,
> From the information of the president of the University of North Carolina, to wit, the honorable David L. Swain, who is willing to aid me himself, I learn that you are a gentleman of philanthropic feeling. I therefore thought it essential to apply to your beneficent hand for some assistance to remove the burden of hard servitude. Notwithstanding, sir, there are many in my native section of country who wish to bring me out, and there are others far too penurious which renders it somewhat dubious with regard to my extrication. It is evident that you have heard of me by the fame of my work in poetry, much of which I am now too closely confined to carry out and which I feel a warm interest to do; and, sir, by favoring me with the bounty of 175 dollars, I will endeavor to reward your generosity with my productions as soon as possible. I am the only public or recognized poet of colour in my native state or perhaps in the union, born in slavery but yet craving that scope and expression whereby my literary labour of the night may be circulated throughout the whole world. Then I forbid that my productions should ever fall to the ground, but rather soar as an eagle above the towering mountains and thus return as a triumphing spirit to the bosom of its God who gave it birth, though now confined in these loathesome fetters. Please assist the lowering vassal arise and live a glad denizen the remnant of his days and as one of active utility.
>
> Yours respect.
> George M. Horton
> Of Colour

On the reverse side of the letter, also in the poet's hand, was "The Poet's Feeble Petition":

> Bewailing mid the ruthless wave,
>   I lift my feeble hand to thee.
> Let me no longer be a slave
>   But drop these fetters and be free.

> Why will regardless fortune sleep
>   Deaf to my penitential prayer,
> Or leave the struggling Bard to weep,
>   Alas, and languish in despair?
>
> As an eagle devoid of wings
>   Aspiring to the mountain's height;
> Yet in the vale aloud he sings
>   For Pity's aid to give him flight.
>
> Then listen all who never felt
>   For fettered genius heretofore—
> Let hearts of petrifaction melt
>   And bid the gifted Negro soar.

Greeley is assumed to have been acquainted with the poet's work and life, not only because of his broad Abolitionist sympathies, but by virtue of a more personal link with the Horton locale. Mrs. Greeley, the former Mary Youngs Cheney of Connecticut, had taught school in 1834 in Warrenton, North Carolina, a favored summer resort of university students from nearby Chapel Hill. From them she learned about the slave poet.

If Horton thus had an advocate in the Greeley household, it did him no good. His letter and the "feeble petition" never reached the New York editor. These, like the communication to Garrison, were filed by Governor Swain and still rest among his papers. Despite this, references have cropped up in literary histories to Greeley's publication of the poetic petition. However, the biographer who did the most extensive research of the poet's life has written: "Several writers on Horton have stated that 'The Poet's Feeble Petition' was used in the *New York Tribune*, but I have not found in Greeley's newspaper either the poem or the letter." Indeed, both are more easily found in the Swain archives at Chapel Hill.

Sharing the same fate, the entreaties to the two editors, Garrison and Greeley, were distinctly different in kind. The first, in 1844, had asked for no more than assistance in the publication of the poet's work. The second appealed for help to secure the poet's freedom. The difference cannot be explained by changes in the political climate; it was not that much better in 1852. What had changed in the interim, as revealed in the poet's subsequent correspondence, was his master's frame of mind. This subsequent correspondence is undated but apparently was written not long after the ill-fated appeals to Greeley. In these letters Swain is cast, not as intermediary, but as recipient. The first letter to Swain reads:

Sir,

I have been some time very anxious for some Gentleman in this place to buy me, and have recently made choice of you, sir, and provided you will accede to the proposition, I am willing to serve you to the best of my ability. Sir my object for this is my distant walk to attend to my business, which chiefly lies on the Hill. The price is $200 50 [250] dollars, which I cannot but think I am worth. Sir I am willing to make you all the possible remuneration which I can, provided I can succeed in the publication of my books which I have in hand. Sir I have from this inconvenience been thrown far behind and provided you buy me I shall be under all obligations to your generosity. Sir you will please write a note to Master when and as you see proper.

Yours respectfully
George M. Horton
Poet

Intriguing questions are posed by the letter. If Hall Horton had agreed to sell the poet, as the letter implies, then $250 seems like a fair price, for twenty-three years earlier, when he was much younger and more vigorous, *Freedom's Journal* had estimated his market value at between $500 and $700. A depreciation of 50 to 65 per cent in the cash value of a slave between the ages of thirty-two and fifty-five is plausible economics. But these reasonable calculations run afoul of another: if the poet was still paying the master 50 cents a day, then returns in two years would exceed the quoted sales price of $250, and it is unlikely that Hall Horton, hard bargainer that he was, would let his property go for so little when it could yield so much. Had the aging poet finally lost the battle of 50 cents a day? It would seem so, for then the proposed sale makes clear economic sense.

Such economic logic is confounded, in turn, by the reference in the letter to "my distant walk to attend to my business, which chiefly lies on the Hill." What does this mean? At first blush it appears to mean that the poet's business was in Chapel Hill but his residence was on Hall Horton's plantation, that he was permitted to hire out, and the question recurs: why would Hall Horton agree to sell him then? The puzzling passage could also mean that the poet had reverted to the practice of this youth; weekdays on the plantation and weekend excursions to Chapel Hill. Or, perhaps, there was some compromise between hiring out full-time and weekend trips on the business of poetry. The one clear point is that the long walk to and from the

To the honorable Governor Swain

Sir,

I have been some time since very anxious for some Gentleman in this place to buy me, and have recently made choice of you sir, and provided you will accede to the proposition, I'm willing to serve you to the best of my ability; sir my object for this is my distant walk to attend to my business, which chiefly lies on the Hill. the price is $200.00 dollars, which I can not but think I am worth. sir I am willing to make you all the possible remuneration which I can, provided I can succeed in the publication of my books which I have in hand sir I have from this inconvenience been thrown far behind and provided you buy me I shall be under all obligations to your generosity sir you will please write a note to Master when and as you see proper

yours respectfully
George M Horton
Poet

Vain Appeals / 147

university town, whatever its frequency, was becoming more taxing for the poet at fifty-five.

Still another possibility is suggested by the reference to "my distant walk." Even when he worked in Chapel Hill, as poet or menial, there were no lodgings for a black slave, or if there were, he could not afford to pay for them, not after his daily remittance of fifty cents to the master, and he was compelled, therefore, to walk eight miles for shelter on the plantation, and back again another eight miles "to attend to my business."

As intriguing as such speculation is, so is speculation about Swain's reaction to the letter, to its self-assurance, to its presumptuousness, tempered only by the most formal politeness. To the Governor it must have bordered on insolence, this notice that he had been chosen by a slave as buyer and future owner, this command, "sir you will please write a note . . ."

The Governor's reaction may be inferred from the next letter. It is not addressed directly to Swain, but to the attention of one John T. Gilmore for transmittal to Swain, and its tone is not so peremptory, for it entertains the prospect of some other purchaser and emphasizes prospective returns to the would-be buyer. In part, this letter says:

> . . . I will endeavor to reward your generosity. . . .
> I now propose to give 2/3 of the whole of the
> proceeds of my new book now preparing for the
> press to you or any other gentleman who will give
> two hundred and fifty dollars for me, and still be
> in obligatory service to you for life. [The phrase "for
> life" was written in, then scratched out.] Provided
> that I can attend to the work at hand, I have no
> doubt but it will soon come forward by the aid of
> subscriptions . . .

The letters to Swain marked a retreat from the communications to Greeley. Writing to the New York editor, Horton aspired to both freedom and poetry; writing to the Carolina Governor, he settled for poetry alone, requesting no more than a change of masters to improve the circumstances for his creative work. Different aspirations but the same result: nothing. He was also disappointed in the anticipation that the book he was then preparing would soon go to press.

Despite the series of frustrations, despite "my distant walk" from the plantation to the campus, which became more distant with the passage of the years—and he now was nearing sixty—he continued to write; to write as well as ever, more aware now of time, of time that was irrevocably past, of time that was passing with increasing swiftness. At sixty he published "What Is Time" in the Chapel Hill *Gazette* (May 9, 1857):

> Time is an eagle's wing
>   That wafts all nature to the final end,
> That bids us either languish or to sing,
>   To sink or to ascend.
>
> Time is the Phoenix bird
>   Collecting branches for its funeral pyre;
> It flaps its wings impatient for the word
>   To set its nest on fire.
>
> Time is a rapid wheel,
>   On which we ride another world to see,
> Whose operations mortals never feel
>   Till in ETERNITY.
>
> Let time the mind concern;
>   It passes quickly like a flash away,
> Alas! and never—never to return.
>   Improve it while ye may.

8

The Eve of War

As the 1850's neared their end the poet was concerned with time, and so the country should have been, especially the ante-bellum South, for its time was running out.

Throughout the last ante-bellum decade, although no volume of his was published, Horton retained his unique status as Chapel Hill's poet laureate and as a campus institution, now hallowed by tradition. Neither he nor the university was untouched by the inexorable march of events toward the dénouement of war, and yet the relationship between the two, between the white campus and the black poet, appeared undisturbed. Tradition, now spanning generations, passed on from old alumni to their undergraduate sons and weighed heavily in a region that cherished tradition to sanctify the status quo. Particularly revealing was a letter from a father to a wayward son who transferred to the University of North Carolina after expulsion from the University of Mississippi because he "had in possession and used a pistol by repeatedly discharging the same in the campus and from the windows of the dormitories." Whatever friction the pistol-shooting escapade created between father and son, the slave poet was a link between them. Wrote the father on October 21, 1859:

> I forgot in my last letter to notice your account of
> the poet George Horton. George and myself used to
> be good friends. I know him well. He has written
> many an acrostic for me and I have loaned him
> many a book to read—always preferring poetical
> works. When I knew him he was unable to write
> though he read very well—Was considered an honest
> humble fellow—was treated with great kindness by
> the students. George no doubt has forgotten me.
> I should like to see him very much.

At the beginning of the decade, in 1852, after a lapse the *University of North Carolina Magazine* was re-established, and once more Horton flourished as a ghostwriter for students whose hankering for literary prestige was greater than their talent. So much of the published verse appeared to have come from Horton's pen that a Southern historian observed: "A glance through the *Magazine*, besides giving weight to the suspicion, suggests that George Moses' efforts were just about on par with the poems appearing in the journals and newspapers of the day. If anything, Poet Horton's are superior."

At the end of the decade, in April, 1860, the *University Magazine* published an article about Horton, which was reprinted in June by the larger and more prestigious *De Bow's Review* (with offices in New Orleans, Washington, and London). The article, after a brief and partial description of the poet's background, went on:

> He has favored us with the sight of the manuscript of another book of his poems, which, from the length of his subscription list, we doubt not he will be able to publish by the next Commencement. It will be rather a large book; the manuscript contains 299 pages letter-paper, closely written.
> His price will be $1 per copy.
> All who have graduated within the last 35 years no doubt remember the sable poet, and will need but the statement above to induce them to send on their names as subscribers.

The announcement concluded with a romantic poem of the sort that he had been selling to students for all those years:

Good-By

I leave thee, with a falling tear
    And mount the fleeting car;
'Tis death to part with one so dear—
For to my view thy charms appear
    Like some revolving star.

I leave thee, but with deep concern
    Which hope cannot remove.
Oh! do not my affection spurn,
But patient wait till my return,
    And prove the truth of love.

I leave thee, but I love thee yet,
    The queen of ev'ry bloom;
I never shall my choice regret,

The Eve of War / 151

>Until the sun of life shall set,
> And love sing in the tomb.
>
>Oh! lady, take these lines to heart!—
> The last fond tale I tell,
>Is that my own dear love thou art;
>Then till we meet no more to part,
> My lady, fare thee well!

The rather large book promised in the spring did not appear. As summer and autumn came in 1860 the passions of politics overshadowed the passion of poetry. It was the year of the fateful Presidential election, and the presentiment was abroad that the irrepressible conflict was nearing a climax. Chapel Hill, for all its apparent moderation and academic detachment, was not insulated from the political turbulence, as was evidenced in the Presidential campaign four years earlier.

In 1856 a professor named Benjamin Sherwood Hedrick announced he would vote for John C. Frémont, the first Presidential candidate of the newborn Republican party. He would cast his vote, said Hedrick, as a protest—not against slavery, but against its extension. Such political apostasy touched off a storm, instantaneous and violent, and it raged in the letter and editorial columns of the Raleigh *Standard*. A typical comment of this newspaper said: "Surely it cannot be expected of us . . . or any citizen in this State, to *argue* with a black Republican. We take it for granted that Professor Hedrick will be promptly removed."

The campus bell tolled mourning for the professor and students burned him in effigy. A faculty committee, headed by the governor of the state, found him guilty of conduct unbecoming a Southerner. When he still refused to resign, his chair was declared vacant.

If this had been the mood in 1856, what was it in 1860? In the intervening four years the United States Supreme Court handed down its Dred Scott decision, legally sanctifying slavery as the immutable condition of those cursed with it, and John Brown's band raided the arsenal at Harpers Ferry, illegally prophesying that if it took war and blood to abolish slavery, so it would be. In the wake of such contradictory portents, a Republican victory, which seemed implausible in 1856, was highly probable in 1860, since the governing Democratic party was fractured.

So it was that in 1860 the country was headed for war—and the poet was entered upon the seventh decade of his life. For a black slave it was a poor time for candor, and only one document survives that affords some insight into his mood toward the end of the 1850's. This is the most curious of the Horton documents, entitled, "AN ADDRESS TO COLLEGIATES of N.C.—The Stream of Liberty and Conscience" by George M. Horton (The Black Bard). The twenty-nine pages, written in pencil and in different hands, bear the prefatory note "Transcribed by the competent 'Amanuensis.'" Students apparently took turns in setting down his oration as he delivered it. There are gaps in the transcript, and despite the claim for its competence, the precision is questionable. In full flight Horton's oratorical prose would have taxed the capacity of a skilled stenographer. To render transcription more difficult, the oration is rambling, a stream of consciousness as well as of conscience, its moral strictures interspersed with ambiguous references to liberty and the condition of the republic. The ambiguities are tantalizing, for they might have been fashioned either by naiveté or sophisticated subtlety. Consider, for example, this passage:

> . . . You should endeavor more faithfully to enlarge the base of the pyramid of your independent republic which has stood the test of almost a century, now tottering beneath the burden on the treacherous pillars of chance, overshadowed with clouds of apprehension, on the dreary verge of destruction, though her protection has long been dwindling at the shrine of depreciation and exhausted commerce, though her public theorists had lost the tapers which led them from the bright fountain of the Union while they went groping their helpless passage through the dark vale of insolvent-bankrupt, while peace sunk into the confusion of parties . . .

Pity the poor amanuensis who seeks to grasp the thread of meaning to help him keep pace with the flow of words. Was this oratorical gibberish or daring double talk? The republic, he was saying, is in a poor way, and his auditors could readily and heartily respond Amen, for they were privileged, young, white Southerners, most of whom would soon be marching in gray uniforms under Confederate colors against the sins of the old republic and to create, so they thought, a new and more perfect one. If, in his verbiage, the orator concealed some shafts against the rebel South, they would be least likely to perceive it, for they were least prone to concede such subtle intelligence and impertinence to the old black slave. He wouldn't dare to allude to John C. Calhoun and other advocates of nullification and secession as "public theorists [who] had lost the tapers which led them from the bright fountain of the Union. . . ." Or would he dare? Was he making a public spectacle of himself while in his inner self relishing the spectacle he was making of the gullibility of prejudice?

This last conjecture is made more credible by his references to liberty:

> To you young gentlemen of the Freshmen class I would tender the following remarks. . . . Improve the time which your liberty affords you to the cultivation of your golden talents with which your poor orator has never been assisted but confined to a horse and tottering plough . . . who has sweated his meagre visage away over the fire at night and almost destroyed his sight in the faithful attempt of arriving to the simple pleasure of reading . . .
>
> The privation of liberty brutalizes human intellect, dulls the enterprizing spirit. . . . It is a death blow to the pleasures of human life.

To be sure, liberty was the watchword of the secessionist South, prepared to shed blood in defense of what it conceived as the most precious liberty of all, the liberty of the white man to enslave the black, but could his audience have imparted this meaning to his use of the word? He was far less ambiguous and far more personal in talking of liberty than in his references to the state of the republic. It was in this oration that he revealed the effort of Governor John Owen to purchase his freedom in 1828, and gave vent to his bitterness over his master's frustration of that venture.

The address to collegiates was an indictment of slavery, and its daring is accented by its timing. The best estimate of historians is that the oration was delivered in 1859, the year of Brown's raid on Harpers Ferry and only two years before John Brown's soul was to be resurrected in a marching song.

His purpose was hinted at in the opening of the oration: "Actuated by innocent motives, I appear before you as a public orator in the cause of liberty and science; but with a degree of diffidence lest I fail to accomplish a task which I feel it my duty to discharge. . . ."

The protestation of "innocent motives" in the very first phrase suggests the contrary, of course. It is intended to disarm, and with the same intention he proceeded. "Yet while you may laugh . . ." Here the transcript was broken off, and what followed was a reference to the "impulse of illiterate genius to expose his jargon to the criticism of the world."

He went on in a personal vein to illustrate his first substantial thesis: "It is obvious that we occupy an age of the world which calls aloud for literary improvement from every quarter and the scientific culture of faculties rational. . . . For impartial genius seems to have looked with indiscriminate eye as touching nations and color. . . ." His personal history is then recited to reinforce his appeal for improvement in *"every* quarter" without discrimination as to nation or color.

The oratorical style ranges from high-flown literary to homespun. A typical juxtaposition:

> But the interrogation follows with regard to the
> misfortune of naked genius by an itinerant muse at
> the foot of a mountain which deserted at the close
> of her incubation and left him without the plumage
> of literary defense waiting in vain for her return
> with a morsel to sustain the infancy of genius . . .

and after that:

> . . . every tub has to stand on its own bottom and
> not on that of another.

He paid his compliments to the influential patrons, who befriended him or offered their assistance, to Dr. Caldwell, to Caroline Lee Hentz, to Governor Owen, and to a Dr. Henderson. He referred to himself as "in the declining sun of life." Such intimate, personal passages, along with the references to liberty and the republic, were heavily padded with others, with generalizations and moralizations couched in obscure rhetoric.

It was a performance, and one Southern biographer of the poet said of it: "Here was the height of the jester, the final glorification of the motley. . . . At the conclusion came lengthy and mocking applause. . . ."

Such a critical judgment recalls the poet's arrival on the campus some forty years earlier, when student pranksters, playing on his vanity, induced him to orate for their diversion. Of this period, it will be recalled, he wrote in his autobiographic sketch of 1845: "I would stand forth and address myself extempore before them, as an orator of inspired promptitude. But I soon found it an object of aversion, and considered myself nothing but a public ignoramus."

Yet the Southern biographer suggests that fourteen years after this perceptive bit of self-criticism the poet reverted to the public self-

The Eve of War / 155

display of his youth simply to play the jester, to bask in mocking applause, to strut the greater virtuosity in the jester's art that could attain "the final glorification of the motley."

Perhaps it seemed so to the students, who may have viewed the performance as nothing more than diversion and entertainment. There is little to suggest that the student crop of 1859 was much wiser, or more sensitive, than the fathers were circa 1817. But the poet was now past sixty, and having spent four decades on the campus he undoubtedly appraised the students far more shrewdly than they did him. He no longer was the young country bumpkin, black and a slave to boot, come to town wide-eyed to peddle fruit and to observe the university citadel of learning and poetry, fair game then for pranking students. As he soon learned to his own humiliation, he was made the butt of the sport. More than forty years later he was not so easily had for mocking, and if in the beginning the jest was at his expense he now had the experience, wisdom, and command of language to repay the young gentlemen. Circumspectly, of course. True, he no longer was a green country youth, but he still was black and a slave, and if he wished to make sport of the young gentlemen, to mock their arrogant self-assurance in relation to a black man, the protective guise of the jester would have been a necessary convenience.

What he meant and what his audience understood was not necessarily the same thing, and he was the more conscious of the potential in such a gap. Maudlin buffoon or deliberately ironic jester? There was enough in the oration, as well as in the circumstances, to make the latter role more plausible.*

Such speculative judgment is buttressed by an incident a decade earlier, when he declined to indulge student expectation of a performance. The occasion was the Fourth of July, 1849, and the site was Gerrard Hall, the auditorium for campus ceremony. Most of the stu-

---

* Among the most vivid expressions in black folklore of the dichotomy between white understanding and black meaning is the folk song "Me an My Captain":

> Me an my captain don't agree,
> But he don't know, 'cause he don't ask me . . .
>
> Got one mind for white folks to see,
> 'Nother for what I know is me;
> He don't know, he don't know my mind,
> When he see me laughing,
> Just laughing to keep from crying.

In a matter of this sort folklore is much more telling evidence than scholarship. Still it is worth citing a scholarly judgment: "The slaves dissembled, they feigned ignorance and humility. If their masters expected them to be fools, they would play the fool's role." (Blassingame, *Slave Community*, p. 208.)

dents went to Hillsborough for the Independence Day celebration, but one who did not, Thomas Miles Garrett, a freshman, recorded in his diary for that day:

> The students who remained on the Hill thought they would not let the Fourth pass without some noise and, accordingly, held a meeting and appointed George Horton, the North Carolina bard, to deliver the oration. This morning the Poet arrived and about 11 o'clock we formed a procession and conducted the orator upon the stage. He made a speech of about five minutes' length, to the great disappointment of all present who expected a long oration. The loud, long, and repeated applause occupied, however, about fifteen minutes. With this the celebration of the day ended.

Prudence, perhaps, precluded outright disobedience of the command to perform, but the performance indicates a distaste for the role. If, then, he orated at great length a decade later, it may be supposed that he did so not simply for the entertainment of the students but to say some things it pleased him to say.

In any event, by 1859 little time was left for the black bard's orations to the collegiates. Two years later Confederate guns fired at Fort Sumter in Charleston harbor.

9

War and Emancipation

Forty days after the opening shots of the Civil War, North Carolina joined the secession parade, following (in order) South Carolina, Mississippi, Florida, Alabama, Georgia, Louisiana, Texas, Virginia, and Arkansas. Of the eleven states that made up the Confederacy only Tennessee was tardier than North Carolina in its formal break with the Union.

At Chapel Hill, a request to suspend classes was rejected by college president Swain, but the students, voting with their feet, marched off to war. By late spring only 75 remained in residence. A year before the university had boasted an enrollment of 460, making it second only to Yale among American colleges. Now, the university was virtually closed, and Horton sank into oblivion for the duration. There is no record at all of what he did during the war; the only certainty is that he survived and when he emerged at war's end he still had poetic manuscripts with him, possibly having added to them during the four years that young men marched, died, and killed in a conflict that was to determine his condition.

Survival itself was no small achievement for the old slave, deprived now of the sustenance, economic and creative, that he derived from the university community. Times were hard in North Carolina. "Nobody has yet starved . . ." said Governor Zebulon B. Vance in his opening message to the 1864–65 session of the General Assembly in North Carolina. Even if the claim was accurate, it denoted that the specter of starvation loomed large enough to disturb the Governor. A North Carolina chronicler recorded on December 31, 1863, that wheat was then $20 and potatoes $8 a bushel, and butter $3 a pound (compared with 12½ cents in prewar days). Another chronicler said of the state's general population: "They couldn't get salt for their food or oil for their lamps; their shoes wore out and their clothes were thin."

If this was the general condition, it was job enough for an aging black slave to root and burrow for subsistence.

Except for a few peripheral skirmishes North Carolina did not become a Civil War battlefield and Union troops did not enter it in force until the final phase of the war. Even if Horton had been inclined to cross over behind the Union lines, there were none within reasonable reach until the spring of 1865. Before 1865 the poet, now well into his sixties, would have had to traverse hundreds of miles through war-torn country to reach the Union lines, either to the west in Tennessee or to the north in Virginia.

It was Sherman's army that finally brought the war's full reality to North Carolina. After his scorched-earth march from Atlanta to the sea, Sherman wheeled northward, sliced through South Carolina, entered North Carolina with the new year of 1865, and occupied Wilmington, the last Confederate seaport, on February 22, 1865. Continuing his relentless push to the north he captured Bentonville on March 19 to 21, and then he paused, grouping his forces for a thrust in one of two directions. His army was poised either to move northward to join General Grant's forces in the Virginia campaign against the armies of General Lee, or to continue the pursuit of General Johnston's army, which had retired westward in North Carolina. With Lee's surrender at Appomattox on April 9, Sherman's choice was clear. He resumed his pursuit of Johnston. From Bentonville to Raleigh was less than forty miles, and from Raleigh to Chapel Hill it was but thirty.

As Sherman neared Chapel Hill his reputation preceded him. "For weeks that spring of 1865," a Southern family chronicler wrote, "the Chapel Hill folks had been in a panic as Sherman marched north from Columbia [South Carolina] into North Carolina driving Johnston's men before him. Everybody knew about his march through Georgia and those who had seen that country and fled into North Carolina said, 'If a crow flew down that valley behind Sherman, he'd sure have to take his breakfast with him.'"

In talking of panic at Sherman's approach the writer referred, of course, to white folks. Another North Carolinian described Sherman's entrance into the state capital: "Raleigh people closed their window blinds and locked their front doors. The dogs crept under shelter; not a human being was visible that bright morning when Sherman's advance guard rode up Fayetteville Street." But black folks did not wait cowering behind drawn blinds and locked doors (for one thing blinds were not customary amenities in slave quarters) for Sherman's men to get to Chapel Hill. Horton did not wait at all. He took off for

Raleigh to meet them there, an enterprising journey—probably on foot—for a man of sixty-eight. His own feelings were recorded later in "The Flag of the Free":

> Lift up thy head, exhausted slave,
>   Nor to the woods for shelter flee;
> Vain shall the threat'ning tyrant save,
>   The flag floats over the free.

For the poet the long march to Raleigh was his own Emancipation Proclamation. For the slave nearing three score and ten it was a daring expedition to explore the realization of the hope of liberty that he had affirmed in verse so many years ago. All his life he had been circumscribed by the restrictions of bondage, confined within the narrow geographic boundaries firmly fixed between the white man's plantation and the white man's university. Now, as he had said, he was "in the declining sun of life," an unseasonal time to shout "Free at last!" and to make a new start in a different world. But he had the spirit for it, and the wit. Amid the thousands of strangers in blue, soldiers scarred and toughened by battle, flushed with victory, bearing the memories of the torch they put to the land they traversed, of Atlanta and Columbia in flames, he looked for a man who would respond to the verse of an old black poet. And not a dilettante or sentimentalist, but a practical man with the initiative or authority to be of practical assistance. He had acquired experience and wisdom in the quest for patrons, but that was in a totally different environment, not in the hectic choas of a strange army on the move through a strange land. He found his man . . .

Meanwhile, Swain, the poet's faithless intermediary, was engaged in some adventures of his own. Quite likely he was affected by the general panic that Sherman's name inspired among white Southerners, but he was not paralyzed by it. As the Yankee troops neared Raleigh, Swain and another former governor of the state, William A. Grant, rode off to intercept the fearsome Sherman and to plead with him that Raleigh and Chapel Hill be spared destruction. According to one historian, this mission was to Swain "the most interesting event in his life. He regarded it as a State negotiation of the greatest significance, and of infinite value to Raleigh and to the University," for by this time the "State Government had collapsed; the State Executive was in retreat. . . ." After a brief visit with the Union general, Swain "was in a buggy on his way to Chapel Hill to prepare for the surrender of his beloved University, and to reassure the hearts of his fellow-townsmen."

Lee had surrendered on Palm Sunday, and so it was through Easter Week that Sherman's columns knifed into the heart of North Carolina.

By Maundy Thursday they reached Raleigh as the Confederate forces continued to retreat without offering battle. On Good Friday (April 14) General Wheeler's cavalry units of Johnston's armies rode into Chapel Hill in their westward withdrawal. That same evening Abraham Lincoln was assassinated and the United States had a new president, Andrew Johnson, native of Raleigh, where Sherman's armies were then encamped. On Easter Sunday morning the last of the Confederate cavalry straggled out of Chapel Hill and the arrival of Sherman's troops was expected that afternoon. Swain and several other leading townspeople patrolled the Durham and Raleigh roads, each armed with a white handkerchief tied to a cane, hoping to meet the Union men with this flag of truce and to remind them of Sherman's promise to spare the university and the town. After a while they returned, mission unaccomplished; they had encountered no one who could accept their token of surrender.

What followed was described by a Chapel Hill resident: "Just at sunset a sedate and soldierly-looking man, at the head of a dozen men *dressed in blue,* rode quietly in by the Raleigh road. Governor Swain, accompanied by a few of the principal citizens, met them at the entrance, and stated that he had General Sherman's promise that the town and the university should be saved from pillage. The soldier replied that such were his orders, and they should be observed. They then rode in, galloped up and down the streets inquiring for rebels; and being informed that *there were none* in town, they withdrew for the night to their camp; and the next morning, being Easter Monday, April Seventeenth, General Atkins, at the head of a detachment of four thousand cavalry, entered about eight A.M., and we were captured."

Local residents attest that the Union troops "behaved with civility and propriety"; instead of engaging in pillage, they quickly thwarted abortive attempts at looting. Men in blue were dispatched to find slaves and to advise them, or to reassure them, that they were free, no longer any man's property. Other Union soldiers set up outdoor classes for the liberated blacks. It was the end of an era in the South, but it did not come as it had been envisioned in the fevered Southern white imagination. Nor did Sherman's arrival confirm the dreadful anticipations inspired by the tales of terror that heralded his advance. Southern white anxiety apparently had not correlated Sherman's prior tactics to any considerations of military necessity, but now that military necessity was no longer operative his march through North Carolina bore little resemblance to the relentless swath he had cut through

Georgia and up the South Carolina coast. By the time Sherman's troops reached Chapel Hill the war was really over except for the formality of General Johnston's surrender, and this formality was consummated on April 26 at Bennett's House, less than ten miles north of Chapel Hill, near the Durham Station in Orange County.

When General Smith B. Atkins rode into Chapel Hill at the head of the 9th Michigan Cavalry, a family chronicler records, "the white people stayed indoors and watched the columns of soldiers ride past behind drawn shades, but the colored folks of the town met their liberators with wild cheers and Union flags miraculously retrieved from places of discard where their masters had tossed them." Horton did not meet the 9th Michigan Cavalry in Chapel Hill, he came with it, having attached himself to this unit during his reconnaissance in Raleigh. More specifically, Horton had attached himself to Will H. S. Banks, a twenty-eight-year-old captain in the Michigan cavalry.

For the young soldier the encounter with the old black poet, forty years his senior, was akin to revelation. "I was astonished at his genius," Banks later recalled. "and more so when he showed me some manuscripts written by himself." A Southern historian wrote that discovery of the poet among the thousands of black refugees who flocked to the Union lines was for Banks the "final justification" of his service in the war, and Banks himself expressed the hope that the poet's creations "may do away with some of the many prejudices so long existing against the poor down-trodden sons of Africa."

In the excitement of the meeting between the young soldier and the old poet a grand project was born. With Banks as patron and promoter they planned to publish a volume that would astound the world with its display of black genius—and, incidentally, make their fortunes. In the military bivouac at Chapel Hill Horton set to "work both night and day composing poems" (as Banks later wrote) to supplement his manuscripts for the projected volume, but he took time out for a familiar exercise. He composed acrostics for Union soldiers on the names of the sweethearts back home. "He takes great delight" in these acrostics, Banks observed, suggesting that he now tossed them off for pleasure, rather than for the pay he had taken from Southern white students.

Even as the volume was taking shape and the long war was ending, Captain Banks was still in uniform, subject to the restrictions of military service. The Michigan Cavalry remained in Chapel Hill for less than two weeks, and on April 30 was ordered to move westward. Horton followed, manuscripts in hand. On July 21, 1865, the troops were mustered out at Lexington, a North Carolina courthouse town, and the strange partners—Horton and Banks—were at last free to effect their grand design.

The poet's conquest of Banks was paralleled by another extra-military conquest by the captain's superior officer, General Atkins. The story of this exploit is told in a Southern family chronicle: "The University buildings and books were neither sacked nor burned as the terrified townsfolk had expected. In fact, General Atkins proved to be both a soldier and a gentleman. . . . So engaging was the Yankee commander that in less than two months after marching into Chapel Hill, he had conquered the daughter of the University's president and won her for a bride. They married in August, 1865. The town was shocked. The wedding caused almost as much of a furor as had Secession. . . ." For Swain the furor occasioned by his daughter's fraternization with the Yankee general was even greater perhaps. In reprisal for this breach of unreconstructed Confederate etiquette he was sacked from the university post he had occupied for thirty-one years.

So Reconstruction began with Swain adding another ex- to his titles—ex-president of the university as well as ex-governor of the state—and Horton embarking on an ambitious venture that, his new mentor hoped, would make him the most renowned poet in the land.

10
Naked Genius

Returned to civilian life, young Captain Banks nonetheless pursued the publishing venture with a cavalryman's dash, guided by two tactical principles he could have learned from his old commander General Sherman: strike swiftly and strike deep in the enemy's territory.

As he saw it, the projected volume was an extension of the just-concluded war. It was to serve as retroactive vindication of emancipation. By revealing to the world the poetic genius of one black man, it would demonstrate the latent genius of all black men for freedom. With this objective in mind haste seemed essential to help dispel the confusion and skepticism in the war's chaotic aftermath. And it also seemed essential to him that the volume be published in the South, where the rationales for slavery were most deeply imbedded. Immediately after demobilization Banks, accompanied by Horton, headed back to Raleigh, to the William B. Smith & Co. Southern Field & Fireside Book Publishing House.

Commanders plan grand strategy, but it is the troops that have to do the marching. In this instance the grand strategy of Captain Banks entailed a forced march by Poet Horton. He was forced to produce much poetry in little time. The old man was as prolific as ever. Between early spring, when the new poetic volume was conceived, and late summer or early fall, when it was given to the Raleigh publisher, the poet's output was prodigious. Indeed, it seems incredible considering that much of the time he was on the move and prior to July 21, even when he lighted somewhere, it was amid the excitements and distractions of a military bivouac.

The manuscript submitted to the printer contained 132 poems, by far the largest number in any of Horton's published volumes. True, 42 of the poems were lifted from the *Poetical Works* of 1845 and a couple from *The Hope of Liberty,* but this still left two-thirds of the poems that had not appeared in any previous volume, and from the subject matter it was manifest that many of these were written after the initial meeting between Horton and Banks. There were three poems on the death of Abraham Lincoln, tributes (one each) to Generals Grant and Sherman, an ironic ballad on the final flight of Confederate President Jefferson Davis, and still others on topical themes: "The Heroes of the Late War," "The Flag of the Free," "The Dying Soldier's Message," and "The Southern Refugee."

The traces of haste in preparation of the volume are also conspicuous in a brief biographic sketch of the poet, compiled by Banks. It is filled with inaccuracies, minor and major, which might have been corrected if he had taken more time to consult with Horton. The purpose of the volume, however, is set forth clearly in an introduction by Banks:

> Having met with the author of these works during the victorious march of our army through the State of North Carolina, he having been one of the many refugees who flocked to our lines for safety, I was astonished at his genius, and more so when he showed me some manuscripts written by himself. Knowing the various objections which many of our citizens, north as well as south, have against the black man being made free, and one of these being that they possessed no genius, I formed the idea that I would revise and compile his works and have them published to the public at large, that all might see that there are erroneous opinions entertained with regard to African genius, and also to show that God in his gifts was in no wise partial to the European, but that he gave genius to the black as well as the white man. With this object in view, I offer this little volume to the public, hoping that it may do away with some of the many prejudices so long existing against the poor down-trodden sons of Africa.

To reassure "those who doubt the author's genius," Banks offered as references four North Carolina "gentlemen [who] have been personally acquainted with Mr. Horton for the last forty years, and can testify to the wonderful genius he possesses, which is purely void of the garb of education." Listed were Ex-Governor Swain and Judge Battle, both of Chapel Hill; Dennis Heartt, editor of the Hillsborough *Recorder* and publisher of Horton's 1845 volume; and Hall Horton, "his late master." (As further evidence of haste and sloppiness, Hall Horton is mistakenly called Hall Hart, and Dennis Heartt's surname is misspelled "Hart.")

To corroborate such Southern testimony, nineteen of Banks's fellow officers in the Michigan Cavalry regiment are listed as additional witnesses. The most prestigious witness was Swain, and by the time the volume appeared he was in the center of the scandal occasioned by his daughter's marriage to General Atkins. By this time, too, he had visited the North and shocked some Chapel Hill residents with tales of having dined with Horace Greeley. One more note: the introduction marked the first time the poet was called "Mr. Horton" in print.

The sociopolitical enthusiasm expressed by Banks in his introduction was matched, and perhaps exceeded, by the commercial exuberance contained in a signed notice at the end of the volume. This was a booster's call to "Energetic Young Men" to make their fortunes by undertaking to sell the book, which was destined "to be one of the most popular the world has ever known," one to be "read with admiration and wonder by all." Banks's sales argument went on:

> The politician, no matter whether he be for or
> against the African, will have a curiosity to know
> what it contains, knowing that the work is backed
> by such proof as to set forever at rest any doubts
> that might otherwise arise in the minds of people as
> to its being the production of one who has spent his
> life until a few short months ago in slavery. The
> philanthropist who inscribes upon his banner
> "Freedom and equal rights to all" will certainly
> want the work, while those whose political training
> has been such as to teach them that the black man
> is not capable of being educated, and having
> therefore no right that white men are in duty bound
> to respect, will dwell over its pages and rejoice that
> those whose liberation they are bound to accept as
> a reality are really possessed of genius, which when
> properly cultivated will elevate and prepare them to
> assume the grave responsibilities of that position to
> which they have lately been called by the
> proclamation of the lamented Abraham Lincoln.

The notice concluded by promising the "Energetic Young Men" that this book for everyman, this gateway to fortune, would have a sequel, that even then Horton was preparing another volume of verse that soon would be published under the title *The Black Poet*.

Between the effusive introduction and appended notice rested the body of *Naked Genius*, a title that bore Horton's stamp. He had referred to himself on occasion as an "illiterate genius" or an "uncultivated genius," but in his prewar address to the collegiates of North

Carolina he had employed the phrase "naked genius"—"naked genius . . . without the plumage of literary defense." The image of nakedness was also conveyed in Banks's introduction, which referred to the poet's "wonderful genius . . . purely void of the garb of education."

Some of the new poems in the volume, especially the topical ones, bore the marks of haste and traces of expedience rather than inspiration. Having composed acrostics and romantic doggerel for sale, Horton was no stranger to hack work, and his familiarity with it is exhibited in some of the verse. Yet, in its totality, the volume attested to Horton's undiminished vigor and humor at sixty-eight and, if anything, revealed a greater range and mastery of style, a greater freedom in form and theme. Many of the poems were, after all, the first he wrote as a freeman, released at last from the strictures and calculations imposed by the circumstance of slavery. In addition, he must have been infected to some degree by Banks's enthusiasm, despite the prudent cautions of age, despite the defense mechanisms fashioned in his long servitude and the many disappointments he had endured. There was reason enough for a mood of celebration, but it was tempered by the knowledge that the past could not be undone and that his own sun was well past its zenith. So he wrote "George Moses Horton, Myself":

> I feel myself in need
> > Of the inspiring strains of ancient lore,
> My heart to lift, my empty mind to feed,
> > And all the world explore.
>
> I know that I am old
> > And never can recover what is past;
> And for the future may some light unfold
> > And soar from age's blast.
>
> I feel resolved to try,
> > My wish to prove, my calling to pursue,
> Or mount up from the earth into the sky
> > To show what Heaven can do.
>
> My genius from a boy
> > Has fluttered like a bird within my heart;
> But could not, thus confined, her powers employ,
> > Impatient to depart.
>
> She, like a restless bird,
> > Would spread her wings, her power to be unfurled,
> And let her songs be loudly heard,
> > And dart from world to world.

Other poems were less somber and introspective, employing the stylistic device of pricking the pomp of conventional poetic form and

Naked Genius / 167

classical allusion with an earthy image. Consider this flight from Roman mythology to the farmyard earth:

> Aurora's smiles adorn the mountain's brow,
> And peasant hums delighted at his plough,
> And lo, the dairy maid salutes her bounteous cow.

Another poem, "The Slave," begins in a conventional style:

> What right divine has mortal man received,
>   To domineer with uncontroll'd command? . . .
>
> If Africa was fraught with weaker light,
>   Whilst to the tribes of Europe more was given,
> Does this impart to them a lawful right
>   To counterfeit the golden rule of Heaven?

Then it veers off into this pigsty image:

> Because the blood-sow's left side pigs were black,
>   Whose sable tincture was by nature struck,
> Are you by justice bound to pull them back,
>   And leave the sandy colored pigs to suck?

All of still another poem, "Death of an Old Carriage Horse," is a single animal image to comment on the slave condition:

> I was a harness horse,
>   Constrained to travel weak or strong
> With orders from oppressing force
>   Push along, push along.
>
> I had no space of rest,
>   And took at forks the roughest prong,
> Still by the cruel driver pressed,
>   Push along, push along.
>
> The order of the day
>   Was push, the plea of every tongue,
> The only word was all the way
>   Push along, push along.
>
> Thus to my journey's end
>   Had I to travel right or wrong,
> Till death my sweet and favored friend,
>   Bade me from life to push along.

In "Jefferson in a Tight Place" he recounts in ballad form the then popular story that Davis was disguised as a woman in his final flight. One verse in this longish poem is:

> But he is now brought to a bay,
> However fast he run away,
> He knows he has not long to stay,
>   And assumes a raccoon's dress.
> Found in a hole, he veils his face,
> And fain would take a lady's place,
> But fails, for he has run his race,
>   And falls into distress.

He felt freer now to write about slavery. *Naked Genius* contained seven poems dealing directly with this theme, five of them new, as compared with three in the 1829 volume and only one in 1845 when the times were more precarious.

In one of the new compositions on slavery, "The Obstruction of Genius," he moved from contemplation of his own experience into a broad generalization:

> No cultivating hand was found,
>   To urge the night improving slave,
> Never by freedom's laurel crowned,
>   But pushed through hardship to the grave.
>
> Why did the Gods of Afric sleep,
>   Forgetful of their guardian love,
> When the white traitors of the deep,
>   Betray'd him in the palmy grove.

Another on slavery, "Negro Speculation," contains the verse:

> We think of the shackles and fetters,
>   And traverse the countries of pain;
> 'Tis written in blood-dripping letters,
>   Whilst struggling, be fast in the chain!
>   Weep, humanity, weep!

Yet another, simply entitled "Slavery," is not confined to a recital of slavery's cruelties but speaks of wrath and vengeance, in apparent reference to the Civil War. This one, too, invokes God. In the beginning God seems asleep or indifferent, as in some other poems, but in this one He finally awakes with thunder:

> Our fathers from their native land
>   Were dragged across the brackish deep,
> Bound fast together, hand in hand,
>   O! did the God of nature sleep?

When sadly thro' the almond grove
    The pirate dragged them o'er the sod,
Devoid of pity and of love,
    They seemed as left without a God.

The maledictions of our God,
    Pervade the dwindling world we see;
He hurls the vengeance with his rod,
    And thunders, let the slave be free.

11

Oblivion and Death

With the publication of *Naked Genius* arranged for in Raleigh, the poet and the promoter headed North, Horton stopping in Philadelphia and Banks going on home to Michigan.

The notice to "Energetic Young Men" advised them to communicate with Banks in Michigan, but it may be assumed that few if any responded to the invitation. In the acquisitive boom that followed the Civil War and later evolved into the Gilded Age energetic young men, bent on making their fortune, were tempted by more promising ventures than the sale of poetry. When the volume did not realize Banks's great expectations he lost his enthusiasm for it and made his exit from the poet's life. Having entered into the poetic realm with the bold charge of the cavalry raid, he now simulated the same maneuver with the abruptness of his withdrawal.

Horton was left with an old predicament, a manuscript in hand and a publisher to find, but he faced it in new and strange surroundings, in a sprawling Northern urban center and not a small university town of the rural South. He was just one more stranger among the slightly more than 22,000 black residents in what then was the country's second most populated city, recording 674,000 inhabitants in the 1870 census. Even the natural climate represented a marked change, from the relative dry in the rolling countryside of the Piedmont plateau to the wet of the coastal plain, exposing him to the damp chill and humid heat of the lowlands at the confluence of the Delaware and Schuylkill rivers. One can only conjecture about the impact of these changes upon a man of sixty-nine, especially the shock of his first encounter with a Northern urban ghetto.

In this new environment the poet did something he had never done before in his long life. He turned to black compatriots for help in the publication of his manuscript, specifically seeking the assistance of one of Philadelphia's established black societies, the Banneker Institute, an exclusive fraternity of thirty educated black men who met at Liberty Hall. The records of this society contain this entry: "A special meeting of the institution was held on the evening of August 31, 1866, the object being to receive Mr. George Horton of North Carolina, a poet of considerable genius, it was claimed. The feasibility of publishing his book was submitted to Mr. John J. Smythe, but found too expensive."

The qualified recognition (the phrase "it was claimed" hanging like an albatross on that other phrase "poet of considerable genius") and the unqualified disappointment (the manuscript—presumably the one Banks had promised to publish under the title *The Black Poet*—was never published) ended the poet's fleeting association with the Banneker Institute. No further reference to him is to be found in the society's minutes.

Horton's principal biographer asserts that the Banneker Institute people found the poet "overbearing, conceited, and offensive," that such "unctuous hauteur" caused the rupture between the poet and the society. No hard evidence is offered to support this harsh judgment, and no such evidence exists, the only tangible evidence of the relationship between the poet and the society being the two quoted sentences from its minutes. Any conclusions about the Banneker incident must rest on inference drawn from the relevant circumstances, and these are exceedingly complex, for they involve not only the poet's character and prior behavior patterns but also the structure and mores of Philadelphia's black community. If it is permissible to conclude that the poet was vain, especially in relation to other blacks, then surely it is a tenable conclusion from even a cursory study of Philadelphia's black community that its aristocracy was not devoid of a social conceit that could be expressed in "unctuous hauteur."

Among Philadelphia's several distinctions in the national history it was also the cradle of black community organization in the country. Here the first black secular organization in the United States, a Free African Society, was formed in 1787. Here, too, the first black church in America, the First African Church of St. Thomas, was founded in 1792, and two years later came the birth of the Bethel Church, which was to grow into the African Methodist Episcopal Church, by far the largest of the black religious denominations.

By the time Horton arrived, social stratification in this old and structured black community had developed the contours that were to be etched at the end of the century by Dr. William E. B. Du Bois in *The Philadelphia Negro*, a comprehensive and pioneering study of a Northern urban ghetto. St. Thomas' Protestant Episcopal Church and the

Central Presbyterian Church, for example, already were the well-established exclusive havens of aristocratic congregations.

"At St. Thomas'," Dr. Du Bois wrote, "one looks for the well-to-do Philadelphians, largely descendants of favorite mulatto house-servants, and consequently well-bred and educated, but rather cold and reserved to strangers and newcomers; at Central Presbyterian one sees the older, simpler set of respectable Philadelphians . . . pleasant but conservative."

Commenting further on this "aristocracy of the Negro population in education, wealth and general social efficiency," Dr. Du Bois observed: "It is natural . . . that . . . the mass of Negroes should look upon the worshipers at St. Thomas' and Central as feeling themselves above them, and should dislike them for it. On the other hand it is just as natural for the well-educated and well-to-do Negroes to feel themselves . . . above the servant girls and porters of the middle class of workers." A concomitant of snobbery is exclusiveness, the point made by Dr. Du Bois in noting the cold reserve of St. Thomas' parishioners toward strangers and newcomers and reiterated by him with the observation that "strangers secure entrance to this circle with difficulty and only by introduction."

Any encounter between this upper stratum of an urban black community and the rustic poet was prone to create tensions, for if Horton was vain, so were his hosts, and few frictions are as abrasive as the friction of contending vanities. If there was indeed a clash of vanities, it was not a contest between equals on a neutral terrain. He was a newcomer and stranger, fresh from the South and the slavery in which he was reared; Philadelphia's black aristocrats were, for the most part, descendants of several generations of freedmen and urban dwellers, a long-evolved and tightly knit social group, self-assured in their claim to greater social polish and sophistication. In such circumstances it is a most dubious presumption to attribute the poet's rupture with the Banneker Institute exclusively to his "unctuous hauteur."

Although the reasons for it are uncertain, the one certainty is that Horton was not admitted into the upper stratum of Philadelphia's black community. Dr. Du Bois estimated that this upper stratum constituted a little more than 10 per cent of the total black population, and Horton vanished into the other 90 per cent. He simply disappeared from public notice into the middle or bottom layers of the ghetto, which burgeoned in the decade of the 1870's, Philadelphia's black population soaring by 43 per cent in those ten years and reaching 31,699 in the 1880 census. It was easy enough for one old black man to be submerged in this tide of newcomers and strangers.

Oblivion and Death / 173

After the Banneker Institute meeting of 1866 no trace of Horton has been found in public annals or private records until one incident in 1883. Since the latter also occurred in Philadelphia, the assumption is that he spent the intervening seventeen years in that city, but no documentary evidence of it has been turned up. Those years, between the ages of sixty-nine and eighty-six, are a mysterious void, and although several claims have been made for what he did during those years, there is nothing to substantiate them, except for that one incident in 1883. This was an interview with the poet by a man named Collier Cobb.

Cobb was a professor of geology at the University of North Carolina, who said he became interested in Horton, a subject remote from his academic discipline, by reading a verse the poet had written for a lady's album in 1840. "The quality of the verse," he wrote, "and the story of its author led me to look into the man's history and to search for his work in the files of the newspapers of his day." The search finally led him to the Philadelphia interview in 1883.

His recollection of the interview is reflected in two documents. One was a paper entitled "An American Man of Letters—George Moses Horton, The Negro Poet," first presented on September 23, 1886, to a meeting of Southern Students of Harvard College in Cambridge, and subsequently published in scholarly journals and presented to other academic groups. The other document was a letter written to a Victor Hugo Palsits of the New York Public Library's Manuscript Department on January 10, 1929.

The paper, it may be noted, was composed only three years after the Philadelphia interview, but contains no account of it. Almost all of the paper is filled with Horton lore and legend on the Chapel Hill campus. At the very end, and very briefly, three assertions are made that bear on the Philadelphia period and conceivably are based on what Cobb learned in the interview. These assertions are:

1. "His later work showed remotely and in some small measure the influence of that group of Elizabethan poets who were wont to meet in the clubroom of the Mermaid Tavern, and, after he went to Philadelphia, he wrote a number of poems in imitation of Marlowe's 'Passionate Shepherd to His Love' and 'The Nymph's Reply' by Sir Walter Raleigh."

(Alas, Cobb quotes no samples from this work—and no one else has found such examples.)

2. "It was in Philadelphia that he developed his gift of story telling, his stories being modelled on the old stories of the East, as he had learned them from the Bible and in many cases being bodily taken from

the Scriptures and made modern as to names and places. In this he was even more successful than was Benjamin Franklin in his famous paraphrase of the Book of Job. The source of Horton's inspiration was always hid from any but the closest students of Holy Writ, and even they did not often recognize their old friends in modern dress."

(Once more the good professor offered neither quotations nor specific references, although his was ostensibly a scholarly paper prepared for an academic audience.)

3. "In yet another respect this poet would be a paradox in our day. He did very little work before reaching the age of 40, and the most productive period of his life began when he was 67 years old, continuing until his death at the age of 85, in 1883."

Curiously, although Cobb asserted that Horton was most productive past the age of sixty-seven, he cites not one work of this most prolific period. Instead, he says, "All the examples of his verse that I have given are selected from his early productions, written when he was still an unlettered slave."

In contrast to the paper of 1886 the letter of 1929 speaks directly of the 1883 interview, but this is forty-six years after the event. Memory is hardly served by such a great lapse in time and by Cobb's own advanced age.

"I called on Poet Horton in Philadelphia in 1883, the very year in which he died," Cobb wrote. "He could then both read and write, and was publishing short stories in a number of newspapers. . . . In addressing Horton in Philadelphia I called him 'Poet,' which pleased him greatly, and he told me that I was using his proper title."

Cobb referred to two Horton manuscripts, but both of these belonged to his Chapel Hill period. The letter sheds no more light on the Philadelphia years and contains no clues as to where such light might be found. Indeed, even the flat statement as fact that Horton died in 1883 is veiled in mystery. There is no record of his death in Philadelphia, either in that year or in the next several years, although the city carefully kept such records at the time. As a consequence Horton's most thorough biographer has written:

> It is not known where or exactly when he made his
> departure. Perhaps it was not even in Philadelphia.
> Perhaps, sensing a need greater than strength, he
> took the weary highway south where, in accordance
> with a resolution made upon leaving North
> Carolina, he breathed out his ultimate moments in
> familiar surroundings.

Oblivion and Death / 175

> "Let this be chased in my breast
> Through this and future years to come:
> My last abode, my final rest,
> Be lodged with thee, my native home."

It is a nice magnolia-scented sentimentality, this speculation that the poet, well into the ninth decade of his life, sensing the proximity of death, resolved to fulfill an old poetic vow to die and be buried in North Carolina. But the nonsentimental fact is that Horton, in death, was treated even more shabbily than Phillis Wheatley. At least her death was noted, its exact date recorded, though the grave was unmarked. Not only is Horton's grave unmarked, but even its locale remains subject to a speculative range with a 360-mile radius, from Philadelphia to Chapel Hill. No public notice was taken of his death when it occurred. If Professor Cobb had access to the precise facts (and he implies that he did with the certainty of his assertion that Horton died in 1883), apparently he did not bother to pursue them, for if he had taken this trouble, it seems unlikely that he would not have recorded his findings.

Somewhere, some time, Horton died, and no one seemed to care. This terrible anonymity in death casts some shadow of doubt on Professor Cobb's testimony about the poet's Philadelphia years. Cobb's statement that the poet "was publishing short stories in a number of newspapers," disguising biblical characters and plots, was subsequently embellished by other Southern writers. It has been said that to realize the maximum cash return, Horton published these stories simultaneously in several periodicals and that "this practice made him a writer of syndicated features at a surprisingly early date." If he did, in fact, publish so extensively, he would have had some relationship with editors and would have established some sort of reputation, so that on both counts—acquaintance with editors and literary reputation —his passing would have occasioned public notice. But it did not. Nor have any samples of his supposedly prolific prose output been discovered, and a search of the most likely sources in Philadelphia and vicinity has not turned up any samples of such work.

Faced with this strange void, a speculative reconstruction of the 1883 interview between the professor and the poet is tempting. The only bit of direct dialogue recalled by Cobb concerns his form of address. He addresses Horton as "Poet," and Horton replies that he is greatly pleased by this use of his proper title. The old black man asserts his pride and dignity in this initial exchange with the inquisitive white visitor from Chapel Hill. He is eighty-five now, and he knows there is not much life left for him, neither time nor energy for new ventures. All that can matter now is the retention of pride and dignity in the encounter with the young white stranger, who will go back to Chapel Hill and relate his impressions of the old poet who for so many years made his mark on the North Carolina campus.

There is some reminiscing about the campus. Yes, says the poet, he wrote verses for Cobb's great-uncle, Fred Henry Cobb, and for his uncle, Colonel John P. Cobb and for his father, the Reverend Needham Bryan Cobb (all this was recalled by Professor Cobb in his 1929 letter). But inevitably the conversation turns to the questions: What are you doing now? What have you been doing since you left Chapel Hill?

Assume then that the poet suffered a shattering disappointment when Captain Banks's grandiose hopes for *Naked Genius* proved to be an illusion. The disappointment is compounded when Banks runs out on his commitment to promote publication of *The Black Poet*. Horton turns to the Banneker Institute for help, and is rebuffed. He is then sixty-nine, an old, black, lonely man, a country man all his life, in a big, strange city. He has too much pride to return to Chapel Hill and parade his failure, and not enough resilience any more to march on to success in the far more competitive environment of a big urban center. He resorts to odd jobs, menial jobs, and somehow ekes out an existence.

Assume all this is so, does he tell it to the visiting professor from Chapel Hill? No, he does not, he has his pride. Yes, he says, I've been doing some writing. No, not poetry, not much of that. I've been writing stories. What kind of stories? Bible stories, dressed up, so people think they're new. He is vague about it, dropping hazy hints about their publication. The poet, practiced in this art of put-on with white folks, is totally plausible. Later the professor fills in the blank spots, turns vague hints into definite assertions, and still later other writers improve on the professor's version, and at the end of the process Horton emerges as one of the first American writers of syndicated features.

This flight of the imagination is credible. Since no sample of Horton's prose work in Philadelphia has been produced, the assumption that such a body of work exists seems to rest solely on what Horton might have said to Cobb in 1883. It may be, of course, that some Philadelphia stories will be uncovered, and then the above scenario will be reduced to poor fancy, but more nagging questions will be magnified.

If Cobb thought it a paradox that "the most productive period of his [Horton's] life began when he was 67 years old," would it not be a greater paradox for the work of this period to be totally buried all these years? By the time Horton arrived in Philadelphia, he already was an authentic pioneer in Afro-American letters, a poet with rare achievements and distinctions; and if, thereafter, he became even more productive, what can be said of a society that ignored him so completely that no readily discernible trace of him in this period can be found in its annals? What can be said of a society that was so indifferent to his death as to leave no record of its place and time?

12

Critical Appraisals

In many respects matters did not improve for George Moses Horton after his death. His body had been buried poorly, maybe in Philadelphia, maybe in North Carolina, maybe somewhere else, and now his memory was buried too well by the patronizations of Southern scholarship.

Professor Cobb, after quoting "The Slave's Complaint" in *The Hope of Liberty*, appended the comment: "George never really cared for more liberty than he had, but he was fond of playing to the grandstand. . . ." This judgment is offered as a parenthetical aside, most casually, without elaboration or argument. In this offhand manner the antislavery poems, the first of their kind by an Afro-American, are dismissed as exhibitionist capers for the gallery, devoid of genuine emotion. The reach of Cobb's cavalier judgment extends beyond Horton. As Vernon Loggins observed in *The Negro Author*, "Negro poetry between 1790 and 1840 is represented mainly by the work of a North Carolina slave, George Moses Horton." Cobb thus denies that in this critical half-century, when the institution of slavery was consolidated in its final forms, there was any authentic poetic outcry against it from among its victims.

Cobb is not alone in his judgment of Horton's desire for liberty. The poet's most comprehensive biographer, Professor Richard Walser, said much the same thing, but his observation was pinpointed in time to the decade of the 1840's, after publication of *The Hope of Liberty* and the failure of the manumission efforts that coincided with it. "No longer did he think of being set free, for he had as much liberty as his simple requirements demanded."

A somewhat more subtle commentary on Horton's relationship to slavery was contained in a biographical essay by Stephen B. Weeks in *The Southern Workman* (October, 1914), published by the Hampton

Normal and Agricultural Institute Press. Weeks also took *The Hope of Liberty* as his point of departure, commenting:

> It is of interest to call attention to the title of this little pamphlet for the important light it throws upon the condition of slaves in North Carolina at the date of its publication. It is usually said that all higher aspiration in the slave was crushed and that those individuals who were intelligent enough to desire freedom were ruthlessly suppressed, but in North Carolina Horton was not only allowed to express his feelings privately on the subject, but even to print and openly publish his desires, and in doing this he was aided and abetted by some of the best men in the state. Not only was Horton allowed to do this in 1829, but he continued to enjoy the same liberty after the enactment of the harder laws that were passed as a result of the Nat Turner insurrection of 1831.

Historically, that final assertion is inaccurate. The guarded restraint in dealing with slavery conspicuously distinguishes Horton's 1845 volume from that of 1829, before the more repressive regime was introduced in 1830–31, and in 1865, after emancipation. From the record it appears that Horton felt he did not continue "to enjoy the same liberty" in the long interval between 1830 and the end of the Civil War.

Objectively, Weeks contradicts Cobb, for he assumes the antislavery poems were authentic expressions of aspiration, intelligence, and desire. This assumption is relevant to the principal thrust of his comment, which poses another issue. Ironically, apologists for slavery, as well as its antagonists, invoked the poetical works of Horton (or of Wheatley) to buttress their position. If Abolitionists argued that black poetry was evidence of black intelligence, sensitivity, and humanity, and, therefore, of the black right to freedom, slavery's apologists turned this argument into its opposite. They contended that a system in which a Wheatley or a Horton could emerge was not, on the face of it, as despotic and dehumanizing as its critics charged. There was flexibility in it, they averred, and some benevolence—as there was, of course, for any oppressive regime strives for maximum stability by mixing acquiescence with repression. However, the attainments of rare individuals in unique circumstances, a classification that embraces both Wheatley and Horton, is no index of the condition of the mass.

Moreover, the celebration of what they managed to do as slaves begs the question: what might they have done if not fettered?

Professor Walser addressed himself to that question, and this was his answer: "That most of Horton's antislavery poems are selfish and unimpassioned, philosophic rather than realistic, is indicative that, while he was taught to resent his status, he did not find it overly tragic or oppressive. Under the system he flourished, as would not have been the case had he been free. . . ."

It is easy to be outraged at this assertion that Horton flourished best under slavery. In an absolute sense the issues posed by this assertion are not, as the lawyers might say, probative. That is, once the hypothetical question is posed—what if he had been free?—a virtually limitless range of contingencies and possibilities is opened up. In what specific circumstances? Under what particular conditions? Such questions are unanswerable, and this imparts a special meretriciousness to Walser's assertion, the more so because it is categorical, and yet on its own specific terms it is even less susceptible of categorical proof than its hypothetical opposite. And outside the specific terms there is only the generalization that men have flourished more in freedom, as relative as that term might be, than under slavery, which is an absolute.

Into this argument Professor Cobb, whose bias is more crude, injects a paradoxical twist with his unsubstantiated testimony. Cobb, it may be recalled, claimed that the most productive period of Horton's life began when he was sixty-seven years old. This coincided with his emancipation. If a man, with freedom, is more productive at age sixty-seven and beyond than he was, with slavery, in his prime years, this says much for the rejuvenating and renaissant qualities of freedom. Yet this same Cobb, who vouches for Horton's miraculous response to liberty, also contends that he really did not care for it.

Two more facets of Walser's statement merit comment. One is the assertion that Horton "was taught to resent his status." Now, Horton learned to read without being taught, and offhand this seems like a more impressive conquest of learning than a slave's cultivation of resentment against his status. Indeed, ante-bellum history suggests that large numbers of blacks, who never mastered the alphabet, managed on their own to acquire a deep and abiding resentment against their status. But in Walser's biography Horton, with his remarkable capacity for learning, does not himself learn to resent slavery, but is taught to do so, and his teacher is Caroline Lee Hentz, the intruder from New England. It is a variation on the stereotype of Northern agitators stirring up the blacks, who otherwise would not have the wit or dignity to be discontented with their condition.

Finally, for the present, there is Walser's assessment of Horton's antislavery poems and the conclusion he draws from it. He says that "most" of these poems are selfish, unimpassioned, philosophic, which means that some are not vitiated by these qualities. Good. Which then are the more self-revelatory, the more authentic expressions of inner emotion and attitude, the few that are imbued with passion, or the "most" that are not? In estimating any poet's work as reflection of the innermost self, what is the yardstick? Is the measure to be sought in some average or median of his output, or is such a mean to be overshadowed by the peaks he attains? As complicating as such questions are for critical judgment in general, in this specific instance the complication is compounded by yet another question. To what degree was Horton influenced, in writing the antislavery poems, by his awareness that he was writing for a white publisher and a white audience in a slave state? The question is especially critical for his first antislavery poems of the late 1820's. By the time of the final volume in 1865 he was nearing seventy and age could in itself account for cooling passion and philosophical detachment; age and the weight of habit patterns molded by his long tenure as a slave.

To pose the questions above is already to ruffle the smoothness of Walser's conclusion from the quality of the poems that Horton did not find slavery "overly tragic or oppressive." That dangling adverb "overly" is a gratuitous annoyance. Strike it. Did the poet then find slavery merely tragic and oppressive, without any indeterminate qualifications of degree?

Other irritants crop up in the Southern literature about Horton. Biographic essayist Weeks offers this picture: "As a slave, George was usually employed on the farm, but besides some personal services to his master it is said that his main occupations in winter were hunting and fishing, and in the summer attending protracted meetings, or, as they were then called, camp meetings." Mind you, these are designated as "his main occupations." Hunting and fishing can be solitary pastimes, but not camp meetings. If he attended such meetings for most of the summer, so did the other slaves, and an idyllic image is conjured up of all those happy-go-lucky darkies singing and stomping and listening to preaching through the long days and balmy evenings of the summer months. It seems almost vulgar to recall that in the summer of 1828 Master James Horton declined to sell the poet because there was work to be done on the farm.

Other dismal samples of historical scholarship and literary criticism can be culled readily from the literature about Horton, but enough has been cited to indicate the posthumous price he has paid in the appropriation of him as a regional ornament of the ante-bellum South.

American regionalism can be a double-edged sword and Horton was cut by both edges, by the embrace of Southern provincialism and by the indifference of Northern parochialism. After the Civil War and Reconstruction he no longer could be a chattel, but he remained a cultural property of the South, such possession being solemnized and shaped by the counterrevolution in the latter part of the nineteenth century. In politics and jurisprudence the counterrevolution was legitimatized by the Hayes-Tilden compromise and the "separate but equal" doctrine. Culture and ideology do not lend themselves so readily to such definite landmarks, but just the same, these, too, were molded by the compacts that tacitly sanctioned the violent and forcible institutionalization of white supremacy. A kind of cultural autonomy evolved, and if the interpretation of the Southern past did not become the exclusive domain of Southern scholars, for a long time they did enjoy a near-monopoly and most certainly commanded the dominant positions in the field. Up to a point, given the regional configurations of the country, this was inevitable, but recognition of this does not mean reconciliation with its consequences. These consequences flow from the truism that the past is seen from the vantage point of the present, being most often employed to justify or rationalize the present, and the specific present in which modern Southern historiography was molded is the present of the late nineteenth century, when segregation and oppression were codified in law and custom. Today, as the centenary of the Hayes-Tilden compromise draws near, the edifice erected by it—political, social, cultural—is being shattered. Out of the rubble, Horton is one of the small trophies that ought to be rescued.

Unlike Wheatley, he never made a splash in London and did not make his mark in a nationally recognized cultural center.* He was not favored by the disparagement of so eminent a critic as Thomas Jefferson and was not defended by other eminent men. By the mischance of his place and time he has remained more obscure than Wheatley. Yet though also a minor poet, historically he is more significant than Wheatley is in the evolution of Afro-American letters. He is more original, more inventive, his range is far broader in form, language,

---

* But eighty years after his death an anthology of American poetry (quoting three stanzas from "On Liberty and Slavery") placed him in illustrious companionship with T. S. Eliot, E. E. Cummings, Countee Cullen, Emily Dickinson Paul Laurence Dunbar, Ralph Waldo Emerson, Langston Hughes, Freneau, Longfellow, Lowell, MacLeish, Poe, Whitman, and Whittier (Sim Copans, ed., *J' Entends l'Amérique Qui Chante: Panorama de la Poésie aux États-Unis* [Paris: Nouveaux Horizons, 1963]).

and theme. Most important, a distinct human personality emerges from his verse, complex and contradictory and fudged at times, but an authentic personality that is self-assertive in its hopes and its commentary on the human condition, that possesses irony and wit, that is, on occasion, bold enough to break with convention. He has a sense of identity that, from the available evidence, Wheatley did not and perhaps could not possess.

On the most elementary personal level her memory of her birthplace, of her kin and her people, was totally obliterated. In his formative years all these things were part of his environment and he always knew where he came from and who he was. As a child prodigy she was sheltered and molded by her Puritan owners, so that what came forth was an artificial, hothouse creation. Her remarkable intelligence and talent became vessels that were filled to the brim with Puritan values and mores. Once her precocity was discovered, the attainment of literacy and knowledge was made easy for her, and the cultivation of her creative talent was facilitated—but toward given ends predestined by others. From the very beginning the cultural influences that shaped her were those of a white Puritan society.

In contrast, Horton was initially shaped in the community of black slaves, and here he was exposed to his earliest cultural influences. He had to struggle against towering obstacles to master the rudiments of reading. By the time he acquired patrons he was no precocious child; he was a young man well into his twenties, who had spent all his formative years on a slave plantation, and himself had made the first and most difficult conquests on the path to his poetic vocation. The wisdom he brought with him to the campus had been learned in the school of slavery. As a black in a white world he had resources for self-reliance that Wheatley did not have, and his relationship with white patrons was different from hers. She, falling into patronage as an unformed child, became, in great measure, its passive object. He was ever a conscious, active protagonist in the relationship with white patronage, knowingly employing wit and charm, artifice and cajolery, supplication and pressure, doing all this with the ever-present awareness that he was black and a slave.

His Southern biographers attempt to portray him as the contented slave, but his Raleigh publishers in 1829 displayed greater perception when they cited his antislavery verse of the time as evidence "that his heart has felt deeply and sensitively in this lowest possible condition of human nature." Some of this verse is animated by a passion that stamps it as the authentic expression of his innermost feeling. Then there are his efforts to secure manumission, abandoned only when they seemed patently hopeless, and his later flight to the Union lines, and finally, his migration to Philadelphia. This last is very telling. A man of his advanced age would hardly have chosen voluntary exile in a strange, forbidding environment if the familiar locales of his youth, to which he could have returned, evoked nothing but memories of happy contentment. If Chapel Hill, set in the natural surroundings he knew and loved, beckoned with nostalgic remembrance of ante-bellum days, the aged wanderer might have found his way back. Instead, it seemed, he remained in Philadelphia.

He extolled liberty in his verse, he strove for it in his life; when it approached he rushed out to meet it, and once it was his he turned his back on the landmarks of his slavery. This aspiration to liberty is one central motif of his life, more muted at times, more pronounced at others, but constant. It is essential first to establish his hostility to slavery before examining its limitations.

He resented the system, but he lived within it, and this entailed accommodation to it, especially for the slave who aspired to be a poet. A slave could not be the dilettante playing with alienation, announcing his withdrawal from the society because he did not share its values. He was an instrument of production, and the system did not provide this leeway for such instruments. It was the premise of slavery that a black man had no rights that a white man need respect, and the white man was master. Beyond passive resistance or a blind, individual outburst of anger (and there are numerous examples of both), uncompromising hostility to slavery could take one of two overt forms: organized revolt or flight. Nat Turner is an example of the former, and Frederick Douglass of the latter, but Horton was neither a Turner nor a Douglass. He was not a militant. He was not a man of action, he was a poet, and given nature's diversity in the making of human beings, there is little point in reproaching him for being the one and not the other.

Moreover, it was his fate to be a black poet when and where the practice of his art, the expression of this innermost bent, was dependent upon white favor in a slave society. One may not be able to delineate all the consequences of this relationship, but surely one must reckon with its pervasive influence upon what he wrote and how he lived. There were two elements in this active equation: The black slave and the white society, and it is no good to depict what the black poet did, as if he were a free agent exercising free choice, without calculating what the dominant society demanded that he do as condition for maintaining his unique and precarious position in the antebellum social organism. It does no good to remark upon the white tolerance, benevolence, and even encouragement that were bestowed upon the poet without inquiring: but what was the implicit price of this largesse?

So we come once more upon Walser's observation that most of Horton's antislavery verse was "selfish," was "philosophic rather than realistic." Imagine then the step beyond the subjective and self-centered. The lines

> Alas! and am I born for this,
> To wear this slavish chain?

are transformed into

> Alas! and are *we* born for this,
> To wear this slavish chain?

The transformation is substantive. The first version is a personal protest, the second is a generic challenge to slavery. In the first the poet speaks for others only by implication; in the second he does so explicitly. The first may evoke the response that this uncommonly talented and sensitive man ought to be free of the slavish chain, without disturbing the chain for others. The second version permits no such inference, for it represents the transition from "let me be free" to "let my people go."

The two lines of verse are only the statement of a theme. Once the theme is cast in collective rather than individual terms, how is it to be elaborated and developed, and with what further implications? Where does it go and where does it end? Individual manumission, although rare and discouraged by law and custom, was occasionally effected in the South, and its selective practice did not shake the system. To leap from manumission for "I" to abolition for "we" is to tread on the dangerous ground of revolution.

Surely Horton must have possessed a sense of what was and was not permissible. Among slaves less gifted than he such a sense was highly developed. It would not have required an extraordinary amount of such sense to perceive that the fine line between "I" and "we," between personal protest and revolutionary challenge, was also the boundary between the permissible and the impermissible. If such suppositions are valid, then what Horton wrote cannot be judged, on its face, as the free expression of his innermost self, but as a delicate balance—a compromise, if you will—between his own feelings and the pressures of the society, which assumed tangible forms in the white publishers and purchasers of his work.

Considering the social constraints upon him, the most reasonable assumption is that he said less than he meant rather than more, as his biographers contend. This assumption is buttressed by delving into one curious aspect of Walser's treatment of the poet. In his biography, Walser reproduced four of the ten stanzes of "On Liberty and Slavery," and all four are hinged on the first personal pronoun, as the first line was. "Alas! and am I born for this . . . ?" However, there is one stanza in which "we" appears, smuggled in, as it were, for throughout the poem the poet speaks as "I." It would seem a significant coincidence that the "we" is tucked away in the most militant stanza, the one that suggests bloody struggle for freedom:

> Oh, Liberty! thou golden prize,
>   So often sought by blood—
> We crave thy sacred sun to rise,
>   The gift of nature's God!

All the dangers that attend a transgression beyond self in the antislavery verse also lurk in a progression from the philosophic to the realistic. Condemnation of slavery in the abstract was not fraught with the revolutionary implications of its exposure in the specific. Simply to dip into the possibilities of realism is already to reveal how unrealistic it is to conceive that he could have written in such a vein. Was he going to publish and sell verse about the rape of black women by white masters? This is realism, treading on the most forbidden ground perhaps, but if one recalls the Southern reaction more than a century later to the physical protest against such small humiliations as exclusion from a lunch counter or relegation to the back of the bus, one should comprehend that any realistic exposure of slavery, in its specific manifestations of cruelty, injustice, and humiliation, would have been an incendiary torch in the slave South of the mid-nineteenth century.

Self-censorship is notoriously the most common form of censorship. His Southern biographers assume, imply, and on occasion assert that Horton had neither wit nor cause to engage in self-censorship; no cause because he had nothing to say that would unpardonably offend white Southern sensibilities. To Cobb's claim that the poet really desired no more liberty than he had, a collateral claim is thus joined: he really wanted to say no more than was clearly permissible for a slave by the prevailing standards of the society. The second claim is as gross and smug as the first.

The societal pressures upon Horton for self-censorship were enormous and many. These involved more than the processing of his poetic collections by white publishers for a white market. His bread-and-butter output consisted of the acrostics and romantic poems he wrote for sale to university students. The reputation and relationships he created on campus were, therefore, indispensable to his survival as a poet. Recalling the white professor, who was hanged in effigy and summarily dismissed for daring to announce he would vote for Frémont, one may readily imagine what would have happened to a black slave who went about the campus spouting poetry that, in realistic terms, indicted the common oppression of slaves. Or can one really imagine it? Would an effigy have been enough for hanging? At its most benign the reaction would have meant farewell to poetry and back to the plantation with an admonition to the master to shape up his uppity and seditious nigger.

If it is not possible truly to weigh his work without throwing into the scales the social restraints of a slave society, this also holds true for any judgment of his personal behavior. Recall his first encounter with the campus, how he was maneuvered into the role of buffoon, the unwitting butt for student amusement. There was no subtlety in this hint of societal expectations. As he became aware of what he was doing and what was being done to him he could have concluded: if this is the kind of game the young gentlemen wish to play, he will play it, not as the unwitting fool, but as the knowing jester. Remembering his initiation at the university, there is gross injustice in the blandness of the assumption by his biographers that the jester's role was his free choice, a voluntary projection of innate character, thereby absolving slave society of this bit of typecasting.

From any proximity to an objective vantage point white society's psychological need for casting him in the role is far more persuasive than his for essaying it. As poet the black slave put in question the cherished assumption of white superiority, the one assumption that was the indispensable foundation for the Southern edifice, social, political, economic, cultural, psychological. Was it not restorative then for the white ego to cast the poet also as a clown? So choosing and commanding the power to control his life and determine his condition, white society surely was positioned to impose its choice to flatter its own sense of superiority.

He made his accommodations to the essential cruelty of the jest, for he had to be ingratiating. It was the condition for his existence on campus. Recognizing the need he met it with a flair. As has been suggested before, when on occasion he appeared to be mocking himself he may have been mocking his auditors. He did not make the rules but he had to play the game, and possibly he came to enjoy some of it, but not all of it, and not without reservation. There is, for example, the edge of bitterness in his recollection of how he first was enticed to perform on campus. In an opposite direction there is the eloquence and the fulsomeness of his tribute to Caroline Lee Hentz, the person who came closest, not only to accepting his talent as a poet, but to respecting his dignity as a human being. He expressed gratitude to others who helped him, but he paid such tribute to no one else. In this revealing reaction to a relationship, which was most free of the humiliating disfigurement of human relationships inherent in slavery, there is a powerful affirmation of his own dignity and aspiration. He asserts a sense of his own worth by so eagerly responding to an acceptance of it. The same assertion is contained in his antislavery poems and introspective verse.

Walser says he performed as "mendicant and fool and poet." True, but the one role that clearly was not imposed upon him, that he chose himself and pursued, despite all the obstacles interposed by a slave society, was that of poet. As for the other two roles, imposition is far more reasonably assumed than denied, and the questionable area is the degree and kind of his compromise in playing them, and what this did to him. It may be said that he became a poet despite his slavery, and a jester and mendicant because of it.

This same biographer refers to him as "George Moses, uncomplicated fellow." The judgment is patronizing, but there is also more to it. To say the poet was uncomplicated is also to suggest several possibilities that singly or in combination might have made him so. It is to suggest, perhaps, a harmony with his environment, or worse yet, a mindless acquiescence to it. (There is an alternate possibility of a single-minded disharmony with his social environment, so total and unalterable an opposition to it as to make for the simplicity that rare revolutionaries achieve, but Horton patently was not of this breed.) Or, perhaps, it is to suggest that his own social condition was uncomplicated, as in the idyllic pattern of benign masters and contented slaves. Still another hypothesis is that his condition might have been beset by complexities, created by slavery and his particular relation to it, but he, simple child of nature, was impervious to such complexities.

None of these possibilities accords with the reality of his work and life, for these abound with the signs of tension between him and his environment. To accept at face value the mask of simplicity (and, on occasion, even simple-mindedness) that he so often wore before white society is like accepting the surface appearance of stark simplicity in the master-slave relationship without probing underneath for all its complicated effects upon the human beings, masters or bondsmen, who were caught in its embrace. Much of black folklore and humor revolves around illusion and reality; the illusion that is created to fit white preconceptions and to mask the reality of black feeling. Under slavery, as in many situations since, such duality was an expedient for survival. That it has become part of folklore attests to the prevalence of the artifice. Given Horton's wit and talent (as jester as well as poet), given too his encounters with white society, which were unique for a slave in their multiplicity and variety, it would seem the assumption that he did not resort to the most common black artifice is burdened with more naiveté than any that may be attributed properly to him.

Horton was, indeed, a complicated fellow, and among the complications was his relationship to the black community. Manifestly he preferred Chapel Hill to the slave quarters on the plantation. His vocation as poet dictated such a preference. The university afforded him the tools of his craft and a market for its products, as distinct from the plantation, where the tools were the hoe and the plough and the marketable products were grain and fruit. The university could tolerate a slave poet as an exotic embellishment; the plantation needed farm hands, not literary ornaments. The fledgling poet sought patrons and teachers, and the campus was where he found them. Poetry, aside from the religious hymn and the folk song, was a white privilege; to be a poet was to seek access to white society. True, some black freedmen in the North, such as Walker, Douglass, William Wells Brown, and others, wrote for a black audience as well as for a white, but the same option did not exist for a black slave in the South. No such publishing facilities were open to him, and between the prevalence of illiteracy and the absence of distributive channels the potential of a black audience was extinguished.

As poet his choice, or more accurately, nonchoice, was determined by conditions that the dominant white society created. However, even as slave a preference for Chapel Hill was understandable. There he was not subject to the kind of surveillance and discipline that were applied to the field hand on the plantation. The small compensations that induced other slaves to seek an opportunity for hiring out also beckoned to him, except that he was more fortunate in his vocation. Moreover, aside from its utilitarian value the university environment, once he was committed to intellectual pursuits, offered other advantages as well. Compared to the plantation the university was an oasis of culture, and a man with a thirst for learning could quench it even if he were limited to sporadic, haphazard draughts in peripheral waters.

He was not, of course, accepted into white society, and at the same time, in large measure, he estranged himself from the black. It would seem that, like Wheatley, he was suspended in a limbo between the two worlds, black and white. But it was not the same. Wheatley was cast into the limbo by her Puritan masters without ever truly having known the black world, and thereafter was quarantined from it. Horton knew that world intimately, knowing no other until he was into his twenties, and his knowledge of it was not dimmed in later years, since he spent much of these shuttling between the two worlds. Consequently, although the occasions were rare, he did draw on shared black experience in his verse, as in the poem on the eve of a slave auction. For that matter, the contrast between Wheatley's solitary, equivocal, and aborted criticism of slavery and his full-throated protest against it also mirrors the difference in their experience. Although his antislavery poems were cast in an individual, subjective mold for the most part, they emerged from the experience whose essence he shared with the community of slaves.

Still, he did occupy a twilight zone between the two worlds, striving to strengthen his contact with the white world for the favors he could extract from it, and to minimize his skin-status tie to the black for the disabilities that went with it. If this be opportunism, as has been noted, it was one price exacted for consummation of his passion to be a poet.

However, another social factor had a bearing on his behavior. This was the character of the black community. Economically rooted in agriculture, slavery dispersed its chattel, atomizing them into plantation units. Fearful of revolt, the slave oligarchy employed its vast powers to block any bond or sense of community among slaves that transcended plantation boundaries. The severe strictures against slave literacy, for example, were designed admittedly to prevent communication. The massive effort to keep the slaves in scattered, relatively small units, cut off and isolated from each other, truncated development of black consciousness and retarded the growth of a culture to reflect such consciousness of a distinct identity. Without the possibilities of cohesion or the opportunities for communication (except for an underground word-of-mouth grapevine) the self-awareness of a people does not flower. This rule held true for the dispersed slaves in the ante-bellum South.

Thus for Horton as a poet the commanding powers of white society were paralleled by the virtual nonexistence of a black constituency. This accentuated his dependence on a white society, which existed economically on the backs of slave labor and ideologically on the premise of black inferiority. That in these circumstances he exhibited symptoms of compromise and opportunism was inevitable. What is truly noteworthy, however, is that he retained so large and hard a core of integrity.

Like any man the poet ought to be assessed within the limitations and opportunities of his time and place. By this standard the judgment of a black contemporary is of special value. The story is told that Bishop Daniel A. Payne of the African Methodist Episcopal Church, a pioneer black educator and himself an author, read some of Horton's poems to Sojourner Truth in 1858, inviting a comparison with his own attempts at verse.

"Dan," she said, "yourn be pretty, but his'n be strong."

The verdict of the fabled conductor on the Underground Railroad carries more authority than the judgment of the poet's Southern white biographers. Sojourner Truth could identify with Horton, and if she felt strength in his verse, then it was indeed strong in his time.

Horton's primary, indeed historic, originality lies in his antislavery poems, but there is also an original vein in the indigenous quality of his work. To be sure, he was also imitative, but he was more catholic in his imitation than Wheatley was. One can readily trace influences of Byron and other romantic poets, and yet some of the poems most closely resemble those of Robert Burns, although there is no evidence of direct influence or conscious imitation. In their proximity to nature, in their closeness to the earth, in their intimate acquaintance with the folk, the slave and the Scot arrived at a similarity of poetic idiom.

In Horton, however, these qualities bear the distinct stamp of rural North Carolina in the first half of the nineteenth century, when the frontier was still more reality than legend. As a result there is a native American strain in his work, and he was conscious of this nativity. One incident is particularly revelatory, both of his awareness and of the less attractive native strain in the Southern white assessment of him.

In 1849 the Hungarian patriot and revolutionary, Lajos Kossuth, visited the United States and was welcomed with great acclaim. This welcome harmonized with the widespread popular enthusiasm in this country for the European revolutions of 1848. To celebrate Kossuth's arrival the Raleigh *Register* published some English verse in his honor, prompting Horton to write a vigorous defense of native American poetry.

"I always have been and am still opposed to every exaltation of foreign over native talent," Horton said in his letter (Raleigh *Register*, December 29, 1849). "I am for developing *our own* resources, and cherishing native genius. I may never be before the People for any office, and therefore cannot be personally affected by any seeming assent to what I do most cordially disapprove. But as a North Carolina patriot, I ask, Why leave our own to stand on foreign soil? Why *go abroad* for poetry when we have an infinitely superior article of domestic manufacture? I am too modest to speak of my own, but surely there *is* poetry of native growth, even of your fair City of Oaks, good enough for a Toast to Lajos Kossuth, without straying off into foreign parts."

Walser surmised that "it was presumption and arrogance—which led him to [this] defense of American writers." The pertinent question is, who is presumptuous and arrogant in this instance, the critic or the target of his criticism? Why is it "presumption and arrogance" to express a sentiment, which had some vogue in the country at the time, having been voiced most notably twelve years earlier by a more eminent personage in the American culture?

There is no way of knowing whether Horton ever read Ralph Waldo Emerson's oration on "The American Scholar," but the spread of seminal thoughts develops a momentum of its own, and surely traces of the New England intellectual's address to the Phi Beta Kappa Society at Harvard may be discerned in the slave poet's letter to the *Register*.

"Our day of dependence, our long apprenticeship to the learning of other lands, draws to a close," Emerson had said. "The millions that around us are rushing into life, cannot always be fed on the sere remains of foreign harvests." So saying, Emerson prophesied a revival of American poetry, singing of actions and events on this continent that will "lead in a new age."

Allowing for differences in polish and in the sweep of conception, the principal thrust of Emerson's oration and Horton's letter was similar. But what has been hailed as prophetic insight in the Northern white thinker becomes arrogance and presumption, it would seem, when uttered by the Southern black slave.

Another aspect of the incident invites intriguing speculation. It might not have been fortuitous that Kossuth's visit was the occasion for Horton's letter. Other black men drew a parallel between the European revolutions of 1848 and the slaves' struggle for freedom. A scant six months before Horton's letter appeared in the Raleigh *Register* an address by Frederick Douglass in Boston's Faneuil Hall emphasized that parallel. In his peroration, having declared that "I should welcome the intelligence tomorrow, should it come, that the slaves had risen in the South," Douglass concluded:

> You welcomed the intelligence from France, that Louis Phillippe had been barricaded in Paris—you threw up your caps in honor of the victory achieved by Republicanism over Royalty—you shouted aloud—"Long live the Republic!"—and joined heartily in the watchword of "Liberty, Equality, Fraternity"—and should you not hail, with equal pleasure, the tidings from the South that the slave had risen, and achieved for himself, against the iron-hearted slaveholder, what the republicans of France achieved against the royalists of France?

Once again there is no way of knowing whether Horton had read Douglass' address as published in the *Liberator,* and there is no way of tracing the journey of such ideas in remote removal from an original source. For that matter, there is no ground for assuming that only an outside stimulus could evoke in a slave a sympathetic response to revolutions waged under the watchword of liberty, equality, and fraternity. What Douglass could say in Faneuil Hall could not, of course, be said by Horton in the Raleigh *Register.* Still the revolutions of 1848, as personified in one of their most popular protagonists, were on the poet's mind. He himself did not offer a toast to Kossuth (would it have been meet for a slave a toast a revolutionary?), he only objected that a toast had been rendered with borrowed wine. As couched, his public protest became an Emersonian call for recognition in general of native poetic genius; yet imbedded in it also was the specific demand for an American response to European revolution.

Unfortunately, Horton's feelings about Kossuth cannot be plucked with any certainty from the realm of conjecture, but the same uncertainty does not attend his espousal of native poetry, for in this the professions in his letter find solid confirmation in the body of his work. He belongs to the company of early American writers who, in Emerson's phrase, heralded the close of "our day of dependence" upon foreign cultures, who found their idiom as well as their inspiration in the American environment.

When Emerson wrote his address the country had just entered into the third generation of its independence. Cultural independence was not so easily or swiftly proclaimed as political independence was in the declaration of 1776. Its attainment was subtler and slower, but a national culture was in the making, and poets did not lag. Several volumes of Bryant's verse had been published by 1837, the year of

Emerson's address. The precocious Edgar Allan Poe had produced a book of verse a decade earlier, when he was just eighteen, and in the ensuing years had established his reputation as poet, critic, and storyteller. Longfellow, Whittier, and Lowell were soon to make their major debuts, and beyond them loomed the figure of Walt Whitman, whose *Leaves of Grass* was to appear in its first, modest edition in 1855. All of these were Horton's contemporaries, but with the possible exception of Bryant, the only one among them who was his senior, it is very unlikely that any made their mark upon Horton in his molding years between the preparation of *The Hope of Liberty* in 1828-29 and the publication of *The Poetical Works* in 1845. Even if it is assumed that he could have gained access to their verse, their major works and reputations might have been too late.

Just to list them, however, is already to indicate that, unlike Wheatley, Horton cannot be sheltered in the mediocrity of his contemporaries. Those white poets were good enough, so if Horton's work was to gain recognition simply on its merits as poetry, it would have had to be much, much better than Wheatley's. It wasn't that much better; the apologia cannot be offered that his was no worse than the best of his contemporaries. Undoubtedly the stiffer competition in his poetic age contributed to his effacement. To any censure for not being better than he was, he might have replied with the words that William Wells Brown once used:

> If you have not liked my grammar, recollect . . .
> that I was brought up where I had not the privilege
> of education. Recollect that you have come . . .
> to hear a Slave, and not a man, according to the
> laws of the land; and if the Slave has failed to
> interest you . . . charge it to the blighting
> influences of Slavery—that institution that has made
> me property, and that is making property of three
> millions of my countrymen at the present day.
> Charge it upon that institution that is annihilating
> the minds of three millions of my countrymen.

With all the truth in that protest, the remarkable thing is not only that Horton achieved the poetic quality he did but that it harmonized with the vital chord of the times that was sounded by Emerson. His letter to the Raleigh *Register*, like his selection of topical themes in his volumes of 1845 and 1865, revealed an interest in contemporary events and personalities far beyond the perimeters of plantation and campus.

The complexity of his relationship with the social environment stands in marked contrast to the simplicity of his relationship with his natural surroundings, to his easy and affectionate familiarity with the woods and hills and pastoral lands of North Carolina. Much about Horton and Wheatley is revealed in their poetic treatment of nature. Both, for example, wrote about the evening and the morning.

This was Wheatley's evening:

> Filled with the praise of him who gives the light,
> And draws the sabled curtains of the night,
> Let placid slumbers soothe each weary mind,
> At morn to wake, more heavenly, more refined;
> So shall the labours of the day begin
> More pure, more guarded from the snares of sin . . .

And this was Horton's evening:

> The night-hawk now, with his nocturnal tone,
> Wakes up, and all the Owls begin to moan,
> Or heave from dreary vales their dismal song,
> Whilst in the air the meteors play along.

This was Wheatley's morning:

> Aurora hail! and all the thousand dyes
> Which deck thy progress through the vaulted skies;
> The morn awakes, and wide extends her rays,
> On ev'ry leaf the gentle zephyr plays;
> Harmonious lays the feathered race resume,
> Dart the bright eye, and shake the painted plume.

And this was Horton's morning:

> Aurora's smiles adorn the mountain's brow,
> The peasant hums delighted at his plough,
> And lo, the dairy maid salutes her bounteous cow.

The difference in style is accounted for in part by the disparity in education. Her disciplined lines march to the commands of a more rigorous and more systematic training in the classics; his are more prone to break ranks, for they were schooled in a catch-as-catch-can self-education. The more significant difference lies, however, in their apprehension of nature—hers formal and pietistic, his free and familiar and playful.

A comparable contrast is exhibited in their treatment of the natural phenomenon of death. In "On the Death of a Young Lady of Five Years of Age," Wheatley wrote:

> Perfect in bliss, she, from her heavenly home,
> Looks down, and smiling, beckons you to come.
> Why then, fond parents, why those fruitless groans?
> Restrain your tears, and cease your plaintive moans.
> Freed from a world of sin, and snares, and pain,
> Why would you wish your daughter back again?
> No—bow resigned; let hope your grief control,
> And check the rising tumult of the soul.

In "The Death of an Infant" Horton also invoked the Christian consolation of resurrection in heavenly afterlife ("O be not disturbed when death is but gain/The triumph of life from the tomb"), and he too referred to the pain of living (the infant "soars from the ocean of pain"), but not to sin or snares. He also included this stanza:

> With pleasure I thought it my own,
>   And smil'd on its infantile charms;
> But some mystic bird, like an eagle, came down,
>   And snatch'd it away from my arms.

It may be recalled that Wheatley, even after the loss of her first two children in infancy, wrote a eulogy on the death of someone else's infant without any discernible allusion to her personal tragedy. Horton personalized an experience he did not have; Wheatley had an experience she could not personalize. It was not simply a matter of personal style, of modesty and egotism. In Wheatley it was not self-effacement; her self was effaced by external forces. In the traumatic transplantation from Equatorial Africa the tender roots were destroyed, and in Colonial New England she was overwhelmed by the graft of alien values and mores, alien not only in relation to the African origins, but also alien in the more immediate sense because they were not the natural outgrowth of her true condition and status as a black and a slave. In consequence the traits of a distinct personality, which are rooted and nourished in human community, were obliterated, and although this may grate on some ears it was a form of spiritual and cultural genocide. There was so little self-assertion because so little self was left to assert.

Even physically she never became acclimated to this American soil. On the elementary physiological plane the divergent histories of Wheatley and Horton are aptly suggestive. She, ever frail and sickly, died in her early thirties; he, possessed of remarkable physical vitality, lived on well into his eighties. Of course, a large element of chance enters into the time of human mortality, and yet there is appropriate symbolism in his genius for survival and her lack of it. He was no transplant, his roots were here, and the marks of North Carolina upon them were far more pronounced than the traces of the unknown African region from which his untraced ancestors were abducted. He was nourished by the sustenance of family, of contemporary community, which represented shared experience and culture, as elementary as this last was at the time.

In his own genius for survival Horton already embodied the first genius of the race and therefore became a pawn in the historical dispute about the why and how of black survival, about its sources and consequences. To his biographers the secret of survival was simple: it was a capacity for accommodation. In this they expressed not only the prevalent white analysis, but also the eternally prevalent white counsel to blacks: accommodate. The simple explanation was never true, and now, more than a century after emancipation and more than three centuries after the first slave auction, its fallacy is egregious. Mere accommodation might conceivably account for survival of a mass of individuals, heterogeneous in all else except the similarity of physical, racial traits, but it cannot explain the proliferating signs and expressions of black consciousness, culture, and cohesion, all these being the configuration of a distinct black identity and common black aspiration. Something other than a heritage of accommodation is at work here, for this is resistance, this is bold, affirmative revolt against the black condition in the United States. If oppression, and a uniquely structured form of oppression at that, is the dominant fact in the common fate of a people, where else but in resistance can this people find the primary impulse for cohesion and self-awareness? The answer to that question is being given with explosive force in the ghettos of the country.

Any stage in evolution is an outgrowth of all that preceded it, and the contemporary stage of Afro-American evolution therefore contains the clues for retrospective examination (or re-examination) of its antecedents. Any full examination of this sort would trace the contradiction between accommodation and resistance, not in static balance or equilibrium, but in ever-changing interaction. It would focus on the paramount phenomenon: the spark of resistance was never so dimmed as to lose the volatility to burst into flame. Such an examination is beyond the purview here. Here, the more modest issue is the relationship of the first two significant black poets in the country to the evolution of the Afro-American community.

Wheatley uniquely epitomized the enormous pressures for erasure of African origins. In her circumstances this left a void that she could not fill with any clear sense of root and identity. Horton, on the other hand, represented, in a still embryonic form, the consciousness and identity that were shaped by the black experience in the United States, which encompassed and filtered what survived of the African heritage. It is necessary to emphasize *still embryonic,* for the historical evolution of a people and its self-awareness is a relatively slow process in the most favored circumstances, and the circumstances for Afro-Americans were least favored. The transcendent fact of the black experience for most of Horton's lifetime was the institution of slavery, and the relationship to this institution, therefore, was the decisive element in shaping black consciousness. Simply by uttering the first black poetic outcry against slavery, he already established himself as an important figure in the tradition that is the most vital substance in the development of black identity; the tradition of resistance to oppression, of refusal to acquiesce in a state of inferiority.

If the first half of the nineteenth century was the flowering period of the American nation, it was also the embryonic period of the "nation within a nation," to employ Martin R. Delany's suggestive phrase. Such diversified black spokesmen as Douglass, Walker, Brown, and Delany among others, were then etching the outlines of black consciousness and identity. These were political men, and freedmen operating in the relative freedom of the North, possessing opportunities for association and communication with black compatriots and white Abolitionists. No black man in a slave state could speak as they did to a public (except, of course, in the language of physical revolt, as did Nat Turner, Denmark Vesey, and some others). Horton is better appreciated by underlining his difference from those others in status and locale, and in temperament as well. Despite all these limitations, he achieved the historical distinction of being a black slave in the South who articulated the black hope for freedom.

Wheatley's life was a tragedy. Horton's, despite the tragic elements in it, especially the terrible anonymity of his death and final years, was an affirmation. The rare distinction he achieved places him in the company of black pioneers who extracted from the common fate of black folk, which was imposed by others, the sense of a common destiny that they themselves will fashion.

Notes

Three volumes of Horton's work are extant: *The Hope of Liberty* (Raleigh: J. Gales & Son, 1829); a second edition was published in Philadelphia in 1837, entitled *Hope of Liberty—Poems by A Slave,* and a third in Boston in 1838 appended to Phillis Wheatley's *Poems,* as noted above. His second volume, *The Poetical Works of George M. Horton* has been mentioned above. The third volume was entitled *Naked Genius* (Raleigh: Wm. B. Smith & Co., 1865). Several of his poems not included in the above appear in various newspapers and magazines to which specific reference is made in the chapter notes.

George Moses Horton's life story has been told over and over, from the short notice "derived from himself" in *Freedom's Journal* (New York, August 8, 1828) to the full-length biography by Richard Walser, *The Black Poet: The Story of George Moses Horton, A North Carolina Slave* (New York: Philosophical Library, 1966). Most of the telling has been by Southern writers to whom reference is made in the chapter notes. For this study Horton's truncated autobiography prefacing *The Poetical Works of George M. Horton, The Colored Bard of North-Carolina* (Hillsboro, N.C.: D. Heartt, 1845) and Walser, *Black Poet,* who filled in details and rounded out as best he could the thirty-eight years remaining after the autobiography, were the chief sources. Walser's book presents in full the autobiography (except for the last couple of lines) and has the virtue of making accessible an otherwise rare-to-find personal history by the poet.

One final word to these general notes: because of the paucity of hard, factual detail about the lives of Phillis Wheatley and Horton, there has been more than a normal resort by biographers to inference and even conjecture, especially in the case of Horton, to fill in the gaps. The same expedients are employed in this study. Any inference or conjecture involves an element of speculation, and its validity may be judged only in its relationship to the available facts and to an assessment of the environmental circumstances. The reader will have to use this frame of reference in judging whether the inferences and conjectures in this interpretive study come closer to the truth than those that hitherto have prevailed.

1. A Natural Poet

The quotations in the first two paragraphs of this chapter are, in order, from: Richard Walser, "A Slave Poet and His Patron," in *The State, A Weekly Survey of North Carolina*, vol. 13, no. 50, May 11, 1946; Edward A. Oldham, "North Carolina Poets—Past and Present—George Moses Horton," in *North Carolina Poetry Review*, vol. 2, no. 4, Jan.–Feb., 1935, issued by the North Carolina Poetry Society at Gastonia, North Carolina; Richard Banbury Creecy, *Grandfather's Tales of North Carolina History* (Raleigh: Edwards & Broughton, 1901), p. 212; Caroline Lee Hentz, *Lovell's Folly* (Hubbard & Edwards, 1833), pp. 259–260; see also Loggins, *The Negro Author*, p. 107; Kemp P. Battle, "George Horton, The Slave Poet," in *North Carolina University Magazine*, May, 1888, pp. 229–232; idem., *History of the University of North Carolina*, 2 vols. (Raleigh: Edwards Broughton Printing Co., 1907), 1:604.

That he was the first black man to earn his living by writing is said in an article by Collier Cobb, "An American Man of Letters—George Moses Horton, the Negro Poet," (this article was originally presented as a paper at a meeting of Southern Students at Harvard, September 23, 1886; published in part in *The State Chronicle*, Raleigh, March 31, 1888; published in full in *The North Carolina Review*, October 3, 1909, and in the *University of North Carolina Magazine*, October, 1909); the remark is repeated by Stephen B. Weeks in "George Moses Horton: Slave Poet," in *The Southern Workman*, published by the Hampton Institute of Virginia, October, 1914, pp. 571–577; and by Walser in *Black Poet*, p. 25. Walser states also that Horton's was the first protest against slavery by a slave and the first book by a black man in the South (ibid., p. 41).

The two lines quoted are from "On Liberty and Slavery" in *Hope of Liberty*.

Horton's pride in his unmixed ancestry is quoted from Cobb; other biographic sketches have also referred to this pride. Weeks says people who knew the poet at Chapel Hill described him as "a full-blooded Negro who boasted of the purity of his black blood," but adds, "on the other hand Negroes who knew him in Philadelphia report that he was of mixed blood." The latter is the only statement of its kind that I found.

The accounts of his childhood and his early efforts at poetic composition are based chiefly on his autobiography, "Life of George M. Horton, The Colored Bard of North Carolina," which prefaces *The Poetical Works*. The earliest record of these subjects is one "derived from himself," which appeared in *Freedom's Journal* on August 8, 1828. The next is the "Explanation" prefacing *Hope of Liberty*. The last one during his lifetime is "Sketch of the Author" by "The Compiler" (Captain Will H. S. Banks), as a preface to *Naked Genius*. Thereafter followed Cobb; Weeks; Oldham; Loggins, *The Negro Author*, pp. 107, 382, n. 43; Walser, *Black Poet*, pp. 5–12.

The fact that he wrote acrostics on girls' names at the request of university students appears in practically all the references mentioned. In addition, this is also mentioned in a letter from an alumnus to his student son at the university (William Thomson to Ruffin Thomson, October 21, 1859, Thomson Papers, Southern Historical Collection, University of North Carolina).

2. The Slave and The Citadel

A description of the early campus was written by Caroline P. Spencer, "Old Times in Chapel Hill," a series of articles appearing in the *North Carolina University Magazine* (specifically here, October, 1887); also, Hugh Talmage Lefler, *North Carolina History, Told by Contemporaries* (Chapel Hill: University of North Carolina Press, 1934); Walser, *The Black Poet*, pp. 19–20.

The reference to the students' disturbances in the town is from Battle, *History*, 1:262.

The personal description of Horton appears in several places, notably Battle, ibid., 1:603; Cobb, "American Man of Letters"; Weeks, "George Moses Horton"; Loggins, *The Negro Author*, p. 107; Walser, *Black Poet*, p. 12.

In this chapter, quotations in the first person, comments made by the poet, and the two poems appearing on pages 91–92, are contained in his autobiography. This matter may also be found in Walser, ibid., pp. 2–24 *passim*.

The acrostic to Julia Shepard is in the Pettigrew Papers, Southern Historical Collection of the University of North Carolina; it is also quoted in Walser, ibid., p. 23, and reproduced as the frontispiece to that book.

The estimate of Horton's birth date springs chiefly from the "Explanation" in *Hope of Liberty*, which, published in 1829, states, "The author is now 32 years of age . . ." Others have accepted this year as correct: James Weldon Johnson, *American Negro Poetry*, p. xxv; Loggins, *The Negro Author*, p. 107; Walser, *Black Poet*, p. 3. *Freedom's Journal*, however, in 1828, says, "He is about 25 years of age . . ." and the "Sketch of the Author" in *Naked Genius* says he was "probably born in the year 1794."

The autobiography lists the slaves on William Horton's plantation, and none of them is an adult male; Walser confirms this by his reference to the 1810 census, which lists only eight slaves belonging to William Horton (*Black Poet*, p. 3). Walser is also the authority for the description of the Horton plantations in Northhampton and Chatham Counties (ibid., pp. 3–5).

Horton's own story of how he learned to read is recounted various times: Battle, *History*, 1:603–605; Cobb; Weeks; Oldham; Walser, *Black Poet*, p. 5. The quotations on this subject are from Weeks.

The reference to the 1840 census is in Samuel Huntington Hobbs, Jr.,

North Carolina, Economic and Social (Chapel Hill: University of North Carolina Press, 1930), p. 248, quoting from R. D. W. Connor, *Ante-Bellum Builders of North Carolina*.

The Wesley hymnal that Horton used to learn to read is mentioned by the poet himself in his autobiography; Walser comments on this (*Black Poet*, p. 8); as do Oldham; Weeks; Battle (*History*, 1:603–605); and Cobb.

The quotation from Goethe is in DeWitt H. Parker, *The Principles of Aesthetics* (Boston: Silver, Burdett & Co., 1920), p. 49, quoting from Goethe's *Poetry and Truth*, English ed., Parke Goodwin.

"George Moses Horton, Myself" is in *Naked Genius*.

"Division of an Estate" is in *Poetical Works* and *Naked Genius*.

The reference to the "Camp Plague" is from Walser, *Black Poet*, pp. 15, 110, n.

The detail of Horton's being inspired by hearing someone read poetry is mentioned by Cobb and Oldham.

Horton himself acknowledges that many persons lent him books; almost all of the biographic sketches also record this fact. The legend about President Polk is mentioned by Battle (*History*, 1:603–605); and repeated and embellished by Walser (*Black Poet*, pp. 21, 72).

That no students appeared on opening day of the university is recounted by Battle (*History*, 1:63); that but a solitary one appeared on February 12, 1795, is also mentioned by him. As to the faculty pay at that time, Battle says $600 per year was offered (ibid., p. 108); the other reference to faculty pay is in Lefler (*North Carolina History*, pp. 157–159).

The campus memoir referred to is Spencer, "Old Times in Chapel Hill," *North Carolina University Magazine*, vol. 7, no. 5, May, 1888.

The description of the graduate's attire at the Commencement Ball of 1818 is from Battle (*History*, 1:268–269); it may also be found in Phillips Russell, *The Woman Who Rang the Bell: The Story of Cornelia Phillips Spencer* (Chapel Hill: University of North Carolina Press, 1949), pp. 14–15. This was the commencement, it will be recalled, at which James K. Polk graduated.

3. Poet Laureate

The reference to Augustus Alton is in Horton's autobiography, and Walser identifies him (*Black Poet*, p. 25).

Practically all of the biographic sketches of Horton are in agreement as to the sliding price schedule for his poems; Walser is the source for the statement that some poems were sold more than once (ibid., p. 26).

"Love" is in *Hope of Liberty*.

The happy effect ascribed to Horton's poems is mentioned by Battle in "George Horton."

The quotation stating the students' usual weekly investment in Horton's poetry is from Creecy (*Grandfather's Tales*, p. 212). Walser is the authority for the statement regarding a student's allowance at that time (*Black Poet,* p. 26). The annual cost of a slave's upkeep is from Kenneth Stampp, *The Peculiar Institution* (New York: Random House, Vintage Books, 1956), p. 406. The figure for wages for Northern white workers are from Philip Foner, *History of the Labor Movement in the United States,* 4 vols. (New York: International Publishers, 1947), 1:99.

The acclaim of Dr. Caldwell is in Battle, *History,* 1:411; the description is by Caroline P. Spencer, "Old Times," vol. 7, no. 5, May, 1888.

The "common saying" is referred to by Cobb; Loggins repeats it (*The Negro Author,* pp. 110, 383, n. 55).

Horton's acknowledgment of his indebtedness to Mrs. Hentz occurs in two places: his autobiography and "An Address to Collegiates of North Carolina: The Stream of Liberty and Conscience" (the latter is in the North Carolina Collection at the University of North Carolina). Others have recounted it: "A North Carolina Poet—George Moses Horton—More Generally Known as 'Poet Horton'," an unsigned article in *De Bow's Review,* June, 1860, vol. 3, no. 6, reprinted from *North Carolina University Magazine,* April, 1860, vol. 9, no. 8; "Sketch of the Author," preface to *Naked Genius;* Weeks; Oldham; Walser, "A Slave Poet"; idem., editor with an introduction, *North Carolina Poetry* (Richmond: Garrett & Massie, 1951), p. 13; idem., *Black Poet,* pp. 28–33; Mrs. Hentz herself refers to it in *Lovell's Folly,* pp. 256–257, n.

The purchase by James Horton of three slaves is mentioned by Walser, *Black Poet,* p. 16.

The statement of the North Carolina Supreme Court is quoted in Stampp, *Peculiar Institution,* p. 199.

"A Slave's Reflection on the Eve before His Sale" is in *Naked Genius.*

James Horton's ignorance of the poet's talents is mentioned in the "Explanation" to *Hope of Liberty;* also by Cobb and Oldham.

Horton's estimation of James Horton is in his "Address to Collegiates of North Carolina."

The stanza quoted is from "On Liberty and Slavery" in *Hope of Liberty.*

4. Hope of Liberty

The "Explanation" that prefaces *Hope of Liberty* states: "Several compositions of his have already appeared in the *Raleigh Register.* Some have made their way into the Boston newspapers . . . ." Loggins quotes from the *Liberator* of March 29, 1834 (*The Negro Author,* pp. 108–109, 383, n. 49, 50). Horton mentions such notices in his autobiography and in the "Sketch of the Author" in *Naked Genius;* and Walser also refers to them (*Black Poet,* pp. 31–32, 35).

"Gratitude" does not appear in any of his three extant published volumes.

Horton's reference to the attempt of Governor Owen and others to buy his freedom is in his "Address to Collegiates of North Carolina." Mention of this is also made in "Sketch of the Author," *Naked Genius,* and in Walser, *Black Poet,* pp. 38–39.

The "Explanation" to *Hope of Liberty* states explicitly that Horton would go to Liberia if freed; Loggins refers to this (*The Negro Author,* p. 109), as does Walser (*Black Poet,* pp. 40, 112, n.).

The statement quoted from *Freedom's Journal* was made by Samuel E. Cornish, then senior editor (Bella Gross, *Clarion Call: The History and Development of the Negro People's Convention Movement in the United States from 1817 to 1840* [New York: Privately Printed, 1947], p. 8). Gross's reference gives no date for the statement made by Cornish.

The quotation from David Walker's *Appeal* is taken from Herbert Aptheker, *One Continual Cry—David Walker's Appeal to the Colored Citizens of the World (1829–1830), Its Setting and Its Meaning* (New York: Humanities Press, 1965), p. 131.

The six-line stanza quoted appears at the end of the "Explanation" in *Hope of Liberty.*

Weeks is the source for the statement that Horton was "aided and abetted by some of the best men in the state."

All of Horton's poems quoted in this chapter are contained in *Hope of Liberty;* "On the Evening and the Morning" appeared also in the *Raleigh Register,* July 18, 1829, under Horton's by-line.

Walser asks the rhetorical question on page 113 (*Black Poet,* p. 42).

Speculation as to why *Hope of Liberty* failed is made by Walser (ibid.).

Hints of financial irregularities in connection with the sale of *Hope of Liberty* might be gleaned from the correspondence that prefaces the 1837 edition; see also Loggins (*The Negro Author,* p. 109); and Redding (*To Make a Poet Black,* p. 15). Walser remains silent on this specific point.

Governor Owen's insistence that the Legislature set a price on David Walker's head is stated by Walser (*Black Poet,* p. 43); confirmation of a similar action in Georgia is in Aptheker, *One Continual Cry* (quoting Henry Highland Garnet's sketch of Walker's life), p. 43.

The "convivial excess" is referred to by Creecy (*Grandfather's Tales,* p. 220).

5. Years of Reaction

The two quotations from David Walker's *Appeal* appear in Aptheker (*One Continual Cry,* pp. 83, 137).

The details of the fate of those caught with a copy of the *Appeal* are related by the editors of *The Negro Caravan* (p. 587); Aptheker (*One Continual Cry,* pp. 46–47); Walser (*Black Poet,* p. 43); Benjamin Quarles, *Black Abolitionists* (New York: Oxford University Press, 1969), p. 17.

The suspicion that Walker was murdered was mentioned by Henry Highland Garnet, "A Brief Sketch of the Life and Character of David Walker," quoted by Aptheker (*One Continual Cry,* p. 43).

The repressive laws referred to are *Laws of North Carolina, 1830–31*, Chap. VI: "An Act to Prevent All Persons from Teaching Slaves to Read or Write, the Use of Figures Excepted," quoted by Lefler (*North Carolina History*, pp. 269–270, 274–275); see also Frank Tannenbaum, *Slave and Citizen* (New York: Random House Vintage Books, 1946), pp. 70–71; Clement Eaton, *History of the Old South*, 2d ed. (New York: Macmillan, 1966), p. 253.

The quotation from Frederick Douglass is in Stampp (*Peculiar Institution*, p. 73).

The legal ban on hiring out time is set forth in Walser (*Black Poet*, p. 50).

Walser authenticates the year of James Horton's death as 1843 (ibid., pp. 59–60, 113, n.). The "Sketch of the Author" (*Naked Genius*) and Weeks had erroneously given it as 1832.

Horton's remark as to the manner in which his age was determined by his purchaser is related by Redding (*To Make a Poet Black*, p. 13).

The characterization of Hall Horton is made in "Sketch of the Author" (*Naked Genius*); and by Weeks.

Walser estimates that Hall Horton could hire two productive field hands by permitting Horton to hire out his time (*Black Poet*, p. 60); see also Cobb; Battle (*History*, 1:603); Oldham; Loggins (*The Negro Author*, pp. 107–108, 383, n. 45).

"The Tippler and His Bottle" appears in *Poetical Works* and *Naked Genius*.

The facts relating to Horton's children are in Walser (*Black Poet*, pp. 57, 113, n.); Battle, "George Horton"; and Weeks.

"On the Consequences of Happy Marriages" is in *Hope of Liberty;* "Fate of an Innocent Dog" is in *Poetical Works*.

6. Poetical Works

The communication by William Mercer Green is mentioned by Weeks; by Loggins (*The Negro Author*, p. 117); and by Walser (*Black Poet*, pp. 60–61).

All poems quoted in this chapter are in *The Poetical Works;* "Division of an Estate," "The Woodman and the Money Hunter," and "Imploring to Be Resigned at Death" also appear in *Naked Genius*.

The advance subscription lists for *The Poetical Works* are mentioned by Walser (*Black Poet*, p. 66).

The title of Bryant's poem is also the first line of that poem: "I Cannot Forget With What Fervid Devotion."

The "old unfortunate bard" ploy is mentioned by Cobb, Weeks, and Walser (*Black Poet*, pp. 69–70).

Walser is the authority relied on for the prices quoted for a copy of *The Poetical Works* (ibid., pp. 69–70).

7. Vain Appeals

The Chapel Hill historian referred to is Caroline P. Spencer; her description of Swain appears in the *University Magazine* for February, 1888, and February, 1883; the alumnus who describes him is Cobb.

Swain's offensive conduct was that he permitted his younger daughter to marry a Union officer and that shortly after the war he visited the North, dined with Horace Greeley as well as the war governor of Massachusetts, and had associated with military notables at West Point "on the pleasantest terms" (Russell, *Cornelia Phillips Spencer*, p. 71).

Garrison's denunciation by press and pulpit are described by Walter M. Merrill, *Against Wind and Tide—A Biography of William Lloyd Garrison* (Cambridge: Harvard University Press, 1963), pp. 53–54; and Oliver Johnson, *William Lloyd Garrison and His Times* (Boston: Houghton Mifflin Co., 1881), pp. 186–187. The quotation from the Richmond *Whig* and the remarks of the Rev. William S. Plummer are in Johnson (ibid., pp. 186–187).

Horton's letters to Garrison, Greeley, the two to Swain, and "The Poet's Feeble Petition" are among the Swain Papers, Southern Historical Collection, University of North Carolina.

In the discussion of Douglass, William Wells Brown, and the literature of the time, reference was had to Loggins (*The Negro Author*, pp. 135, 139 [re Douglass], 156, 160, 165–169 [re Brown], 215, 219, 227, and 176–211, *passim*).

Brown's elegy to his mother is quoted in William Edward Farrison, *William Wells Brown—Author and Reformer* (Chicago: University of Chicago Press, 1969), p. 138.

On the subject of the various kinds of meetings and associations of the black writers of the time, reference was had to Farrison (op. cit., pp. 78, 116, 262–264, 345).

Walser assumes Horton was ignorant of his recognition in the North in the latter half of the 1830's (*Black Poet*, p. 57). Horton's earlier awareness of such recognition is demonstrated by the assertion in his autobiography that Mrs. Hentz had sent "the blast [of his fame] on the gale of passage back to the frozen plains of Massachusetts."

Cobb, Weeks, Loggins (*The Negro Author*, p. 111), and Walser (*Black Poet*, p. 77) mention Mrs. Greeley's knowledge about Horton.

Walser is the authority that "The Poet's Feeble Petition" was not printed in the New York Tribune (ibid., p. 114, n.).

8. The Eve of War

The wayward son was Ruffin Thomson and the letter is from his father, William H. Thomson (October 21, 1859). The letter is among the Thomson Papers, Southern Historical Collection, University of North Carolina.

It is Walser who finds Horton's poems superior to most that appeared in the university magazine (*Black Poet,* p. 75).

The account of the case of Professor Benjamin Sherwood Hedrick is written by Battle (*History,* 1:654–657); it is repeated by Walser (*Black Poet,* pp. 81–82).

The manuscript transcript of "An Address to Collegiates of North Carolina" is in the North Carolina Collection at the University of North Carolina.

The poem "Me and My Captain" is quoted from *The Negro Caravan,* p. 471.

The writer who estimated the "Address" and its effect, and who related the July 4, 1849, incident is Walser (*Black Poet,* p. 84); the quoted passage from Thomas Miles Garrett's diary appears in Walser (ibid., p. 73).

9. War and Emancipation

Hobbs is the authority that the university was virtually closed with the advent of the war (*North Carolina,* pp. 249–250); Battle states: "It is believed that the University of North Carolina was the only institution of rank . . . which had commencement exercises in the terrible year of 1865" (*History,* 1:749); Russell states that in 1865 there were but four graduating seniors (*Cornelia Phillips Spencer,* p. 58).

The prices for staple foods are given by Russell (ibid., p. 49).

The narration of the shortage of necessities and of the panic caused by Sherman's advance is quoted from Pauli Murray, *Proud Shoes* (New York: Harper & Bros., 1956), pp. 161–162.

Except where otherwise indicated the description of Chapel Hill's occupation by Union troops is by Caroline P. Spencer, "Old Times," in the *North Carolina University Magazine,* May, 1888. Battle says that she "is our authority for the incidents connected with the occupation of Chapel Hill by the Federal troops" (*History,* 1:741); she wrote a book on this subject entitled *The Last Ninety Days of the War* (New York: Watchman Publishing Co., 1866), dedicated to Swain.

"The Flag of the Free" is in *Naked Genius.*

Pauli Murray's family chronicle is the source for the statement that "the white people stayed indoors," etc. (*Proud Shoes,* p. 162).

Banks's recollection of his meeting and friendship with Horton is in his introduction to *Naked Genius.* It is Walser who feels that Banks found justification for his service in the war (*Black Poet,* pp. 91–92).

Pauli Murray describes General Atkins and his behavior (*Proud Shoes,* p. 163).

10. Naked Genius

The references and the poems quoted in this chapter are in *Naked Genius.*

11. Oblivion and Death

The description and opinion of Horton's attitude at the meeting of the Banneker Institute is from Walser (*Black Poet*, pp. 104, 115, n.).

The quotations from W. E. B. Du Bois appear in *The Philadelphia Negro* (New York: Benjamin Blom, 1899; reissued 1967), pp. 203, 317, 318.

The quotation regarding lack of any information as to where Horton died is from Walser (*Black Poet*, pp. 106, 115, n.).

Those who mention Horton's prose are Cobb, Weeks, and Walser (*Black Poet*, pp. 104–106, 115, n.). In the hope of finding anything that was published under Horton's by-line in Philadelphia, I consulted the following libraries: Philadelphia Free Library; University of Pennsylvania; Haverford College; Pennsylvania Historical Society; and the Library Company of Philadelphia, which houses, among its special collections, American newspapers and periodicals of that time. I discovered not even a reference to any prose by Horton at any of these libraries.

12. Critical Appraisals

Loggins makes the statement that Horton is the main representative of Negro poetry between 1790 and 1840 (*The Negro Author*, p. 104).

Walser's statement that Horton required no more liberty than he had, his estimation of Horton's antislavery poems, and his opinion that Horton was "taught to resent" his slave status are in his main work on Horton (*Black Poet*, pp. 72, 70). In connection with the latter point, cf. Redding: "Later Horton learned to hate" (*To Make a Poet Black*, p. 14); and Benjamin Brawley: "His work was infused with his desire for freedom . . ." and "The passion in the heart of this man . . ." ("Three Negro Poets: Horton, Mrs. Harper, and Whitman," *Journal of Negro History*, vol. 2, no. 4, October, 1917, pp. 384–386).

The phrases "overly tragic," "mendicant and fool," and "uncomplicated fellow" are Walser's (*Black Poet*, pp. 70, 72, 32).

The reference to Daniel A. Payne and Sojourner Truth is in J. Saunders Redding, *The Lonesome Road: The Story of the Negro's Part in America* (New York: Doubleday, 1958), p. 81.

Walser's is the reference to Horton's "presumption and arrogance" (*Black Poet*, p. 73).

The quotations from Emerson's "The American Scholar" appear in *The Portable Emerson*, selected and edited by Mark Van Doren (New York: Viking Press, 1946), p. 23.

The quotations from Frederick Douglass appear in *The Negro Caravan*, quoting the report of his speech in the *Liberator*, June 8, 1849 (p. 621).

The quotation from William Wells Brown is from "A Lecture Delivered before the Female Anti-Slavery Society of Salem" and may be found in Loggins (*The Negro Author*, p. 159).

"A Hymn to the Morning," "A Hymn to the Evening," and "On the Death of a Young Lady of five years of age" are in Wheatley, *Poems*. "On the Evening and the Morning" and "Death of an Infant" are in *The Hope of Liberty*.

Martin Robinson Delany's phrase is in *The Condition, Elevation, Emigration, and Destiny of the Colored Peoples of the United States, Politically Considered* (Philadelphia: Published by the Author, 1852; reissued New York: Arno Press and *The New York Times*, 1968), Appendix, p. 209.

Index

Addison, Joseph, 133
Aesop, 82
Alton, Augustus, 97, 202
Aptheker, Herbert, 69, 204
Atkins, Smith B., 160–162, 165, 207
Attucks, Crispus, 26, 72

Banks, Will H. S., 161–166, 170, 171, 176, 200, 207
Banneker, Benjamin, 17–18, 71
Banneker Institute, 170–171, 172, 173, 176, 208
Bargar, B. D., 73, 75
Battle, Kemp P., 164, 200, 201, 202, 203, 205, 207
Beecher, Mrs. William, 43, 44, 45, 75
Blassingame, John W., 36n, 141n, 155n
Blumenbach, Johann Friedrich, 54, 77
Boston Daily Advertiser, 74
Boston Evening Post & General Advertiser, 48–49
Boston Gazette, 34–35
Boston Independent Chronicle, 51
Boston Magazine, 51, 76
Bowdoin, James, 34
Bradstreet, Anne, 16, 71, 78
Brawley, Benjamin, 69–70, 71, 72, 73, 74, 75, 77, 208

Bronson, Eli, 17
Brown, Henry Box, 141
Brown, John, 115, 151, 153
Brown, Sterling, 71
Brown, William Wells, 141–142, 189, 194, 198, 206, 208
Bryant, William Cullen, 131–132, 193, 194, 205
Burgoyne, John, 39
Burns, Robert, 81, 113, 191
Burritt, Elijah H., 116
Bush, Douglas, 78
Byron, George Noel Gordon, Lord, 81, 99, 112–113, 191
Byrum, Rhody, 122

Caldwell, Joseph, 99–100, 102, 113, 119, 135, 136, 154, 203
Calhoun, John C., 152
Chapel Hill Gazette, 148
Chase, Samuel, 17
Clarkson, Thomas, 54, 77
Clay, Henry, 128, 136
Cobb, Collier, 173–176, 178, 179, 180, 186, 200, 201, 202, 203, 205, 206, 208
Connor, R. D. W., 202
Cooper, Samuel, 49, 67, 76
Copans, Sim, 182
Cornish, Samuel E., 204
Cornwallis, Charles, Lord, 41
Creecy, Richard Banbury, 200, 202, 204

INDEX / 212

Cullen, Countee, 182
Cummings, E. E., 182

Dartmouth, Earl of, 27–29, 30, 62, 71, 73, 78
Davis, Arthur P., 71
Davis, Jefferson, 164, 167–168
Deane, Charles, 68, 73
De Bow's Review, 150, 203
Delany, Martin Robinson, 141, 142, 198, 209
Demosthenes, 133
Dickinson, Emily, 182
Douglass, Frederick, 36n, 120, 121, 141, 142, 184, 189, 192–193, 198, 205, 206, 208
Du Bois, W. E. B., 18, 171–172, 208
Dumas, Alexandre, 60–61
Dunbar, Paul Laurence, 182n
Dunmore, Lord, 8–10, 69

Eaton, Clement, 205
Eliot, T. S., 182
Emerson, Ralph Waldo, 182, 192, 193, 194, 208
Equiano, Oloudah, 12–13, 25, 71, 72

Farrison, William Edward, 206
Foner, Philip, 203
Fontenelle, Bernard le Bouvier de, 54
Ford, Worthington Chauncey, 69
Franklin, Benjamin, 25, 28, 48, 72, 174
Freedom's Journal, 105–107, 108, 109, 145, 199, 200, 201, 204
Frémont, John C., 151, 187
Freneau, Philip, 182

Gales, Joseph, 109, 130, 137, 199
Gales, Weston R., 109, 113, 114, 130, 137, 199

Garnet, Henry Highland, 142, 204
Garrett, Thomas Miles, 156, 207
Garrick, David, 25
Garrison, William Lloyd, 137, 138–141, 142, 144, 206
George III, 26, 28, 33, 73
Gilmore, John T., 147
Giraud, M., 45
Goethe, Johann Wolfgang von, 92, 202
Goodwin, Parke, 202
Grant, Ulysses S., 158, 164
Grant, William A., 159
Greeley, Horace, 143–144, 147, 165, 206
Greeley, Mary Cheney, 144, 206
Green, William Mercer, 126, 205
Greene, Lorenzo Johnston, 18, 70, 71, 75, 76
Grégoire, Henri, 45, 53, 70, 76, 77
Gross, Bella, 204

Hale, Edward D., 42, 75
Hammon, Jupiter, 16, 49, 76–77
Hancock, John, 34, 35–36
Heartman, Charles Frederick, 69, 71, 73, 75, 76, 77, 78
Heartt, Dennis, 126, 164, 199
Hedrick, Benjamin Sherwood, 151, 207
Henson, Josiah, 141
Hentz, Caroline Lee, 100–101, 113, 119, 131, 138, 154, 180, 188, 200, 203, 206
Hentz, Nicholas, 100
Hill, George Birbeck, 72
Hillsborough Recorder, 126, 164
Hobbs, Samuel Huntington, Jr., 201–202, 207
Homer, 55, 99, 133
Horton, George Moses, 61, 62, 63–64, 67, 68, 78; birth and childhood, 86–87; learns to read, 88–90; first poems, 91–

92; first appears on University of North Carolina campus, 84–85, 93–94; composes acrostics, 85; "won" by James Horton in a lottery, 93; sells romantic verse to students, 97–98; assisted by students, 99; relation with Dr. Caldwell, 99–100, 119; and with Mrs. Hentz, 100–101, 119; assesses slave owners, 87–88, 102; anti-slavery verse, 81, 103, 106, 110–112, 159, 167–169, 185–186; described in novel by Mrs. Hentz, 100–101; efforts to buy his freedom, 105–108; publication of *The Hope of Liberty*, 109–114 passim; hires out, 120–121; bought by Hall Horton, 121; problems with alcohol, 81, 121–122; his marriage, 122–123; publication of *The Poetical Works*, 126–134 passim; compared with Bryant, 131–132; his verse analyzed, 131–134, 166–167, 181, 185–186; relations with Swain, 135–147 passim; correspondence to Garrison, 138–141; and to Greeley, 143–144; isolation from black literary surge of 1840's and 1850's, 141–142; "An Address to Collegiates of N.C.—The Stream of Liberty and Conscience," 152–155; July Fourth oration, 155–156; journey to meet Sherman's troops in Raleigh, 158–159; meets Captain Banks, 161; publication of *Naked Genius*, 163–169 passim; settles in Philadelphia, 170; encounter with Banneker Institute, 170–172; interviewed by Cobb, 173–176; death, 174–175, 177; appraisals of, by Cobb, Weeks and Walser, 178–181, 185–186, 188, 192; and by Sojourner Truth, 191; defends native poetry in letter to *Raleigh Register*, 191–192; relation to his time, 193–194; and to the black community, 190–191.

Horton and Wheatley, comparisons and contrasts, xi-xiii passim; 61, 62, 63, 87, 91, 92, 175, 182–183, 190, 191, 194, 195–198

Horton, Hall, 120–121, 145, 164, 205

Horton, James, 93–94, 102–103, 106, 108, 109, 114, 118, 120, 137, 181, 203

Horton, William, 86, 87–88, 93, 102, 140, 201

Hughes, Langston, 182

Huntingdon, Selina Shirley, Countess of, 24–26, 28, 31, 32–33, 40, 49, 50, 72, 73, 75

Hutchinson, Thomas, 34, 36

Jackson, Andrew, 128
Jackson, Sara Dunlap, 73
Jefferson, Thomas, 18, 53, 54, 77, 95, 182
Johnson, Andrew, 160
Johnson, James Weldon, 59, 68, 77, 78, 201
Johnson, Michael, see Crispus Attucks
Johnson, Oliver, 206
Johnson, Samuel, 25, 72
Johnston, Albert Sidney, 158, 160, 161
Journal of Negro History, 73, 208

Knapp, Isaac, 137, 138
Kossuth, Lajos, 191, 192, 193

Lancaster Gazette, 138

INDEX / 214

Lathrop, Mary, see Mary Wheatley
Lee, Charles, 37–38, 74
Lee, Robert E., 158, 159
Lee, Ulysses, 71
Lefler, Hugh Talmage, 201, 202, 205
Liberator, 137, 138, 142, 193, 203, 208
Light, George W., 67–68
Lincoln, Abraham, 10, 160, 164, 165
Locke, John, 133
Loggins, Vernon, 67, 70, 72, 73, 74, 75, 76, 77, 78, 178, 200, 201, 203, 204, 205, 206, 208
Longfellow, Henry Wadsworth, 182, 194
Lossing, Benson J., 68
Louis Phillippe, 193
Lowell, James Russell, 182, 194

Mannix, Daniel P., 70, 71
Marlowe, Christopher, 173
Mason, Julian D., Jr., 68, 70, 71, 72, 73, 74, 75, 76, 77
Massachusetts Spy, 72
Mather, Cotton, 39
Mazyck, Walter H., 68–69
MacLeish, Archibald, 182
Merrill, Walter M., 206
Milton, John, 32, 52, 99
Monthly Review (London), 74–75
Morel, E. D., 73
Murray, Pauli, 207

Nell, William C., 141, 142
Newton, Sir Isaac, 56, 78, 133
New York Tribune, 143, 144, 206
North Carolina Poetry Review, 200
North Carolina University Magazine, 94, 150, 200, 201, 203, 206, 207
North Star, 142

Occum, Rev., 34
Odell, Margaretta Matilda, 11, 68, 69, 70, 71, 73, 74, 75, 76, 77
Oldham, Edward A., 200, 201, 202, 203, 205
Ovid, 15, 55, 133
Owen, John, 107–108, 113, 114, 116, 153, 154, 203, 204

Paine, Thomas, 7, 37
Palsits, Victor Hugo, 173
Parker, DeWitt H., 202
Payne, Daniel A., 191, 208
Pennsylvania Magazine, 7, 37, 69
Peters, John, 43, 45–47, 51, 52, 75, 76, 77
Peters, Phillis, see Phillis Wheatley
Pickman, Dudley L., 52
Plato, 133
Plummer, William S., 139, 206
Poe, Edgar Allan, 81, 182, 194
Polk, James Knox, 95, 202
Pope Alexander, 8, 15, 21–23, 25, 29, 37, 56–58, 72, 77, 78, 133
Prince (Wheatley), 20–21
Pushkin, Alexander, 60–61, 73

Quarles, Benjamin, 204
Quincy, Mr., 46, 76

Raleigh Register, 109, 112, 191–192, 193, 194, 203, 204
Raleigh Standard, 151
Raleigh, Sir Walter, 173
Ransom, Stanley Austin, Jr., 77
Rebecq, Constant de, 54
Redding, J. Saunders, 59, 61–64, 70, 71, 73, 78, 204, 205, 208
Reed, Joseph, 4–7 passim
Richmond Whig, 139, 206
Rush, Benjamin, 49, 74
Russell, Phillips, 202, 206, 207

Saintsbury, George, 56, 72, 77

Schomburg, Arthur A., 58–59, 76, 77, 78
Scott, Dred, 151
Seeber, Edward D., 77
Sewall, Joseph, 75
Shakespeare, 99
Shepard, Julia, 85–86, 201
Sherman, William Tecumseh, 158–161, 163, 164, 207
Shurtleff, Nathaniel B., 74, 75, 77
Smith, Samuel Stanhope, 53, 77
Smythe, John J., 171
Snipes, Franklin, 122, 123
Snipes, Free, 122
Southern Literary Messenger, 126
Southern Workman, 178, 200
Sparks, Jared, 69
Spencer, Caroline P., 201, 202, 203, 206, 207
Stampp, Kenneth, 203, 205
State (The), A Weekly Survey of North Carolina, 200
State Chronicle, 200
Stowe, Harriet Beecher, 141
Swain, David L., 135–137, 138, 140–141, 143–147, 157, 159, 160, 162, 164, 165, 206, 207

Tannenbaum, Frank, 205
Tanner, Obour, 32, 35, 36, 40, 42, 44–45, 48, 65, 73, 74, 75–76
Terence, 55
Terry, Lucy, 16–17, 71
Thatcher, B. B., 68
Thomson, Ruffin, 201, 206
Thomson, William, 201, 206
Thomson, James, 99
Truth, Sojourner, 141, 191, 208
Turner, Nat, 115, 118, 119, 137, 179, 184, 198

Van Doren, Carl, 69, 74
Van Doren, Mark, 208

Vance, Zebulon B., 157
Varick, Richard, 68–69
Vassa, Gustavus, see Oloudah Equiano
Vesey, Denmark, 198
Virgil, 55, 99
Voltaire, Francois Marie Arouet, 54, 77

Walker, David C., 107–109, 114, 115–118, 119, 137, 142, 189, 198, 204
Walser, Richard, 178, 180–181, 185, 186, 188, 192, 199, 200, 201, 202, 203, 204, 205, 206, 207, 208
Ward, Samuel Ringgold, 142
Washington, George, 3–10, 29, 33, 37, 38, 49, 50–51, 58, 68, 69
Watson, Brook, 32, 52
Weeks, Stephen B., 178–179, 181, 200, 201, 202, 203, 204, 205, 206, 208
Wegelin, Oscar, 77
Wesley, Charles (Hymnal), 88, 89, 91, 202
Wheatley, John, 3, 5, 8, 11, 24, 26, 27, 34, 38–39, 41, 44, 50, 60, 63, 69–70, 74, 75
Wheatley, Mary, 11, 15, 18, 19, 22–23, 41, 60, 63, 74, 75
Wheatley, Nathaniel, 11, 32, 41, 60, 63, 74
Wheatley, Phillis, visit to George Washington, correspondence and ode to him, 3–10 passim; purchased by Susannah Wheatley, 11–12; speculation about African origins and abduction by slave traders, 12–14; child prodigy, 15–21 passim; education, 15–16; unique status in Wheatley household and Boston society, 18–23; Puritan influence, 18, 19, 22,

Wheatley, Phillis (*Cont.*)
23, 55, 57, 65, 66; success of elegy to Rev. Whitefield, 24–26; Boston Massacre, 26–27; response to Stamp Act repeal, 28; ode to Lord Dartmouth and her one qualified protest against slavery, 28–29, 62; journey to London, 31–36 passim; reception in London, 32; correspondence with Countess of Huntingdon, 32–33; publication of *Poems on Various Subjects, Religious and Moral*, 33–35; death of Susannah Wheatley, 36; the Revolutionary War, 37–42 passim; ode to General Lee, 37–38; baptism in Old South Church, 39; freedom and marriage, 40–41; correspondence with Obour Tanner, 32, 35, 36, 40, 42, 44, 48, 73; estimates of her marriage to John Peters, 42–47 passim; plans for second volume of verse, 48–49; last poems, 49–50; poverty and death, 50–52; critical appraisals of—by Jefferson, 53, Dr. Smith, 53, Abbe Grégoire, 53, Voltaire, 54, Blumenbach, 54, Clarkson, 54, British periodicals, 54, Schomburg, 58–59, Johnson, 59, Wright, 60–61, Redding, 62–63; her poetry analyzed, 54–58; see also 87, 91, 92, 113, 131, 137, 138, 175, 179, 182, 183, 190, 191, 194, 195–198, 199

Wheatley and Horton, comparisons and contrasts, see Horton and Wheatley

Wheatley, Susannah, 8, 11–12, 15, 18–21, 22–23, 26, 27, 30–32 passim, 35, 36, 44, 46, 48, 50, 60, 63, 69–70, 73, 74

Wheeler, Joseph, 160

White, Elizabeth Wade, 71, 78

Whitefield, George, 24–26, 27, 28, 72

Whitman, Walt, 182, 194

Whittier, John Greenleaf, 182, 194

Woodson, Carter G., 70

Worster, Dr., 139–140

Wrazell, Sir Nathaniel William, 73

Wright, Richard, 59–61, 62, 78

Young, Edward, 99

KIRN MEMORIAL LIBRARY

NO LONGER THE PROPERTY OF
NORFOLK PUBLIC LIBRARY
STORAGE

KIRN MEMORIAL LIBRARY

DEMCO